lynn bowen walker

Queen
of the
Castle

52 weeks of encouragement

for the uninspired,
domestically challenged
or just plain tired
homemaker

INTEGRITY®
PUBLISHERS
Nashville

Cover Design: Brand Navigation, www.brandnavigation.com
Cover Illustration: Ed Goble
Interior Design: Susan Browne Design

Library of Congress Cataloging-in-Publication Data

Walker, Lynn Bowen.

  Queen of the castle : 52 weeks of homemaking encouragement for the uninspired, domestically challenged, or just plain tired / by Lynn Bowen Walker.

       p. cm.

  Summary: "Help and hope for every women who isn't homemaker of the year"--Provided by publisher.

  ISBN-13: 9-781-59145-474-8

  ISBN-10: 1-59145-474-3 (tradepaper)

  1. Housewives--Religious life. 2. Homemakers--Religious life. 3. Home economics. I. Title.

  BV4528.15.W35 2006

  248.8'435--dc22

                          2006013036

Printed in the United States of America

06 07 08 09 10 VG 9 8 7 6 5 4 3 2 1

To all the women who are

faithfully tending their homes and families.

Do not grow weary in doing good.

You are doing such important work.

contents

Acknowledgments

Thank you: To my mom and dad, Carolyn and Jim Bowen, for always telling me I could accomplish anything I set my mind to; to my in-laws, Mary Ann and John Walker, for raising such a terrific son; to Pam Ryder, for her unwavering support and enthusiasm; to Ron Lee and Annette LaPlaca, for encouragement so many years ago; to Robert and Bobbie Wolgemuth, for taking the time for one more writer; to Mark, Ben, and Jake, for providing me with so much joy. I love you high as the sky. And to my Lord Jesus Christ, who, in spite of knowing everything about me, loves me completely and irrevocably. Lord, to whom shall we go? You and You alone have words of eternal life.

week 1

Who, Me?
A Homemaker?!

OK, so let's get this out of the way right up-front: I am not homemaker of the year. A bag of peeled carrots on the dinner table is often the closest I get to a side dish. I've been known to make my children snack outside in the rain after I've just done my biyearly kitchen floor mopping. Our house was robbed once, and it took me more than an hour to notice that the disarray was someone else's handiwork.

My homemaking sins are like scarlet.

So what am I doing writing a book about homemaking?

Actually, my plan A was not to write a book for homemakers but to *read* one. I was looking for a book that would help me figure out something special to surprise my family with on Valentine's Day—a book with ideas on when and how to plant bulbs (pointy side *up*, in case you're wondering) and some hints on getting my kids to help with chores when I wasn't even sure I knew how to do chores myself. Seeing as home economics classes went out with the Nixon administration and nearby grandmas with a hankering to teach knitting were in short supply, I needed advice on all kinds of homemaking skills, and I needed it fast. I didn't have the time or energy to search out a hundred different books to help me get good at my job.

new word
for the week:

Ululate (yōōl′ yə-lāt′)
To howl, hoot, wail, or lament loudly. Surprise your friends and family by using your new word today. As in, *"Quit your **ululating**. Three bites of broccoli won't kill you."*

alternate
new word:

Whiffle (wǐf′ əl).
To move or think erratically; waver. As in, *"OK, you only have to eat two bites of broccoli. You're lucky I'm willing to **whiffle** on this one."*

The thing that is so important for us to keep before us is that if we choose not to do this very special job, it will simply not get done. The mothering, the nurturing, the comforting and caring that fills the committed homemaker's day will simply be lost, and society will be impoverished. . . .

Women can give up their jobs as clerks, engineers, salespeople, doctors—other people will step in and the world will go on as smoothly as before. . . . The groceries will still be sold, trucks loaded with merchandise will still roll across our highways, and Wall Street will carry on. Not so with homemaking. We are the

cont. ⇒

What I found in my quest for that just-right homemaking book was a shelf full of books on becoming the perfect parent. I found books on making my own cleaning products with ingredients found in my very own cupboards. (Oh, joy.) I found books on organizing my piles of paper, baking with my bread machine, and cooking gourmet French dinners from scratch.

What I couldn't find was a more encompassing, more inclusive book that recognized I am more than just the family dinner wizard. I am more than just the laundry-stain getter-outer, the head muffin maker, the sibling squabble solver. I am more than just seeker of bargain outlet stores, overseer of the family calendar, and consultant for cheesy junior high science projects that promise results in twenty-four hours or less. My job includes zillions of tasks, some creative and some mundane. I wanted a book that recognized all this and would still help me figure out how to get dinner on the table when my fanny's stuck to the driver's seat most afternoons between 2 and 7 p.m.

Though I read many good books along my journey—the best of which I've quoted here in sidebars—I finally decided that in order to read the book I was looking for, I would have to write it. So here it is. I hope this book encourages you, as writing it has encouraged me, to love your family with your whole heart and serve them with as much joy as you can squeeze forth after the day's fifth load of laundry. As King Solomon said three thousand years ago, "The wise woman builds her house, but the foolish tears it down with her own hands" (Proverbs 14:1).

Solomon was right. Let's be wise women who commit ourselves to building our homes. Then we can watch in wonder as God turns them into the strongest, sturdiest dwellings imaginable.

When I was in college, I worked as an intern at a maga-zine. I will never forget the comment of a coworker near my own age as she eyed the engagement ring on my finger. In a voice dripping with condescension, she asked, "Are we supposed to congratulate you?" The clear message, in that I-am-woman, hear-me-roar era, was that graduation and career were laudable, but graduation and marriage were not.

Several years later, as I found myself at home, chang-ing diapers and blotting baby spit-up from my shoulder, I had to swat the nagging invisible voices of disapproval that floated around my brain like unwelcome gnats. *Is this all you're doing with your Stanford degree? What about the profession you trained for?*

It took me years to realize that though I was not going to an office every day, I still had a profession. In fact, I had an incredibly demanding profession, one with twenty-four-hour days, no sick leave, and eternal consequences.

"Homemaking is a proud profession," says a bumper sticker in my collection.[1] Homemaking is a proud pro-fession. It's an honorable profession. It's an important profession. As homemakers, you and I set the tone for our homes. We have the potential to make them warm and inviting. We can create wonderful environments where friends and family can thrive.

The world sends the message that being home is a foolish waste of a woman's time and talents. The home-maker's heart tells her that nurturing her family is one of the most fulfilling, creative endeavors she could imagine.

There have been moments in these at-home years when I've been enticed by the thought of escaping to the grown-up world of the workplace—the world of dry-clean-only clothes, complete sentences, and a paycheck that you can trade in for actual money. (You've probably had those moments too.) But always after about five seconds, I realize no babysitter could have ever treasured my sons the way I do. And no amount of financial rewards or professional pats on the back could have ever come close to the joy of watching my children grow and making a home for our family. Home, with the family God has blessed me with, is where I want to be. And now as I see my boys becoming young men, with the young motherhood years fading into the background and the empty nest not too far in my future, I thank God once again for these treasures—my husband and two sons—and for the precious, irretrievable joy and privilege of being there to take care of them.

You may wonder sometimes if patching one more pair of worn-out knees or making one more peanut-butter-and-jelly brown bag lunch really matters. Let me tell you: it matters. If you are home raising your family, you are doing important work. By loving the family God has given you, you are making an impact not only on this generation but also on the one after and the one after that. As a homemaker, your work has eternal consequences.

That's something no paid position can touch.

I love the sound of the word *homemaker*. To me, it resonates warmth, nurturing, and the ability to take an impersonal dwelling and, with diligence and love, transform it into a home.

In a magazine article I wrote once, I identified myself as a homemaker. To my dismay, the editor changed the word to "housekeeper." I am the *last* person who deserves the title of housekeeper, as anyone who's gotten past my front door can attest. I give new meaning to the phrase "You could eat off my kitchen floor." Cobwebs flourish, dust bunnies spawn more dust bunnies, and a closed door at my house should be treated the same as a friend's hatchet-job haircut—discreetly ignored. The job title "housekeeper" implies I clean house all day. (I don't.) It implies the structure itself is what I'm tending, in a janitorial capacity.

Though as homemakers we can't completely escape the occasional run-in with Mr. Clean—even if it's just to slam the cupboard door before he escapes from his little bottle—our job involves far more than keeping house.

Homemaking involves people. It encompasses loving our children, nurturing their creativity, and helping them recognize their unique gifts. Homemaking is encouraging our husbands, admiring their finer qualities, and praying for them when they're going through a rough time. Homemaking is being a people tender, a "family manager,"™ as author Kathy Peel calls it. It's caring about the people who enter our world and nourishing them with kind words, food perhaps, and a listening ear. You and I change the lives we touch. We have the capacity to bring love and laughter and encouragement to those who enter our homes. It's a huge job.

In truth, *every* woman is a homemaker, whether she wants to be or not. Young or old, single or married, childless or with a house full of kids, if she has a home, be it three thousand luxurious square feet or a single-room apartment, she is most likely the one in charge of keeping it running.

My hope is that even if you've never owned a peppy little apron and wouldn't dream of donning yellow rubber gloves, you will come to embrace homemaking as the vital, life-changing work that it is. As author Linda Weltner says in her book *No Place Like Home: Rooms and Reflections from One Family's Life*, "In a world filled with peril, what greater gift than to have the power to make a home out of what would otherwise have been merely living quarters."[4]

Let's cherish that very great gift. ♔

"Discipline yourself for the purpose of godliness; for bodily discipline is only of little profit, but godliness is profitable for all things, since it holds promise for the present life and also for the life to come." (1 Timothy 4:7–8)

prayer LORD, PLEASE ENCOURAGE ME IN MY WORK AT HOME. HELP ME TO LOOK PAST MY LESS-THAN-SPOTLESS HOUSE AND SEE MY MANY DAILY TASKS AS OPPORTUNITIES TO LOVE MY FAMILY AND TO HONOR YOU. HELP OUR HOME TO BECOME THE STRONG, HEALTHY PLACE YOU WANT IT TO BE. THANK YOU FOR THE OPPORTUNITIES YOU GIVE ME HERE.

week 2

new word

for the week:

Gawp (gôp).
To stare with mouth open in wonder
or astonishment; gape. As in,
*"No need to gawp. We'll have these
spilled groceries cleaned up in no
time."*

alternate

new word:

Ineffable (ĭn-ĕf' ə-bəl).
Beyond expression; indescribable.
As in, *"I am looking forward to
grocery shopping without the
children; it will be an ineffable
delight."*

Giving Homemaking Our Best

A friend who's been home raising kids and now grandkids for more than thirty years shared that one of her most discouraging moments was being asked by a young girl, "Do you work *at all*?" My friend was so stunned she couldn't give an answer.

Being a homemaker in our culture is not a valued position. Though the job involves incredible amounts of physical, mental, and emotional energy, it can still be trivialized by those who've never done it. When our work isn't valued by others, it is only with great effort that we value it ourselves.

When my sons were two and three, I took a trip by myself to visit my sister, who lives in Norway. For the week I was gone, my husband took time off from work to care for our boys. Seven days later when I returned, I was greeted by a man who was utterly exhausted. "I don't want you to ever have to go grocery shopping with the kids again," he panted. "From now on, I'll watch them while you go." Apparently a tipped-over cart, food strewn everywhere, two howling children, and glares from elderly ladies gave him an empathy for my job that all the play-by-play description in the world couldn't have won. "I could get the laundry washed and dried," he said, eyes glazed from no sleep, "but I couldn't get it folded. When they napped, I napped."

Those of us who run a home every day have a thorough appreciation for the enormity of the task, even when our children no longer ride around in grocery carts. Counters do not wipe themselves, socks do not wash themselves (or turn themselves right side out), mail does not answer itself, and, as a college friend discovered to her dismay, "You mean you have to *buy* toilet paper?!" Those of us who run a home know there is always more to be done.

But to those who have never attempted it, homemaking appears to involve no work at all. If that special someone in your life hasn't yet had the opportunity of running your home for a time—even if it's just a day or two—consider going on a weekend women's retreat or maybe a short visit to a relative. Give him the gift of discovering just what a homemaker's job entails. Attitudes around your home may never be the same.

Pam Young and Peggy Jones, real-life sisters and authors of the wonderful book *Sidetracked Home Executives* (see week 17), once calculated that in their jobs as mothers and homemakers they had

- been pregnant for 54 months;
- been in labor for 52 hours;
- produced 821 gallons of mothers' milk (8 oz. of milk, 6 times a day, for 365 days, times 6 kids);
- changed 78,840 diapers;
- spent 6,000 hours in the laundry room;
- run 14,965 dishwasher loads;
- waited at the orthodontist 144 hours;
- gone to 1,008 school conferences;
- chaperoned 1 junior high dance;
- broken up 105,850 fights (10 fights a day times 365 days times 29 years with fighting-aged kids);
- made 14,000 peanut-butter sandwiches;
- baked 47,232 chocolate-chip cookies;
- made 1,044 gallons of Kool-Aid®;
- paid $34,580 in allowances;
- spent 1,800 hours helping with homework;
- spent 7,800 hours at soccer games, football games, basketball games, and lessons.[1]

I don't know about you, but it seems to me that the soccer-game figure is a mite low.

Let any man of sense and discernment become the member of a large household, in which a well-educated and pious woman is endeavoring systematically to discharge her multiform duties; let him fully comprehend all her cares, difficulties, and perplexities; and it is probable he would coincide in the opinion that no statesman, at the head of a nation's affairs, had more frequent calls for wisdom, firmness, tact, discrimination, prudence, and versatility of talent, than such a woman. [2]

**Catharine E. Beecher
and Harriet Beecher
Stowe,**
American Woman's Home

"You were born fifty years too late," a friend tells her married daughter, who, though still childless, is tired of the working world and wants to be home.

Our culture so esteems those who work for pay that those of us who work at home for no pay feel obliged to answer the do-you-work question with a no. My husband, when he hears me being asked that question, often breaks in by answering, "She has the hardest job in the world—and also the most important. She's home raising our two boys." I love his acknowledgment that though I don't spend the bulk of my waking hours off in some rented building doing tasks that have nothing to do with nurturing my family, I do indeed have a valid and incredibly valuable career.

Sometimes it's tempting to take on more public commitments than we can really handle. Let's face it: clearing the same old clutter off the same old counters and slicing up enough lunchtime apples to circle the globe can get tiresome. The family is not likely to burst into spontaneous applause at the sight of (yet another) clean bathroom sink.

But if organizing the bake sale or directing the Christmas play come at the expense of dirty laundry that's beginning to emit interesting smells from our back room, it may be time to back off from some of our more public activities. Our families pay a price when we are overcommitted. As homemakers, we need to be careful we don't give away so much of ourselves to the outside community that we have nothing left for those at home.

Dr. Mary Ann Froehlich, in her book *What's a Smart Woman Like You Doing in a Place Like This? Homemaking on Purpose*, says, "The godly professional seeks God first, then cares for her family, and then serves the community. Each is an outflow of the other. But many well-meaning women fall into the trap of serving the community first, then fitting in their family's needs, and finally having a few minutes left over to spend with God. They are always fighting burnout because their resources are constantly running dry. Life is running backwards!

"Consider the following 'log in the eye' situations," she continues. "Sally teaches gourmet cooking classes two evenings a week. Her family is home eating TV dinners. . . . Sue is a successful music teacher. She is based at home and has a large number of students. By the end of the day, she is too tired to give her own children music lessons. Kathy diligently prepares and teaches two Bible studies a week. She does not have devotions with her own children."[3]

We need to be careful to give our families our best, not our leftovers (dinners excepted!). Homemaking is a challenging profession, and to do it well demands our best efforts—especially if we're domestically challenged. Some things just can't be squeezed in like one more person in a restaurant booth.

"So much depends upon the homemakers. I sometimes wonder if they are so busy now with other things that they are forgetting the importance of this special work." These words were written by Laura Ingalls Wilder. The year was 1923.[4]

As I sat on the gym floor waiting for my son's wrestling practice to finish, I read a magazine article about women who own their own businesses. Each had a specialty. A niche. Something that made her company different from all the others.

I got to thinking about that in light of homemaking. Isn't that true of us too? Aren't we all keepers of the home differently, depending on our interests, our energy level, the ages and number of our children, our family's priorities?

Our spiritual gifts, too, help determine our niche as homemakers. If God has gifted us with hospitality, our homes might draw friends for warm chocolate-chip cookies, a homey atmosphere, a cup of tea, and a listening ear.

If God has gifted us in serving, our homes might be bustling hubs of meal preparation for the sick in our congregation or places where baby clothes are laundered and readied to be brought to crisis pregnancy centers. If God has given us gifts of knowledge and wisdom, our homes might be quiet places where we study God's Word and perhaps lead others in Bible studies.

Our job descriptions and our homes will look different than those of every other homemaker. The problem comes when we begin to compare, to think that because someone else's home is straight out of a magazine, complete with hand-spun dog-hair blankets, prize-winning begonias, and her own flock of grain-fed geese, our homes should mimic that. We are each unique, "immaculately unique," as one author puts it. God has given us "varieties of gifts, but the same Spirit. And there are varieties of ministries, and the same Lord" (1 Corinthians 12:4–5). We have different gifts and different ministries. Why do we think our homes should look the same?

So give it some thought. Ask God. What is your niche as a homemaker? How should your home be unique as a result? Dwell on the wonder that, just as each person's thumbprint carries swirlies and whirlies unique to its owner, so our homes carry one-of-a-kind impressions simply because our touch leaves an imprint that no one else can duplicate. ♛

"Do you not know? Have you not heard? The Everlasting God, the LORD, the Creator of the ends of the earth does not become weary or tired. His understanding is inscrutable. He gives strength to the weary, and to him who lacks might He increases power. Though youths grow weary and tired, and vigorous young men stumble badly, yet those who wait for the Lord will gain new strength; they will mount up with wings like eagles, they will run and not get tired, they will walk and not become weary." (Isaiah 40:28–31)

prayer THANK YOU, FATHER, THAT I DON'T HAVE TO BE A HOMEMAKER QUITE LIKE ANYONE ELSE, THAT YOU MADE ME AN ORIGINAL AND THAT MY LIFE AND MY HOME CAN REFLECT THAT. HELP ME TO COUNT ON YOU FOR THE STRENGTH TO DO MY BEST AS I SERVE MY FAMILY.

week 3

Achoo! I Feel Fine: Fostering Our Health

Here's a quiz:

· ·

I take my child to the doctor when he:

   (a) has a raspy cough

   (b) complains of a painful earache

   (c) comes home with a note from school saying he's been exposed to scarlet fever, strep throat, or chicken pox

Now part 2:

· ·

I take myself to the doctor when I have:

   (a) broken my leg

   (b) thrown up for fourteen straight days and fear I may have to miss driving the morning carpool

   (c) Doctor? Do I even have a doctor?

Not to be a nag here, but I'll bet your kids get eye exams, dental checkups, orthotic shoes, and fruity cartoon-character vitamins. Meanwhile, you schlep along with a loose filling, last decade's glasses, dilapidated tennis shoes, and throat lozenges so gummy they have to be scraped off the wrapper with a knife.

Is this any way to treat a queen?

new word

for the week:

Logy (lō′ gē).
Sluggish; lethargic. As in, *"I'm sure I wouldn't feel so logy if I'd gotten more than five and a half hours of sleep last night."*

alternate

new word:

Salubrious
(sə-lōō′ brē-əs).
Conducive to health or well-being; wholesome. As in, *"Getting to bed by nine o'clock on weeknights would be a salubrious habit for our family to get into."*

So here's the deal. This year, let's resolve to take as good care of ourselves as we do of our families. Let's get that checkup. (All women should get a complete physical at age forty.) Let's schedule that mammogram. Let's make that Pap smear appointment. It's nobody's idea of a good time, but you make your kids get shots, don't you? No whining.

And make sure you're getting enough calcium. You need 1000–1200 mg per day.[1]

Now get cracking.

Osteoporosis Facts

2 ounces swiss cheese = 544 mg calcium
1 cup yogurt = 300–450 mg
2 ounces cheddar cheese = 408 mg
1 cup milk (whole, low-fat, or non-fat) = about 300 mg
1 cup ice cream = 176 mg
1 piece cheese pizza = 144 mg
1 ounce canned sardines = 100 mg
1 medium artichoke = 61 mg
1 tablespoon instant nonfat dry milk = 52 mg

Most common in women with small frames, osteoporosis is characterized by weak bones that are likely to fracture. Though the condition often doesn't appear until a woman is post-menopausal, it develops over a number of years, and typically shows no symptoms until it's too late.

Women in their middle years are advised to take steps to prevent it: engage in weight-bearing exercise (such as walking, running, or aerobics), reduce or eliminate smoking, and make sure you're getting enough calcium.

Deborah Shaw Lewis, in her book *Motherhood Stress*, says, "It seems so obvious I almost hesitate to say it. But experience . . . tells me many mothers need to hear it: *Taking care of yourself physically needs to be a high priority if you have any hope for surviving motherhood stress.*"[2]

A key area we often neglect is exercise. Before you clutch your heart and claim you have a certifiable allergic reaction to sweat, dating back to junior high and those awful green "pennies" you wore for PE (think kelly green prison jumpers with shorts, only uglier), stop for a second and rewind that mental movie. Exercise is not torture that you hate; it is movement that you love.

Think back to when you were a kid (before the dreaded "pennies"). What kinds of activities did you love? Floating to music and pretending to be a ballerina? Whacking a tennis ball against a garage wall? A tap dance class? Roller-skating at the local rink? Jumping rope? Incorporate that activity into your life again, as part of a three-times-a-week exercise routine. Start small. If twenty minutes riding your bike around the neighborhood is too much, start with five.

Sneaking in Some Calcium

If you don't like milk, here are a few ways to sneak extra calcium into your diet:

- ◊ Plop plain yogurt onto a baked potato.
- ◊ Add 2 T. instant nonfat dry milk to cold cereal before you add the milk.
- ◊ Add 1 T. dry milk to oatmeal, then add milk, brown sugar, and raisins, as desired.
- ◊ Look for foods with calcium added, such as orange juice and breakfast cereals.
- ◊ Take a daily supplement such as Viactiv, a chewy chocolate square that tastes like candy and gives you 500 mg of calcium.

Your kids need plenty of calcium, too, by the way—between 800 and 1300 mg a day, if they're four to eighteen years old—so keep that in mind as they beg for sodas and you steer them toward chocolate milk.[3]

I've discovered that a morning aerobics class makes me feel better the rest of the day. Some friends who love to walk circle the track at a local school in the afternoons, their little ones in strollers while their older kids play on nearby swings. Another woman spends early mornings reacquainting herself with her playful dolphin side by heading to a local pool for some "masters" swimming. At-home exercise videos work too; leg lifts using your baby as

PURPLE MOO

In blender, blend:

1/2 cup milk

1/2 cup frozen blueberries

1 T. sugar

Drink.

FUN FACTS

⥻

Kids between the ages of five and twelve need at least ten hours of sleep a night; teenagers need nine hours and fifteen minutes a night. So your kids might want to chart their sleep time too.

⥻

Napping for twenty-five to ninety minutes in the afternoon can revive you. But nap any longer, say the experts, and you may not be able to sleep at night.[4]

"weights" give you a good workout and the added bonus of gummy baby smiles.

The idea is not to beat ourselves up that we don't have perfectly toned, twelve-inch thighs. The idea is to take care of ourselves so we'll be refreshed enough to give to our families. Remember the Proverbs 31 woman? "She girds herself with strength and makes her arms strong" (v. 17). That's so she can lug the forty-pound bag of dog food home from the warehouse store.

Remember: we're not being frivolous when we schedule exercise into our week. We're being responsible.

As I drove my kids to school recently, weary from too little sleep for too many nights, a little voice came to me: "Listen to your body." It was the voice of my exercise teacher of Christmas past, the one whose class I took while pregnant with my first son. Over those prenatal months, she'd often exhorted us expectant mommies to pay attention to what our bodies were telling us, to have the good sense not to go any further when our bodies had had enough.

It's a wonderful theory. But just like "I'll never use television as a babysitter," in real life it's awfully hard to make it stick. My body was telling me it needed more than six hours of sleep. But how can you listen when you have two science-fair projects looming and an elaborate Styrofoam model of the temple of Solomon due on Friday? (Actually, they are neither my science-fair projects nor my temple, but as any mother knows, that is a mere technicality.)

I would like to listen to my body and take a nap. But I have paid for a twice-weekly exercise class that meets this morning and have promised to meet a friend afterward. I cannot listen to my body. I must ignore it as it sags into the bucket seat of the car, eyes scratchy from not enough rest.

Studies show that most Americans are chronically sleep

deprived, with the majority of the population sleeping sixty to ninety minutes less than we should.[5] In fact, since Thomas Edison invented the light bulb in 1879, our nightly sleep has dropped from an average of nine hours to seven.[6] It almost makes you want to go back to candles and whale oil lamps.

The tricky part is no one can tell you exactly how much sleep you need. The range is six to nine hours each night, with most adults falling in the seven-to-eight-and-a-half range. One sign you're probably not getting enough is if you fall asleep within five minutes of your head hitting the pillow.

To see how you're doing, chart your sleep time for a couple of weeks, keeping track of when you get to bed and how long it takes you to fall asleep. When you wake up, see how you feel. How are you doing after only six hours of sleep? How about after eight hours?

Once you figure out your sleep needs, count backward from when you have to get up and see when you should be getting to bed. Set that as a goal—at least once that science-fair project is turned in. ❤

"For Thou didst form my inward parts; Thou didst weave me in my mother's womb. I will give thanks to Thee, for I am fearfully and wonderfully made; Wonderful are Thy works, and my soul knows it very well." (Psalm 139:13–14)

prayer LORD, THANK YOU THAT YOUR WORKS ARE WONDERFUL, AND THAT INCLUDES ME! HELP ME REMEMBER TO TAKE BETTER CARE OF MYSELF, SO I'LL BE BETTER ABLE TO TAKE CARE OF THOSE YOU'VE ENTRUSTED ME WITH.

week 4

Delighting in the King: Building Healthy Spiritual Habits

For years, I had an old water-stained magazine clipping on my refrigerator. The clipping discouraged me from trying to muster up enthusiasm for God's Word on my own; instead, it exhorted me to pray that He would plant that desire in me and make it so strong I couldn't resist.

When I remember to ask, God has been remarkably faithful to answer that prayer. "Lord," I sometimes pray at night, "help me tomorrow to have no peace until I've spent time with You. Give me such a hunger for You and Your Word that I can't go on in my day until I've read Your Word." God is faithful. He longs for intimacy with us (see Isaiah 43:1; 49:15–16; 58:9; Matthew 23:37). He will answer that prayer.

Second Timothy 3:16–17 says, "All Scripture is inspired by God and profitable for teaching, for reproof, for correction, for training in righteousness; so that the man of God may be adequate, equipped for every good work." Without His Word, I won't be equipped for my work. I'll stumble along, following my own misguided priorities, my own treasure trove of wisdom (yikes!), and drawing on my own resources that are about as abundant as a dried-up sponge's excess water. God doesn't want me to live that way.

In contrast, "How blessed is the man who does not walk in the counsel of the wicked, nor stand in the path of sinners, nor sit in the seat of scoffers! But his delight is in the law of the Lord, and in His law he meditates day and night. He will be like a tree firmly planted by streams of water, which yields its fruit in its season, and its leaf does not wither; and in whatever he does, he prospers" (Psalm 1:1–3). That's the life God wants for me and for you: a life flowing with blessing and delight and fruit.

Spending time reading the Bible is one of the best things we can do for ourselves, even in the midst of the flurry of family life. We may think a busy day means we don't have time for God, but the truth of the matter is, as author Joanna Weaver puts it, "The rougher the day, the *more* time I need to spend with my Savior."[2] Even if it's only five minutes, or three. Those few minutes can reframe our entire perspective, and give us the nourishment we need to grow strong.

> ## Quotable
>
> *There are Christians who think they can live a Christian life without ever reading their Bibles, but it is impossible. Our memories do not retain and maintain what we need to know. We are built in such a way that we need refreshment and reminder—again and again.*[1]
>
> **Ray Stedman,**
> *Secrets of the Spirit*

After several years of attempting to read through the Bible in one year—usually abandoned in the first week of January, since it was apparent I was already hopelessly behind —it finally dawned on me that perhaps I was aiming too high. Given the two young superheroes who resided at our house and spent every waking moment searching for ever more creative ways to wangle a visit to the emergency room, I did not have a lot of time for reading. In fact, I did not have a lot of time for basic grooming. It was a good week when I could get my hair washed, and a biyearly visit to the dentist, I'm afraid, became the impossible dream. It stood to reason I was probably not going to get through the Bible in twelve months either.

Cut to six or seven years later, years filled with ear infections, the tooth fairy, chicken pox, and more Little

League practices than you could waggle a bat at. I had finally done it. Over the span of those years, with the help of devotional material from The Navigators (called *Daily Walk*³), I had read through the entire Bible, start to finish. My pace would impress absolutely no one; in fact, there were entire seasons when I made no progress at all. But little by little, step by step, I inched my way through the most important book there is.

That experience taught me that drawing near to God doesn't depend on big, flashy gestures like selling the house and moving to Africa. It depends instead on the small, daily choices we make Monday through Friday.

My favorite answer to "How do you find time to read the Bible?" came from a gal in Bible study class years ago. Her response was, "You have time to go to the bathroom, don't you?" She suggested keeping a Bible in the bathroom and reading a verse while you're there. This may not be the optimum plan for a lifetime of spiritual growth, but at some stages it may be the best you can do.

I believe it was Billy Graham's wife, Ruth, who, when her kids were young, kept a Bible open on the kitchen counter and read a couple of verses whenever she could. Index cards with Bible verses posted around the house work, too, either by the sink, on the washing machine, or on the dashboard of your car.

It may go against every go-for-the-gusto television commercial you've ever seen, but aiming small is sometimes the wisest shot you can take. And it's certainly better than aiming so high that your inner failure monitor is poised to pounce, delighted at the first sign of weakness. (That's why I appreciate so much my friend Kathie's attitude. "Got any New Year's resolutions?" I asked her one January. "No," came her cheery reply, "but I have some New Year's intentions!")

We can drink in God's Word, even when it's only a verse or two at a time. It may seem like an inconsequential choice. But if we repeat that choice over and over, day after day, our lives will be transformed.

THY WORDS WERE FOUND, AND I ATE THEM, AND THY WORDS BECAME TO ME A JOY AND THE DELIGHT OF MY HEART. —JEREMIAH 15:16 RSV

Meeting weekly with others for Bible study is a great way to motivate yourself to read the Bible. See if your church or one nearby offers a women's Bible study. Many provide child care as well.

If you can't find a Bible study group, consider starting your own. Christian bookstores carry Bible study guides on all sorts of topics (I especially liked *Homemaking* by Tjitske Lemstra and Baukje Doornenbal.[4]) A wonderful mail-order source is Joy of Living, (800) 999-2703. Prices are reasonable, and materials include in-depth questions and detailed background notes on the book of the Bible you're studying. Delivery is fast too; I've ordered lessons by phone on Monday, and by Wednesday the study was here.

It all started with a hat. My son wanted to wear his new baseball hat to school, the hat he would need all Little League season long.

"I'm not telling you that you can't," I said, "but if I were you I wouldn't. You might lose it or it might get wrecked. But that's just my advice." I chuckled. "And you know what they say about advice."

As if on cue, both my boys chorused in unison, "What?" By now we were in the car on the way to school—my son, incidentally, hatless.

"That it's worth what you pay for it. So since it was free . . ." I didn't go any further.

My younger son thought for a minute. "That's not necessarily true, Mom. You could pay three thousand dollars for advice and it might not be right."

I had to admit he had a point. And so began our discussion about wisdom.

We talked about the book of Proverbs and its admonition to listen to wise counsel from others. ("The way of a fool is right in his own eyes, but a wise man is he who listens to counsel" [Proverbs 12:15].) We talked about the importance of finding wise people, and where wisdom comes from. ("The fear of the Lord is the beginning of wisdom, and the knowledge of the Holy One is understanding" [Proverbs 9:10].)

We talked about life decisions being like airports. ("It's like we're the pilots but God's the control tower," noted son number one, recently returned from aviation camp. "He's really the One controlling what goes on; we're just following His orders." "Right," I answered. "And we can choose to ignore the control tower if we want, but there will be terrible consequences.")

Before long we were onto other topics—most notably, older son's displeasure at having to spend time at younger son's basketball practice that afternoon—but later, as I reflected on the morning, I was thankful that even a discussion about a hat could bring about valuable lessons from God's Word.

We need to look for opportunities to share God's wisdom with our children. Deuteronomy 6:6–7 tells us, "These words, which I am commanding you today, shall be on your heart. You shall teach them diligently to your sons and shall talk of them when you sit in your house and when you walk by the way and when you lie down and when you rise up."

And, don't forget, when you ride in the car. With or without a hat. ♛

"The law of the LORD is perfect, restoring the soul; the testimony of the LORD is sure, making wise the simple. The precepts of the LORD are right, rejoicing the heart; the commandment of the LORD is pure, enlightening the eyes. The fear of the LORD is clean, enduring forever; the judgments of the LORD are true; they are righteous altogether. They are more desirable than gold, yes, than much fine gold; sweeter also than honey and the drippings of the honeycomb. Moreover, by them Your servant is warned; in keeping them there is great reward." (Psalm 19:7–11)

prayer FATHER, THANK YOU FOR THE DELIGHTS OF YOUR WORD. THANK YOU THAT I DO NOT HAVE TO DRUM UP THE DESIRE TO READ IT ON MY OWN. IF I WILL ONLY ASK, YOU ARE FAITHFUL TO STIR IN ME THE DESIRE TO KNOW YOU BETTER. PROMPT ME, LORD, WHEN OPPORTUNITIES ARISE FOR ME TO SHARE YOUR WORD WITH MY CHILDREN, EVEN IN THE CAR.

CHOCOLATE BREAK! Stop!

CHOCOLATE S'MORE PIE

Speaking of chocolate . . .

There is a book out entitled *Why Women Need Chocolate*,[6] and frankly, the title tells me all I need to know. Apparently chocolate is the number one food women crave,[7] and there is a scientific reason for it. That's good enough for me.

To remind you of summer nights by the campfire, here's a rich and wonderful recipe from Sharon Tyler Herbst's book, *The Food Lover's Guide to Chocolate and Vanilla*.[8] It doesn't take long to make, but start early in the day, as it needs to refrigerate a few hours to firm up. And be careful as you're broiling the marshmallow topping. If you turn your back for twenty seconds, say, to argue with your children over whether a glass of V8® juice counts as a serving of vegetables, the pie can catch on fire. Trust me on this.

Whenever I've made this, I inevitably make another one before the week is up. Because it really is hard to stop at just one.

S'MORE PIE

Crust:
1 ½ cups graham cracker crumbs (half of a 13 ½ ounce box)
6 T. butter, melted

Filling:
1 ½ cups whipping cream (one pint gives you two cups)
2 cups chocolate chips
2 t. vanilla
1 ½ to 2 (7-ounce) jars marshmallow crème

To make crust, preheat oven to 350 degrees. Butter a nine-inch metal pie pan. (Don't use glass, as it may break when going from refrigerator to broiler.) In medium bowl, combine crust ingredients. Press into bottom and sides of pie pan using back of a large spoon. Bake ten minutes, then cool before filling.

To make filling, heat cream and chocolate in medium saucepan over medium-low heat, stirring often until chocolate is melted and mixture is smooth. (I use a wire whisk for thorough blending.) Stir vanilla into melted chocolate mixture, blending well. Pour into cooled crust; *refrigerate for at least four hours*. (If you don't, pie will be soupy.) If you have too much filling for your crust, pour the extra into a small bowl and chill; serve later as pudding.

After pie is cooled and firm, heat oven to broil, positioning rack four inches from broiling unit. Spoon dollops of marshmallow crème over surface of pie. Gently spread to within one inch of edge of crust; marshmallow spreads when heated. (You may want to place pan on a baking sheet in case any marshmallow overflows.)

Broil pie until marshmallow surface is browned to your liking. Watch closely; this takes somewhere in the vicinity of a minute. (Picture the campfire marshmallow smoking then bursting into flames and you get the idea.) Serve immediately or refrigerate until ready to serve.

Yum.

week 5

Celebrating Creativity in Small Snatches

With my penchant to bake first, think later, I don't often take the time to organize my surroundings before moving on to the more fun, more creative parts of my job. I may spend spare minutes enthusiastically paging through magazine clippings looking for a recipe for Festive Holiday Pull-Apart Buns. Meanwhile, the breakfast dishes bond to the sink, and I haven't given a flying thought to what I'll serve for dinner. (Would Festive Holiday Pull-Apart Buns be a good dinner?)

Perhaps instead I should take a closer look at my Creator and try to pattern my work habits after His. In Genesis 1, God imbued the entire creation process with order. What started as utter chaos, an earth that was formless and void, progressed to an earth that was divided into light and dark (v. 4); waters below heaven and waters above (v. 7); and a division of dry land and the seas (vv. 9–10). Once a basic order was in place, He created a multitude of plants (v. 12), fish (v. 21), birds (v. 21), and animals (v. 25). Throughout the entire process, God followed a logical, orderly progression. He didn't say, "Kazaam!" and zap the whole earth into being at once. He took it step by step, introducing each element one at a time, providing

new word

for the week:

Celerity (sə-lĕr'ə-tē).
Swiftness; speed. As in, *"If I exercise celerity in getting this kitchen clean, I may have time to bake a quick batch of cookies."*

alternate

new word:

Obviate (ŏb' vē āt').
To anticipate and prevent. As in, *"And if I wash the dishes as soon as I'm done baking, I will obviate the need for severe scrubbing later."*

the proper environment before adding plants, creatures, and people.

I can follow God's lead, dividing light from dark as I sort my laundry and choose which pile to leave on dry land and which to heave into the sea (er, the washing machine). I can clear off the kitchen table before making the food I hope to fill it with. I can bring about a touch of order in my environment before prematurely pursuing creativity.

But I still can't wait to make those pull-apart buns.

Quotable

Homemaking is the most creative job there is— we're always making something from nothing! It's cooking, decorating, gardening, arranging and planning—not to mention child care, which requires a Michelangelo of Creativity —all true arts.[1]

Susan Branch,
Girlfriends Forever

When I get frustrated that I'm so busy with carpooling and laundry that I don't have time for making quilts or baking wonderful desserts, I turn to Ecclesiastes 3, which reminds me that over the course of our lives there is time for many things. "There is an appointed time for everything. And there is a time for every event under heaven," says Ecclesiastes 3:1. There is "a time to plant and a time to uproot what is planted" (v. 2). "A time to tear down and a time to build up" (v. 3). "A time to throw stones and a time to gather stones" (v. 5).

At this point in my life, taking care of my family involves many mundane tasks and not nearly the time for creative pursuits that I'd like. "It's the season for carting kids around," agrees my husband.

The "excellent wife" described in Proverbs 31 (vv. 10–31), who is the archetype of feminine virtue, didn't achieve all that she did in one day or even one year. Her accomplishments, which include looking for wool and flax, working with her hands in delight, giving food to her household, considering a field and buying it, planting a vineyard, and extending her hands to the poor, represent the work of an entire lifetime. When I remember that there will be more time for creativity down the road, God willing, I can be content that for now my season includes more rising while it is still night (v. 15) and looking well to the ways of my household (v. 27) than it does creating with fine cloth (v. 24). Days are coming when I will have more free time. And when they come, I'm assured by a friend whose children are grown, I will miss these busy, happy days filled with children and bedlam and dirty jeans with muddy football stains.

As writer Valerie Schultz expresses in her essay "Reckless Abandon," "Jump into the life-medium of the moment, whether it's oatmeal or beach sand or Dr. Seuss' rhymes or the soup you're making for dinner." Schultz, a mother of four, says, "You will have no greater manifestation of the creative urge than your child. . . . Give your all, freely, wholeheartedly, and unconditionally. You will get it all back. Your child will grow up confident of your love. Your child will be so secure that his or her gradual but oh-so-quick independence will shock you. And again there will be time for essays or stories or pitchers or pots, all of them bursting with fresh insight and raw creative power."[2]

I may not have time right now to crochet a blanket, or even to make a nice meal on most days. But I do have time to crochet a hat if I bring it in the car and work on it in odd moments, parked and waiting for the kids to finish band or sports practice. I do have time to display a woven runner on my dining room table as I serve my family frozen pizza. I can manage small-scale creativity, as long as I am alert for opportunities.

The other night I leafed through *Beating the Winter Blues: The Complete Survival Handbook for Moms*, by Claudia Arp.[4] In the index, Arp lists "super easy activities . . . great when you are exhausted and are willing to invest ten minutes or less to have your child busy for twenty minutes or more!" My goal wasn't so much to keep my children busy but to take a few minutes to do something fun with them.

I decided on Arp's suggestion of a treasure hunt. I hid twenty coins in our living room area and told the boys they could keep whatever they found. I gave "Ooh, you're getting warmer" clues, and we enjoyed some fun minutes together on a drizzly Saturday afternoon. (My son had been sick for three days; we needed some fun.) The boys were thrilled, and even my husband joined in the merriment.

I want to be creative in my home and with my family, even if my time is limited.

A few more ideas:

◇ Grab a sketch pad and some pencils or pastels, and retire to a spot in your home you think is especially beautiful (if nothing inspires, sit by a window and scan for an outdoor patch of beauty). Pick one small detail and spend a few minutes drawing it. Recruit any willing family members to draw with you. Color your picture, if you have time, and maybe add to it another day.

◇ You probably have scads of pictures of the family cutting down the Christmas tree but none of the everyday, card-playing evenings. Pull out your camera and chronicle the ordinary, peanut-butter-and-jelly moments of your family's life. "A day in the life of . . ." might make a fun couple of pages in the photo album. Start by chronicling the morning's activities, and proceed throughout the day, from "how I spend my free time" to dinnertime and bedtime routines. You could make a page for each member of the family. Don't forget one for yourself too—a shot of the inside of the van or laundry room may someday bring back vivid memories.

◇ If you have any half-done Christmas projects you didn't quite finish, pull one of them out and get going on the next step. Let the February weather work to your advantage as you snuggle up to the fire and make progress.

According to *Prevention* magazine, needlework can be a real stress reliever. Its repetitive nature breaks your conscious train of thought, decreases blood pressure and heart rate, slows breathing, and provides feelings of calm. The magazine suggests you "write yourself a daily 'needlework prescription,'" and practice your craft at least twenty minutes a day.[6] ♣

"He has made everything beautiful in its time. He has also set eternity in the hearts of men; yet they cannot fathom what God has done from beginning to end. I know that there is nothing better for men than to be happy and do good while they live. That everyone may eat and drink, and find satisfaction in all his toil—this is the gift of God." (Ecclesiastes 3:11–13 NIV)

prayer DEAR LORD, THANK YOU SO MUCH FOR MY CHILDREN AND MY HUSBAND. THANK YOU FOR DIRTY BLUE JEANS AND SPILLED CEREAL AND THE PEOPLE I LOVE WHO ARE CONNECTED WITH THEM. HELP ME TO APPRECIATE THIS SPECIAL SEASON OF MY LIFE AND LOOK FOR SMALL OPPORTUNITIES TO BE CREATIVE IN THE MIDDLE OF THE CRAZINESS.

week 6

Valentine's Day

new word

for the week:

Beneficence

(bə-něf′ə-səns).

The quality of charity or kindness. As in, *"This Valentine's week is the perfect opportunity to show beneficence to my family."*

alternate

new word:

Factitious (făk-tĭsh′ əs).

Lacking authenticity or genuineness. As in, *"But if my beneficence is factitious, my family will figure out quickly that I am a fraud."*

One year, our women's Bible study group seized upon the idea of acting as our husbands' "secret pals." In the weeks leading up to Valentine's Day, we were to shower our men with sweet little notes, surprise gifts, encouraging words—anything we could think of to brighten their days. February 14 was to be the grand unveiling, where we'd reveal that we had been the source of all those beneficent deeds.

Fun idea, right?

Truth is, it was awful. During all those weeks of trying to be way more thoughtful than I really am, my brain, I'm embarrassed to admit, decided to keep score. Though I wouldn't have put it in such crass terms, on some level I was convinced that my kind acts were going to get me something. Surely after so much goodness, my generosity would be reciprocated! I could hardly wait.

What I remember most about that Valentine's Day was not the card or the gift my husband did ultimately give me (fortunately for both of us, as he'd had no inkling of my good-deed project or my inflated expectations). What I remember most is the eventual sure and sinking knowledge that I had completely missed the point. I should have given to my husband freely, with the sole motivation of bringing him joy. I should never have allowed the thought of being repaid to enter my kitchen. Love, after all, "does not seek its own" (1 Corinthians 13:5).

The moral is one I hope I never forget: don't give a gift expecting to get something in return. If I'm going to give, I need to do it with no expectations attached. And if I *must* have a gift, I'd better buy it for myself!

Here are a few ideas for surprising your family this Valentine's Day:

- Sneak into their rooms in the dark of night and leave a bag of treats by their beds.
- Tint the breakfast oatmeal pink. Throw in a few red cinnamon candies.
- Tuck a surprise valentine into a cereal box or ice cream carton. Reclose with stealth.
- Tie a red balloon to each person's kitchen chair.
- Write a greeting to your hubby on the coffee filter.
- Make an all-red dinner: spaghetti or pizza, strawberries, jellied cranberry sauce (canned) that's sliced and cut into heart shapes, berry yogurt, fruit punch.
- Secretly turn on the tape recorder during dinner; play it back for everyone later. Consider sending the tape to a faraway grandma.
- Make heart-shaped muffins or cupcakes by placing a cupcake paper into each compartment of a muffin tin, then popping a marble in between the tin and the paper. Fill with batter and bake.[2]
- Page through your wedding album or watch your wedding video with your husband.
- Listen with your husband to "your" song.
- Give your husband a massage as he watches TV. Make sure he has custody of the remote.

Quotable

When Mother Teresa received her Nobel Prize, she was asked, "What can we do to help promote world peace?" "Go home and love your family" was her answer.[1]

Bruce Larson,
My Creator, My Friend

For my husband's valentine gift one year, I asked my boys, then preschoolers, some leading questions about love. "Why do Mommy and Daddy love each other?" "Because you think each other looks handsome," came the earnest reply.

Once I had my responses, I sat the boys one at a time on a chair beside a blank wall, where I had taped a large sheet of poster board. With a reading lamp shining on the side of their bright cherub faces, a perfect shadowed profile appeared; it was easy to trace their profiles, facing each other, onto the board.

Later, I filled in the silhouettes with the questions I'd asked them and their answers. The poster made a wonderful Valentine's Day gift for my husband, and the memory of it still makes us smile as each year Mark and I remind one another that no matter what the rest of the world may think, we do indeed still think each other looks handsome.

Valentine's Day is a perfect low-key holiday to toast not only your immediate family but also others who might need a lift: young adults who are away at college, a friend who's gone

Some quotes about love:

"One of the deep secrets of life is that all that is really worth the doing is what we do for others." —LEWIS CARROLL

"Perfect love sometimes does not come till the first grandchild." —WELSH PROVERB

"Many waters cannot quench love, neither can the floods drown it." —SONG OF SOLOMON 8:7 [KJV]

"Love is what you've been through with somebody." —JAMES THURBER

"Like everything which is not the involuntary result of fleeting emotion, but the creation of time and will, any marriage, happy or unhappy, is infinitely more interesting and significant than any romance, however passionate." —W. H. AUDEN

"An archaeologist is the best husband any woman can have— the older she gets the more he is interested in her." —AGATHA CHRISTIE

"The worst reconciliation is better than the best divorce." —CERVANTES

"Women like silent men. They think they're listening." —MARCEL ACHARD[3]

GIANT POPCORN HEARTS

Giant popcorn hearts make great Valentine's Day gifts for teachers, neighbors, or friends. This recipe makes about five large hearts that taste like popcorn balls, or twenty small hearts, perfect for classroom treats.

Lightly grease a large roasting pan (the kind you cook your Thanksgiving turkey in).

Make **about 20 cups popped popcorn**. (It took me about 6 bags of microwave popcorn to get enough; if you have a hot-air popcorn popper, pop about ¾ cup of kernels.)

Spread popped corn in roasting pan and place in a 200-degree oven. Tear off a large piece of wax paper and set aside. In heavy two-quart saucepan, combine:

1 cup sugar	**2 T. water**
1 cup light corn syrup	**½ t. salt**
1 T. white vinegar	

Cook over medium-high heat, stirring often, until mixture reaches 230 degrees on a candy thermometer (about five minutes). Stir in **¼ cup butter.**

Keep cooking until mixture reaches 260 degrees or soft crack stage.
Add **1 ½ cups dry-roasted peanuts** (optional).

Then return temperature to 260 degrees. Remove from heat and blend in:

1 t. vanilla
½ t. baking soda

Immediately pour over popped corn and stir with a wooden spoon until popcorn is evenly coated. Generously grease hands with butter and, working as quickly as possible, shape mixture into a heart; turn onto wax paper. Repeat until all popcorn has been used. If the mixture hardens before it's shaped, you can set it in warm oven until mixture holds its shape when pressed together.

Cool hearts thoroughly; wrap in clear plastic wrap.[4]

through a particularly tough year, grandparents, singles, widows or widowers from church. If you're crafty, buy heart-shaped stickers and candies and make some valentines of your own. Cut pictures of your kids into heart shapes and send them on. Trace the kids' handprints or footprints and include them in the greeting.

If thoughts of doilies and hot-glue guns make you break out in a rash, however, let the stationery companies do the hard part and simply purchase an inexpensive box of already-made valentines to send off. Dig out your sealing wax, if you have any, to give your greetings a special touch.

 For enduring all the family's winter colds and science-fair projects, you deserve a valentine yourself. Repeat after me:

❋ *I am doing an important job by loving and serving my family.*
❋ *I am demonstrating to my family what love is.*
❋ *The service I am providing my family is priceless.*
❋ *I am helping my family members know they are precious and loved.*

Taking care of our families can be exhausting work (I don't have to tell you that). But I believe God will bless our efforts in ways we can't even imagine. By devoting our energies to our families, we are giving them a gift of love and security beyond measure.

C. S. Lewis once said, "A housewife's work . . . is surely in reality the most important work in the world. What do ships, railways, mines, cars, government, etc. exist for except that people may be fed, warmed, and safe in their own homes? . . . We wage war in order to have peace, we work in order to have leisure, we produce food in order to eat it. So your job is the one for which all others exist."[6]

On his *Sowin' Love* CD, country artist Paul Overstreet sings a beautiful song that celebrates the homemaker. Called "Homemaker," the song, written by Paul Overstreet and Dan Tyler, commends the woman whose heart's desire is to stay home, raise a family, and make her house a home. As Overstreet himself says in his book *Forever and Ever Amen*, "One of the hardest jobs on the face of this planet is being a homemaker, and we all should respect anyone who chooses that as an occupation and life's calling. After staying home and taking care of our kids by myself a few times, I was whipped, worn-out, 'stick a fork in me' done! It is no job for wimps!!"[7]

Give yourself a valentine today and get a copy of *Sowin' Love* (your local library may have it). And happy Valentine's Day!

THE TRUTH ABOUT LOVE: "WE KNOW LOVE BY THIS, THAT HE LAID DOWN HIS LIFE FOR US" *(1 John 3:16)*. ♥

"Love is patient, love is kind and is not jealous; love does not brag and is not arrogant, does not act unbecomingly; it does not seek its own, is not provoked, does not take into account a wrong suffered, does not rejoice in unrighteousness, but rejoices with the truth; bears all things, believes all things, hopes all things, endures all things." (1 Corinthians 13:4–7)

prayer LORD, THANK YOU FOR GIVING ME MY FAMILY. PLEASE WORK IN ME TODAY AS I TRY TO SHOW THEM LOVE. HELP ME NOT TO EXPECT ANYTHING BACK BUT TO SIMPLY LOVE BECAUSE YOU LOVED ME FIRST.

week 7

new word

for the week:

Pertinacious

(pûr′ tə-nā′ shəs).
Stubbornly or perversely persistent.
As in, *"Kids, I wish you wouldn't be
so pertinacious in leaving your trash
in the car."*

alternate

new word:

Intractable

(ĭn-trăk′ tə-bəl).
Difficult to manage. As in, *"I want
to make sure my schedule doesn't
become so intractable that I don't
have time to occasionally make
some cookies."*

It's OK to Say No: Managing Our Time as Homemakers

After reading all kinds of books on time management, I have decided it's all just a lot of hooey about nothing.

Just kidding.

What I have really decided is we all want more time than we have, and there are a couple of ways for us to cope with the realization it ain't gonna happen:

1. Schedule yourself ever more stringently, cutting people off midsentence because their three minutes are up.
2. Accept the fact that you can't do everything.

Some time management tools are helpful, such as calendars, planners, and charts. Mostly what helps, though, is to think about your life and what's important to you. In other words, try to shape your time to fit your goals, instead of allowing your life to fill up with someone else's priorities. The organizer of the book club wants you to commit to Monday mornings. The PTA president thinks you ought to give up Thursday nights. But what do you think? Do those activities really reflect your goals?

Ruth Bell Graham, in her book *Legacy of a Pack Rat*, notes, "God does not promise strength for uncommanded work." Deciding her own schedule was overcommitted, Graham cut back on writing projects and board and committee memberships in order to better put God first in her life and then to "be liberated to be a wife, a homemaker, a mother, and a grandmother."[1]

Graham's example is a good one. As we figure out God's priorities for us, we can pare down our schedules to meet those priorities. The process may be painful—the book club and PTA might be fun—but if we are too busy to do our primary jobs well, those of child of God, wife, and mother, then we are too busy.

Often our efforts at time management result in packing our schedules ever more tightly so we can squeeze in even more activities.

The real key to managing our time, however, might be exactly the opposite: attempting fewer activities so we can better focus on those that matter. It's what Anne Ortlund, in her classic book *Disciplines of the Beautiful Woman*, calls "eliminate and concentrate." The idea is to eliminate from our lives those activities that don't bring us in the direction God is leading. Then we'll have more time to concentrate on what He does want us to do.

Ortlund cites a trip she once took on a ship in the Mediterranean. "The captain long before had laid out the itinerary. He knew where we were to go each day of the trip, and how to get there. . . . Then, along the way, all kinds of contrary winds and cross currents were trying to take us off-course. The captain had to be continually refocusing, redirecting, recentering us on our destination. Otherwise we wouldn't have ended up in the right place at all.

"This is what life-planning is all about," she continues. "We need to decide where we suspect he'd like us to go. . . .

> ## Quotable
>
> *Time is the coin of your life. It is the only coin you have, and only you can determine how it will be spent. Be careful lest you let other people spend it for you.*[2]
>
> **Carl Sandburg**

> ## Quotable
>
> *Not everything that cries the loudest is the most urgent thing.*[3]
>
> **Gordon MacDonald,**
> *Ordering Your Private World*

Quotable

Beware the tyranny of the telephone! From time to time an urgent call brings you a request for which you have no budgeted hours. The pleading voice assures you of the importance of this impending task and how well-qualified you are to take it on. It may be difficult to decline, especially if it seems that the activity can be squeezed in. But no matter how clear the calendar looks, tell the person that you want to think it over. Surprisingly, the engagement often appears less important after the pleading voice has become silent. If you withstand the urgency of the moment, you can weigh the cost and discern whether the task is God's will for you. . . .

cont. ⇒

Then we need to say 'no,' 'no,' 'no,' daily all the rest of our lives to everything that would get us off-course."[4]

It's not easy to say no. Often we're turning down good opportunities. But if we remember that we're declining the good in order to accept the best, we will be able to stay on course, reaching the destination God has mapped out especially for us.

Recently, I accepted an invitation to a girls' night out that I really had no business going to. My week was already packed with extra commitments. Though the get-together sounded fun, that didn't change the fact that I really didn't have time for it.

A week later, as I was putting my house back in order, I realized once again that every time I say yes to something, I'm saying no to something else. I can't add an activity into my schedule without subtracting another activity. My hasty yes (added to a few other "yeses" that week) had cost me, and in the days that followed I had so much catching up to do on dishes, laundry, and errands that I had no time for some important projects I felt God wanted me to do. I'd given away my time to something good, but it wasn't God's best.

I'd been blown off course. By a simple Bunco game.

Have you ever heard the phrase, "the urgent versus the important"? It's about our ability to distinguish between something that demands our immediate attention (a ringing phone, for example) versus something that's of true value (Bible study).

"Some things that are urgent are also important," say Dorothy Lehmkuhl and Dolores Cotter Lamping in their book *Organizing for the Creative Person*, "—a fire alarm or a summons to the boss's office. But others are not. That ringing telephone may just be a salesperson or a friend calling to gossip—something you can deal with later, or not at all."[5]

Take a look at these categories:

Urgent & **Important**	**Urgent &** **Not Important**
Not Urgent & **Important**	**Not Urgent &** **Not Important**

In the first box go activities that are both urgent and important. These are easy to figure out: a voice on the other end of the phone tells us our child is sick and needs to be picked up from school. The baby is crying and needs to be comforted.

Another category that's self-evident is the last box, where we put those activities that are not urgent and not important: sorting through the box of ski clothes, for example, or mending pants that already sport patches on patches. We can let these things slide forever, really, and never face dire consequences. So what if the ski clothes never get sorted? Unless we're going skiing next week, it likely doesn't matter.

What tend to stump us most are the activities that fall into the other two boxes. Those activities that are urgent but not important tempt us by their mere immediacy. We've been invited to a luncheon or committee meeting next Wednesday, for example; the need to give an answer and the built-in deadline make it urgent. But is the activity really important to us? That's a distinction we may need to ponder for a while. In this category can fall telephone calls, mail, some errands, some housework.

Not urgent but important activities include long-term goals—getting a college degree, for example, or putting together a family photo album—as well as our relationships with God, family, and friends. Most of these carry no built-in deadlines or immediately visible consequence for neglecting them; who's going to complain if it's been months since we played a board game with our kids? These activities may not be urgent, but according to our own values, they are important; we need to make time for them.

Luke 10:39–42 is the perfect illustration of a woman who confused the urgent with the important. A woman named Martha welcomed the traveling Jesus into her home. "And she had a sister called Mary, who moreover was listening to the Lord's word, seated at His feet. But Martha was distracted with all her preparations; and she came up to Him, and said, 'Lord, do You not care that my sister has left me to do all the serving alone? Then tell her to help me.' But the Lord answered and said to her, 'Martha, Martha, you are worried and bothered about so many things; but only a few things are necessary, really only one, for Mary has chosen the good part, which shall not be taken away from her.'"

Most of us can identify with Martha. We feel frantic at deadlines such as mealtimes or holidays or company coming but may neglect to examine whether we're focusing on what's really important.

Jesus' response to Martha shows that He viewed spending time with Him as far more important than worrying about how dinner was to be served. Martha needed to keep the urgent—the upcoming meal—from getting in the way of the important—spending time with Christ. It's a good lesson to remember. ♛

"Therefore be careful how you walk, not as unwise men but as wise, making the most of your time, because the days are evil. So then do not be foolish, but understand what the will of the Lord is." (Ephesians 5:15–17)

prayer LORD, PLEASE GIVE ME DISCERNMENT WITH MY TIME. HELP ME TO SEE PAST THE URGENT TO WHAT'S REALLY IMPORTANT. HELP ME TO SLOW DOWN LONG ENOUGH TO ASK YOU FOR GUIDANCE. SHOW ME HOW YOU WANT ME TO WALK, AND HELP ME TO FOLLOW WHERE YOU LEAD.

week 8

Pray First, Act Later

Scripture tells us that after a busy time of serving those around Him, Jesus departed and retreated to a "lonely place" (Mark 1:35 RSV). He went there so He could be alone with His Father and pray.

Departing to a "lonely place" is just what my soul craves after a hectic week of serving my family. When I spend too many days running from sports awards ceremonies to band concerts to school open houses to orthodontist appointments, I feel my resources depleting. I airmail a quick, desperate request: "Please, Lord, help me get through these next weeks." Though not by choice, they are overflowing with commitments.

What a relief it is to steal an hour or two of retreat to a lonely place while the rest of the family is occupied. I drink in time with my Father the way a dog laps water after a long run. I am like a teakettle that has boiled for too long, empty of peace, joy, and patience until I take time to be refilled by my Father.

It's when I'm busiest that I most need to take the time to be with God and to pray. Circumstances may demand my "lonely place" be an unorthodox location (the car, for example, while waiting for my kids in parking lots around

new word
for the week:

Huzza (hə-zä').
A shout of encouragement or triumph; a cheer. As in, *"Huzza that God wants us to pray to Him! Huzza that He delights in giving us what we need!"*

alternate
new word:

Piffle (pĭf' əl).
Foolish or futile talk or ideas; non-sense. As in, *"The idea that I'm too busy to pray is sheer piffle."*

Quotable

*I used to think that if one were an "owl," talking with God in the morning wasn't necessary. But one day, as I was reading Psalm 5, I saw something for the first time. I said to Chris, "Hey, it's really scriptural to talk to God first thing in the morning." In all the times I had read that psalm, it had never really hit me before. "Give ear to my words, O Lord, consider my meditation. Hearken unto the voice of my cry, my King, and my God; for unto Thee will I pray. My voice shalt Thou hear in the morning, O L*ORD*; in the morning will I direct my prayer unto Thee, and will look up" (Psalm 5:1–3 K*JV*).*

cont. ⇒

town). But no matter how I manage it, I desperately need that time to communicate with Him.

When we pray in the middle of our busyness, God can give us direction for how to best spend our energies. Our own plans might look good to us, but they may not match what God has in mind. Read what happened in Mark 1:32–38:

> When evening came, after the sun had set, they began bringing to Him all who were ill and those who were demon-possessed. And the whole city had gathered at the door. And He healed many who were ill with various diseases, and cast out many demons; and He was not permitting the demons to speak, because they knew who He was. In the early morning, while it was still dark, Jesus got up, left the house, and went away to a secluded place, and was praying there. Simon and his companions searched for Him; they found Him, and said to Him, "Everyone is looking for You." He said to them, "Let us go somewhere else to the towns nearby, so that I may preach there also; for that is what I came for."

If Jesus had not gone to His Father that morning and asked for direction, He could easily have stayed in Capernaum. After all, when your friends say, "Everyone is looking for You" (note the urgency), the natural response would be to do what they want and to stay. But God's plan was different. Jesus was to pick up and head for the next town. If He hadn't asked His Father for guidance, He'd never have known.

How often I make my daily plans without talking to God first. I have an agenda in mind, and if unexpected circumstances get in the way I'm peeved. But if I haven't gone to my Father and asked for His direction in the first place, I have no right to be irritated. He has a plan, and it's my job to follow. Even if He takes me where I didn't expect to go.

"I don't know what's wrong," I said to my husband recently as I worked in the kitchen. "I'm feeling kind of blue."

"That's because you're mourning," he answered.

He's right. Friends and family have experienced more than their share of troubles lately, and it takes its toll.

My husband has been studying the Beatitudes in his Bible study group, the "blessed are the . . ."'s found in Matthew 5:3–11. "Blessed are those who mourn, for they shall be comforted," says Jesus in Matthew 5:4. I need to recognize my mourning. I need to see my sadness for what it is: a valid, hurting response to pain experienced by people I love. And I need to bring my mourning to the God of comfort, so He can wrap His loving arms around me as I turn to Him in prayer.

First Thessalonians 5:17 tells us to "pray without ceasing." As homemakers, we can pray as we do our never-ceasing housework. We can pray as we do our dishes and fold our laundry, for an atmosphere of peace in our homes and in the homes of others. For every sock we turn right side out, we can pray for its owner. As we drive on our rounds of errands we can pray for our marriages, that God would make them strong and help us to be the wives He wants us to be. As James 5:13 says, "Is any one of you in trouble? He should pray" (NIV).

It is an amazing privilege to have unlimited access to the Creator of the universe, to be able to talk to our Father in heaven throughout our day whenever a person or situation enters our minds. As Ray C. Stedman says in *Jesus Teaches on Prayer*, "Prayer . . . is simply the expression of human need to an eager Father—the cry of a beloved child to a Father who is ready to pour out all that he has to give."[2]

When I think of prayer, I usually think of coming to God with requests. "There's this thing I want, Lord. Can You give it to me? I'm not too happy about this circumstance, Lord. Can You change it for me?"

When I look at the Lord's Prayer and how Jesus instructed His followers to pray, I see a different focus. He says almost nothing about earthly concerns. Most of His prayer is about God, about honoring Him and living according to His plan. Matthew 6:9–13 (KJV) says, "After this manner therefore pray ye: Our Father which art in heaven, hallowed be thy name. Thy kingdom come. Thy will be done in earth, as it is in heaven. Give us this day our daily bread. And forgive us our debts, as we forgive our debtors. And lead us not into temptation, but deliver us from evil: For thine is the kingdom, and the power, and the glory, for ever. Amen" (see also Luke 11:1–4).

I need to ask myself, when I pray, do I praise God? ("Hallowed be thy name.") When I pray, do I ask for His plan to prevail? ("Thy kingdom come, thy will be done.") When I pray, do I ask that the needs of the day be met, just this day, or am I worrying already about tomorrow? ("Give us this day our daily bread.") Do I ask for forgiveness for the wrongs I've committed and acknowledge that I, too, need to forgive others? ("Forgive us our debts, as we forgive our debtors.") Do I ask for protection from sin? ("Deliver us from evil.") When I pray, do I give God the honor that is due Him? ("For thine is the kingdom, and the power, and the glory, for ever.")

The God of the universe wants us to come to Him with our concerns. "You do not have because you do not ask," says James 4:2. He wants us to share with Him our troubles and pain.

But He doesn't want it to end there. Making requests should be just one part of what I talk to my Father about. After all, how would I like it if the only words I heard from my children were requests for things they wanted?

Quotable

You need not cry very loud; He is nearer to us than we are aware of.[3]

Brother Lawrence,
The Practice of the Presence of God

Prayer ideas:

. . . .

⬦ A friend who teaches at a Catholic school tells me that before the staff prays together each morning, their leader asks them to observe a few moments of silence to prepare themselves for prayer. What a good idea, to settle into an awareness of God's presence before launching into words.

⬦ When life's burdens squish you with heaviness and you can't find the words to express your feelings, try listening to music as a way to come into God's presence. (A great place to start is composer John Rutter's breathtaking work "Gloria," which repeatedly brought audience members to tears when my son's marching band performed it.[4])

⬦ In *What Happens When Women Pray*, author Evelyn Christenson (with Viola Blake) suggests writing out prayers and dating them so you can look back later and see that God's timing is perfect.[5] I have done this only sporadically over the years but have been incredibly encouraged to stumble across old prayer requests later and see how many of them God has answered. It's a wonderful reminder of His faithfulness.

⬦ Gladys Hunt, in *Honey for a Woman's Heart*, advises, "If you have trouble praising God or being thankful, get a hymnbook and keep it handy. It's helpful to read thoughts of praise and faith that have come out of another person's spiritual walk. . . . Singing the words is best of all!"[6]

A BEAUTIFUL PRAYER OF PRAISE FROM KING DAVID IS FOUND IN 1 CHRONICLES 29:10–13:

So David blessed the LORD in the sight of all the assembly; and David said, "Blessed are You, O LORD God of Israel our father, forever and ever. Yours, O LORD, is the greatness and the power and the glory and the victory and the majesty, indeed everything that is in the heavens and the earth; Yours is the dominion, O

LORD, and You exalt Yourself as head over all. Both riches and honor come from You, and You rule over all, and in Your hand is power and might; and it lies in Your hand to make great and to strengthen everyone. Now therefore, our God, we thank You, and praise Your glorious name."

If you want to make Easter celebrations more of a priority in your home this year, check your calendar and note when Easter falls. Count backward by three weeks and note that date on your calendar too. Read through any books or magazines you may have with Easter ideas (start with weeks 13 and 14), and think about which activities you may want to try. Pencil them in on your calendar. Because if you wait until the last minute you might have time to throw a few eggs into dye, but you won't have time to fully appreciate all that Easter means. ♛

"Therefore let us draw near with confidence to the throne of grace, so that we may receive mercy and find grace to help in time of need." (Hebrews 4:16)

prayer THANK YOU, LORD, THAT YOU WHO MAKES THE SUN TO RISE AND THE SUN TO SET EACH DAY, WHO MAKES SPRING AND SUMMER AND AUTUMN AND WINTER, WHO PROVIDES ALL I NEED, ARE THE PERFECT PICTURE OF FAITHFULNESS. THANK YOU THAT I CAN BE TRANSPARENT BEFORE YOU; I CAN ACKNOWLEDGE WHEN I'M HURTING AND WHEN I NEED HELP, AND YOU ARE SO WILLING TO MEET THOSE NEEDS. HELP ME TO REMEMBER AS I PRAY JUST WHO IT IS I'M TALKING TO.

CHOCOLATE BREAK! stop!

CHOCOLATE OATMEAL COOKIES

Here's a great chocolate recipe that's quick, for those times when you need choco-late and you need it now. It's a no-bake cookie. You simply boil the first few ingredi-ents, add oatmeal and vanilla, then drop spoonfuls onto wax paper until the cookies harden. Unfortunately, the wax paper leaves evidence of how many cookies used to be there and are there no longer. (Burp! Pardon me.) So when the kids get home from school and start counting, you may be in trouble. But you can always transfer the cookies to a plate and hide the evidence.

These make great lunchbox cookies, too, on the chance they last that long. Now go. Cook.

MY GRANDMOTHER'S CHOCOLATE OATMEAL COOKIES

Put in large pan:
   2 cups sugar
   ½ stick butter (¼ cup)
   4 T. cocoa
   ½ cup milk

Bring to a boil, stirring constantly. Boil at hard boil 1 ½ minutes.
Remove from heat.

   Add **2 ½ cups quick oats** and **1 t. vanilla**.
   Mix well and drop onto wax paper.
   That's it. I thank you, and Mimi thanks you.

(Note: occasionally these don't "set," and we end up scooping them off the wax paper with a spoon. I'm not sure why this happens; it may have to do with the hu-midity. But if it happens to you, don't give up; try them another day. These are the second-most-requested cookies in our house, next to chocolate chip.)

week 9

new word
for the week:

Ineluctable
(ĭn′ ĭ-lŭk′ tə-bəl).

Not to be avoided or overcome; inevitable. As in, *"With Little League season upon us, and two teams, two practice schedules, two sets of snack shack duties, and two mounds of dirty baseball pants and wadded-up blue socks, I am faced with the **ineluctable** fact that we will not be eating the finest homemade cuisine these next few months."*

alternate
new word:

Putative (pyoo′ tə-tiv).
Generally regarded as such; supposed. As in, *"From a Little Leaguer's point of view, dinner from a fast-food restaurant is **putatively** far superior to any onion-harboring casserole that Mom might concoct."*

When There's No Way Around the Busyness

With all the duties of homemaking, sometimes it feels like I'm a circus performer who spins a plate at the top of a tall skinny pole, then runs and adds another plate to another pole, then another, eventually barreling from the first pole to the last, desperate to keep the plates from crashing to the floor. I sprint from duty to duty, often leaving one half-done as I rush onto the next.

Today, as I stewed over the dirty laundry I didn't get to and the carpet that begs to be vacuumed, I stopped myself. Just what had I done during the day?

When I looked back, I realized it had been a good, productive day. I had spent time reading my Bible and praying. I had visited with a friend from across the country who was briefly in town. I had completely unpacked from a recent weekend away (a job I usually leave half done for days). I'd sorted laundry, planned menus, put gas in the car, brought my son to Little League practice, bought groceries, took my son to get a book-report book, cleaned the kitchen, and hauled in a load of firewood so my husband wouldn't have to. My priorities had been right. There were no activities that gobbled more time than I can spare right now, no schedule that reflected someone else's priorities but not my own.

I have to conclude that there are times in life when, no matter how much we've pared down our schedules, nothing more can be cut. The children need to go to the eye doctor and the orthodontist and the math tutor. For now, life is simply bursting with necessary activity. It just is.

Next time you're tempted to grow discouraged at all the work still to be done, I hope you stop and reflect on all that you did get done. If you spoke encouraging words to a child, if you communicated with God, if you lent your husband a supportive ear and provided breakfast, lunch, and dinner, you have put in a good day's work.

No matter how much is still on your to-do list.

In her book *How to Have All the Time You Need Every Day*, author Pat King points out that as busy as Jesus was, in His life here on earth He never seemed rushed. "He was very tired at times. He was sorrowful at times, even discouraged, it appears, but He was never in a frantic hurry. For every person He healed, thousands never met Him and so remained unhealed. For every person He taught, thousands did not hear His teaching. Yet He did not hurry. We never hear Him say, 'There is not enough time for My work.' He had come into the world for one purpose, to save the world, but He did not take it upon Himself to be more or to do more than the Father asked."[1]

If we're following God's agenda, for our life and for our day, we may be very busy, but we should have peace as we go. We shouldn't feel pressed and frantic. I've noticed that the times I feel most rushed are when I have neglected to ask God for direction but simply start flinging myself in all directions.

When I do take the time to consult Him, life has a completely different flavor. There are days I feel I have His blessing not to answer the phone, to let the answering machine take the messages while I concentrate on more

Quotable

"Today you might be tired because someone was up all night with an earache. You might be looking at four loads of laundry and the dryer just broke and Sears can't come out until Thursday. . . . The phone is ringing and you wanted the answering machine to get it, but your son is bringing it to you proudly and it is on. Someone has a poopy diaper (at what point in our lives can we stop saying the word poopy?) . . . You need to go to the grocery store, but the baby's asleep, but by the time the baby wakes up, your husband will be home expecting dinner. Do you dare serve him fish sticks again?"[2]

Barbara Curtis
Lord, Please Meet Me in the Laundry Room

pressing matters. Some days I feel directed to be "productive," to get the house ready for company, to plan a child's birthday party, or simply to catch up on the dirty clothes pile. Other days I sense it's important to leave room in my schedule, to be there to talk on the phone or to make plans to meet a friend who needs a friend. The only way to know which kind of day it is is to take time at the start to ask.

I like what author Joanna Weaver says in her wonderful book *Having a Mary Heart in a Martha World*: "Ask God to reveal the next step. As you go through your day, keep asking the Lord, 'What is the one thing I need to do next?' Don't let the big picture overwhelm you. Just take the next step as he reveals it—wash one dish, make one phone call, put on your jogging clothes. Then take the next step . . . and the next."[3]

A common metaphor is that there are seasons to life, different phases in our lives when we focus on different things.

I maintain that not only does each life contain different seasons, but each twelve-month period contains different seasons, too, depending on our families' activities.

Right now I am in the frozen-food season.

Since most days during football, basketball, and baseball seasons I am on the road with my kids from 2 to 7 p.m., I am not home during prime dinner-making hours. It has taken me years to realize it doesn't have to be all or nothing, a fancy three-hour made-from-scratch gourmet dinner or eating at McDonald's. I have finally discovered . . . ta da! . . . the frozen-food aisle.

While I'd much prefer to make my own braised ribs with homemade barbecue sauce, I simply can't during sports seasons. I need to accept that I can't always live up to my own standards and recognize that some seasons are frozen-food seasons. There'll be time to do my kind of cooking again during summer or on an occasional free weekend. There'll be time for it again when my sons are no longer so heavily involved in after-school sports.

For now, for this time in my life and this time of the year, you'll find me meandering down the frozen-food aisle, trying not to feel guilty about buying something I know I could make myself. And will again, in some other season.

When you just can't face another McDinner, try:

◊ chicken salad from the deli;

◊ Chinese takeout;

◊ Subway sandwiches;

◊ already-roasted chicken from the grocery store;

◊ canned ravioli, a bag of salad, and ready-to-bake garlic bread.

Take a Quick Busyness Break

When you find yourself in the middle of "one of those weeks" (or months) and need to see your way clear to the next blank calendar square, take even two minutes to do something nice for yourself. While there may not be time for a long bubbly soak in the tub, you can still spritz on your favorite perfume. You may not have a spare hour to curl up with a great new library book, but you can light a scented candle as you sort through mail.

One of my favorite fast treats when I'm running on empty is to use the "satin hands pampering set" I bought from a friend who sells Mary Kay cosmetics. As I head for my bathroom and pull out the special plastic case, a delicious feeling of anticipation comes over me. I take off my rings, roll up my sleeves, and slather onto my hands the emollient cream, the scrub, the gentle cleanser, then the hand cream. It takes only a few minutes, but the difference in my frame of mind is dramatic. As I dry my hands afterward on a soft, fluffy towel and put my rings back on my finger, I hum. I smile. The world looks happier than before.

Even if you have only a minute, take care of yourself. You matter. You are worth pampering.

More quick pampering ideas:

. . . .

- ◇ Give yourself five minutes to enjoy a cup of tea or the glass of juice you didn't have time for at breakfast. Sit at the kitchen table and do nothing but enjoy your drink. (You can set the timer to make sure you get your full five minutes!)
- ◇ Find a classical or jazz CD and listen as you make dinner, fold laundry, or drive.
- ◇ Take deep breaths through your nose. Exhale.
- ◇ Hug someone. If no one's around, hug the dog. Or yourself.
- ◇ A friend with a bad back told me about this relaxing stretch: Lie on the floor on your back, scoot your bottom as close to the wall as you can, and put your legs straight up in the air, touching the wall. Let your arms rest however feels most comfortable, and relax there for a couple of minutes. ♛

"Then you will call, and the Lord will answer; You will cry, and He will say, 'Here I am.' . . . And if you give yourself to the hungry and satisfy the desire of the afflicted, then your light will rise in darkness and your gloom will become like midday. And the Lord will continually guide you, and satisfy your desire in scorched places, and give strength to your bones; and you will be like a watered garden, and like a spring of water whose waters do not fail." (Isaiah 58:9–11)

prayer THANK YOU, LORD, THAT YOU WATER ME IN THE DRY SEASONS OF LIFE. SHOW ME MY DAY'S ASSIGNMENT, AND STRENGTHEN ME AS I ATTEMPT TO DO IT. HELP ME TO FULLY APPRECIATE THIS BUSY TIME OF LIFE AND THE JOY THAT COMES FROM WATCHING MY CHILDREN PARTICIPATE IN THEIR ACTIVITIES.

week 10

Taking a Sabbath

The biggest danger I find in being extraordinarily busy is that God's voice is so quiet I am liable to miss hearing Him. He speaks to me in a steady whisper, always there but easily drowned out by the noise of the world. When I'm consumed by my calendar and list of to-dos, I'm not able to hear Him, to tune in to the real, unseen things that matter most.

Often, in the middle of an especially busy stretch, I think, *I just don't have time to read my Bible and pray right now. Maybe later this week.* Then I wind up directionless, marching off in total ignorance like a soldier heading east while his commander is leading the troops north.

When I'm too busy for God, I am almost certainly too busy for people. As I rush off to attend a meeting or drop my kids somewhere, my mind is on me, me, me, and getting to the next item on my list. I'm not alert to the needs of those around me. Sometimes I think a hurried state is more an attitude that's conveyed to others ("I'm too busy for you") than an actual number of available minutes. A gracious person never gives you the feeling you're keeping her from something more important. She takes that extra moment (and it really does take only a moment) to look you in the eyes, call you by name, and let you know she's glad to see you before she heads off to her next destination.

Jesus was a wonderful example of one who regularly stepped out of life's busyness to spend time apart with God (see Luke 4:42; 5:16). He encouraged His disciples to do the same. After a busy time of preaching and casting out demons (Mark 6:12–13), the disciples desperately needed rest. So Jesus directed them to change course. "And He said to them, 'Come away by yourselves to a secluded place and rest a while.' (For there were many people coming and going, and they did not even have time to eat.) They went away in the boat to a secluded place by themselves" (Mark 6:31–32).

Doesn't that sound like our lives as homemakers at times? Many people coming and going? Not even enough time to eat?

God knows that we can't go on in this state of busyness for too long. So He lovingly encourages us to come away and rest so He can restore and renew us, giving us the strength we need to carry on.

Taking an occasional break from our work is such an important concept that God commanded it. It's the fourth of the Ten Commandments: "Remember the sabbath day, to keep it holy. Six days you shall labor and do all your work, but the seventh day is a sabbath of the Lord your God; in it you shall not do any work, you or your son or your daughter, your male or your female servant or your cattle or your sojourner who stays with you. For in six days the LORD made the heavens and the earth, the sea and all that is in them, and rested on the seventh day; therefore the LORD blessed the sabbath day and made it holy" (Exodus 20: 8–11).

According to the *Holman Bible Dictionary*, the word *Sabbath* comes from the Hebrew word *Shabbat*, which means to cease or desist. "The primary meaning is that of cessation from all work."[1]

As homemakers, we may not be able to cease from "all work" every seven days, especially if we have young children who can't yet dress or feed themselves. But in this Scripture, God makes it clear that we still need a time of rest, that the world will not fall apart if we step aside for a short while and just . . . relax.

So how do we do this? How, right in the thick of family life and all of our home responsibilities, are we supposed to set aside time for rest?

Author Lauren F. Winner, in her article "In Today's Culture, What Does It Mean to Keep the Sabbath Holy?" notes that "honoring the Sabbath was easier in Puritan New England, where almost everyone took the Sabbath seriously. Shops weren't open on Sundays, businesses closed their doors, and everyone headed to church. Sabbaths are much more difficult in contemporary America. In fact, in a society that values busyness and productivity, observing the Sabbath is downright countercultural."[2]

One option is going on a weekend women's retreat, which many churches offer annually and where women can attend workshops or simply sleep. Mom's Morning Out is another, more regular way to get a break, if such a program is offered in your area.

You can lean on relatives or your husband to watch the kids occasionally so you can rest. And it goes without saying that if your kids are young enough to nap, you should nap too. You may also want to set a "quitting time" for yourself every evening, where you are off duty whether there are still dishes in the sink or not.

Once your kids are school-aged, it's much easier to take a break. In especially hectic stretches, when my calendar shows that even Saturdays and Sundays are booked solid with commitments such as kids' sports and band activities, I occasionally get the kids off to school on a weekday and then crawl back into bed and spend several hours talking to God then snoozing. I'll eat a leisurely lunch, spend much-needed time reading my Bible, and drive off to get the kids and begin the hectic afternoon with peace. I am rested. I've taken my Sabbath.

In Mark 2:27, Jesus says, "The Sabbath was made for man, and not man for the Sabbath." God has given us this day of rest and spiritual focus not as an obligation, but as a gift. Take the opportunities that come your way this week to rest. You need it, physically, spiritually, emotionally. Don't feel guilty. Your body wasn't designed to continue nonstop, seven days a week. Shalom.

> ## Quotable
>
> *We need to change our paradigm by giving more value to the sacredness of rest. If we begin by seeing it as a part of our design, part of our spiritual DNA, we will feel more permission to enter into it and cease our running.*[3]
>
> **Kim Thomas,**
> *Even God Rested*

"We do not rest because our work is done; we rest because God commanded it and created us to have a need for it," says Gordon MacDonald in his book *Ordering Your Private World*.[4] Maybe it's precisely because our work is unceasing that we need a Sabbath rest. If we wait until our work is done, we'll never get there.

Psalm 23:1–3 tells us, "The LORD is my shepherd. . . . He makes me lie down in green pastures; He leads me beside quiet waters. He restores my soul."

I find it fascinating that God doesn't merely suggest we lie down in green pastures. He doesn't hope we lie down in green pastures. He makes us lie down in green pastures. He knows that I am ignorant as a sheep, that I will sometimes overdo. I will sometimes keep too busy a schedule, attempt more projects than I have time for, deprive myself of sleep, and neglect to take the time I need to be with Him. So what does He do? My Shepherd gently takes hold of me and makes me lie down.

Have you ever noticed a tendency of yours to get sick at the busiest times? When you're preparing for company, maybe, or right before a holiday? I wonder if that's God's way of making us lie down for a while, because He knows we need it.

In his book *Traveling Light for Mothers*, Max Lucado says, "Can you imagine the satisfaction in the heart of the shepherd when, with work completed, he sees his sheep rest in the tender grass? Can you imagine the satisfaction in the heart of God when we do the same? His pasture is his gift to us. . . . He wants you to lie down. Nestle deeply until you are hidden, buried, in the tall shoots of his love, and there you will find rest."[5] ♛

cont. ⇒

"So there remains a Sabbath rest for the people of God. For the one who has entered His rest has himself also rested from his works, as God did from His. Therefore, let us be diligent to enter that rest." (Hebrews 4:9–11)

praer THANK YOU, LORD, FOR LOVING ME ENOUGH TO MAKE ME LIE DOWN WHEN THAT'S WHAT I NEED. THANK YOU FOR CREATING THE SABBATH SO I CAN ENJOY REFRESHMENT AND FELLOWSHIP WITH YOU.

week 11

Celebrating St. Patrick's Day and Purim

Q. What's Irish and sits out in the rain?
A. Paddy O'Furniture

It's that time o' year again when, Irish or not, we pull out the green socks to keep from getting pinched and head to the grocery store to bag ourselves a corned beef and some cabbage.

The funny thing is, St. Patrick's Day, March 17, commemorates a man who wasn't even Irish. He was an Englishman who was kidnapped by pirates at sixteen and brought to Ireland as a slave. He later escaped, and then years later went back to Ireland as a Christian missionary in AD 432. According to historical records, St. Patrick converted many and baptized more than 120,000 people.

Legend has it that the shamrock, the national symbol of Ireland, was originally used to explain the Trinity, with the three leaves symbolizing the Father, Son, and Holy Spirit. Today, many people in Ireland celebrate St. Patrick's Day by wearing a sprig of shamrock, and also by attending church.

Here in the United States, St. Patrick's Day may be celebrated with parades. In Chicago and San Antonio, people dye the water in local rivers green, according to *St.*

Patrick's Day by Dorothy Rhodes Freeman. And "the Empire State Building lights the night sky with green lights for the holiday."[1]

You may decide it's a bit excessive to dye the family water supply green. But you might put a wee bit o' green dye in the water glasses at dinner (or offer limeade or lemon-lime soda, if you're feeling especially munificent). Serve an all-green meal: green pasta with pesto sauce, salad with avocado, marinated cucumbers, and garlic toast sprinkled with dill—trimmed to resemble shamrocks if you're in an ambitious mood. Or you could serve traditional Irish corned beef brisket, boiled with quartered cabbage, potatoes, and carrots. If you're in a real rush but still want something festive, try warming up canned beef stew (as a substitute for authentic Irish stew, made with lamb) and serve in small hollowed-out rounds of bread, one per person.

See who in the family can dress most garishly in green, from head to toe, and take a vote after dinner with the winner getting first pick at dessert —apple pie is traditional, or you can make cupcakes and sprinkle the frosting with dyed green coconut.

And don't forget the Celtic music. Anything by The Chieftains or Eileen Ivers will have you and your laddies ready to jig in no time.

You might never have thought to send St. Patrick's Day cards, but it's a perfect occasion to mail a green greeting to a far-off relative or a friend whose day you'd like to brighten. If you've never checked out your local stationery store's selection, you might be surprised at the beautiful Irish blessings and prayers some of them contain.

CROCK-POT CORNED BEEF

Making a corned beef dinner is simple with your trusty Crock-Pot. Simply put the **corned beef** in the pot, barely cover it with water, and cook on low for about eight hours. Corned beef usually comes with a **packet of spices**, so toss those in. Make sure to add some **potatoes** too. (For my family of four, I use about eight small red potatoes, or two baking potatoes, well scrubbed and quartered.) If your family likes them, you can also add **carrot chunks** and **cabbage wedges** (my family votes no). Serve corned beef with a sauce made of **sour cream** mixed with a teaspoonful or two of **horseradish**.

You can make your own cards, too, nabbing some of the kids' green construction paper and cutting it into shamrock shapes. Inscribe with a blessing like the one on the next page, or an Irish proverb. Here are a few to consider:

◇ "Firelight will not let you read fine stories, but it's warm and you won't see the dust on the floor."

FUN FACT

↶

Today, in the United States, there are more people of Irish descent than there are in Ireland.[6]

Cead mile failte! is Gaelic for "A hundred thousand welcomes!"[7]

- ◇ "It's no use carrying an umbrella if your shoes are leaking."
- ◇ "A silent mouth is sweet to hear."
- ◇ "Bare is the companionless shoulder."
- ◇ "There's no point in keeping a dog if you are going to do your own barking."
- ◇ "Two shorten the road."
- ◇ "It is a lonely washing that has no man's shirt in it."
- ◇ "If you do not sow in the spring, you will not reap in the autumn."
- ◇ "As the big hound is, so will the pup be."
- ◇ "Put silk on a goat and it is still a goat."
- ◇ "The man with the boots does not mind where he places his foot."[2]

My dad's Irish cousin, who was a nun, sent these proverbs a few years ago: "Don't break your shin on a stool that is not in your way." And "A good retreat is better than a poor fight."[4] Share them at dinnertime, and see if they elicit interesting discussion.

And two final Irish blessings, in honor of this St. Patrick's Day holiday:

"That the sons of your sons may smile up in your face." And "That the frost might never afflict your spuds."[5]

Another holiday you may want to celebrate is the Jewish holiday of Purim (po͝or ĭm), which occurs each year in February or March (it's the fourteenth day of the Hebrew month of Adar; check your calendar for this year's date). Purim is the holiday that commemorates beautiful Queen Esther of Persia, who was Jewish, and her brave stance that ultimately saved the Jews of her day. (To read the complete story, see the book of Esther.)

In a nutshell, the story's about an evil man, Haman, who held high political office around 400 BC under King Ahasuerus. Haman was incensed when Mordecai, a local Jew, refused to bow to him as he passed the king's

IRISH SODA BREAD

I find most traditional Irish soda breads a little boring. But this recipe, with caraway seeds and raisins as well as yeast, is wonderful. It's adapted slightly from a recipe in *The Bread Machine Cookbook* by Donna Rathmell German, which contains instructions for all kinds of unusual, tasty breads.[8]

If you have a bread machine, give this a try. It's delicious toasted and buttered for breakfast or a snack.

Place in bread machine:

1 cup water	**3 cups bread flour**
2 T. butter	**2 ½ t. yeast**
2 T. sugar	**½ cup raisins** (I use golden raisins; add at the machine's
1 t. salt	"beep" if you're home. Otherwise add at the same time as the
½ t. baking soda	rest of your ingredients, and the raisins will be itty bitty by the
2 t. caraway seeds	time the bread's done.)

Push the "start" button. In a few hours, slice yourself a delicious slab of bread.

gate. "Filled with rage" (Esther 3:5), Haman sought to destroy not only Mordecai but all the Jews throughout the whole kingdom.

Esther, Mordecai's niece, found out about the plan. When her uncle urged her to go to the king and plead for her people's lives, she reminded Mordecai of the danger: by appearing before the king unsummoned, she could be put to death. Nonetheless, Mordecai encouraged her to go, emphasizing that since she was Jewish, her life was already in danger. "And who knows whether you have not attained royalty for such a time as this?" (Esther 4:14). So Esther fasted and called upon all her courage, then risked her life by approaching the king. Ultimately, the king saw things Esther's way, the Jews were saved, and Haman was hanged on gallows he'd had constructed for Mordecai.

Esther's courage in the face of peril is an inspiration for all of us who want to trust God even when our circumstances look bleak. God is at work, even when we are fearful. When we hope in God, He'll carry us through.

CHOCOLATE HAMANTASHEN

Like any cookie that's rolled out and cut before baking, *Hamantashen*, a favorite Purim treat, take a bit of effort to make. And, truth be told, they don't look all that pretty when they come out of the oven (a little issue with spreading). But these are fun to make each Purim season, providing the perfect opportunity to talk with your children about the story of Esther. The cookies' three corners are said to represent Haman's hat or, alternatively, the three founders of the Israel nation, Abraham, Isaac, and Jacob. They taste wonderful, too, like a fudgy brownie with jam on top.

I usually make the dough one day, refrigerate, then bake a day or two later.

In large mixing bowl, beat:

1 1/3 cups butter

with mixer on high speed until butter is softened. Add:

1 ¼ cups flour

1 ½ cups sugar

⅔ cup unsweetened cocoa powder

2 eggs

1 t. baking powder

½ t. salt

and beat until thoroughly combined. Mix in:

1 ¼ cups more flour (may want to do this by hand as the dough is quite stiff at this point). Divide dough in two, cover with plastic wrap, smush into flat disks, and chill until easy to handle, perhaps a couple of hours or as long as a couple of days.

When ready to bake, mix together for filling:

½ cup of a thick jam (I use olallieberry)

¼ cup chocolate chips

Set filling aside.

Remove dough from refrigerator. Roll out one disk at a time on floured surface, to ¼-inch thick. (Keep flouring the rolling pin and your work surface if the dough sticks.) Using a two- to three-inch round cookie cutter, cut dough into circles. Place two inches apart on wax paper-lined cookie sheet. Plop ½ to 1 teaspoon of the jam/chocolate chip filling into the center of cookie. Lift up three edges of the dough round and fold toward center, pinching the three outer points together tightly so not much jam is showing. (Here's where they should look like three-cornered hats.) Reroll scraps and continue until all dough is used. Bake at 350 degrees for eleven to fourteen minutes.

Jews today celebrate Purim with much joy. They read the story of Esther from a scroll in the synagogue. Each time the name "Haman" is read, the children stomp their feet, hiss or boo, and whirl or bang their noisemakers (called *gragers*) to drown out his name. They dress up like characters from the story, march in parades, and hold carnivals. They also send gifts of food—*schlach manot*—to friends and neighbors, or give money to those in need. The most popular of the food gifts are three-cornered cookies called *hamantashen*, which resemble Haman's hat.

If your family has time, read Esther's story aloud from the book of Esther this week, stomping and hissing each time Haman's name is read. Celebrate God's protection of His people. Celebrate Purim (see Esther 9:19–28).

Spring is here!

⬥ Paint your toenails bright red.

⬥ Get out the self-tanning lotion and try not to end up with striped legs (don't forget the tops of your feet).

⬥ Bring your Bible outside for some warm-weather reading.

⬥ Dig out short-sleeved shirts and sandals.

⬥ Start doing those push-ups and sit-ups.

⬥ Discuss summer vacation plans with your family.

⬥ Don't forget sunscreen, especially on necks, ears, backs of hands.

⬥ Make a list of Easter activities you want to include in this year's celebration. Write them on your family calendar. (Blow out eggs! Look for lamb cake pan! Check out Easter music from library!)

"Call upon Me in the day of trouble; I shall rescue you, and you will honor Me." (Psalm 50:15)

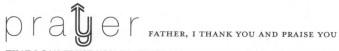

prayer FATHER, I THANK YOU AND PRAISE YOU THAT I CAN TRUST YOU IN WHATEVER CIRCUMSTANCE I FIND MYSELF. GIVE ME COURAGE, LORD, WHEN I NEED IT, AND IN EVERY SITUATION HELP ME TO ACT IN A WAY THAT BRINGS GLORY TO YOU.

week 12

new word

for the week:

Stentorian

(stĕn-tôr′ ē-ən).

Extremely loud. As in, *"Let's all try to be a little less stentorian, shall we? It will be more peaceful around here."*

alternate

new word:

Dulcet (dŭl′ sĭt).

Pleasing to the ear; gently melodious. As in, *"Now we'll put on some dulcet piano music and enjoy a soothing evening. Shall we light candles for dinner?"*

In Search of the Peaceful Home

When I asked my kids a few years back what makes for a peaceful home, my ten-year-old wanted clarification. "Looks, or real?"

He explained that a home can look peaceful on the outside, with clean floors and "nothing dented." (Yes, he was a handful.) But it can be quite unpeaceful if there's a lot of fighting going on, or if people are unwilling to talk out their differences.

"Peacefulness is on the inside, not on the outside," he added. "To look peaceful you clean your house. To be peaceful is to be content about how things are."

My eleven-year-old added that to look peaceful, "Just throw a bunch of lamb pictures on the wall. But being peaceful is having Him."

A friend who's recently received her family counseling degree tells me the first thing an infant requires in order to successfully develop is a sense of safety. When babies have parents who love them, feed them, change them, and keep them warm, they learn that the world is a safe place and that people can be trusted.

I want my home to reflect that feeling of safety. I want my family to have a deep sense that home is a haven, that we can trust each other, that inside these four walls is a safe place to be.

As Christians, we have a perfect Parent who provides us with that security. Our heavenly Father loves us. He feeds us. He changes us (thank goodness). He is the source of peace, which we can then pass on to our family and to others.

In his book *As for Me and My House*, author Walter Wangerin Jr., says "*Peace* is, in Hebrew, *shalom*: wholeness, health, well-being."[1] *The Holman Bible Dictionary* adds that spiritual peace is a "sense of well-being and fulfillment that comes from God and is dependent on His presence," and that "God alone can give peace in all its fullness."[2]

As we turn our thoughts toward God, we can experience peace in our homes, "the peace of God, which surpasses all comprehension" (Philippians 4:7). Even if there are a few dents here and there and we're fresh out of lamb pictures.

John 16:33: "These things I have spoken to you, so that in Me you may have peace. In the world you have tribulation, but take courage; I have overcome the world."

Colossians 1:2: "Grace to you and peace from God our Father."

Luke 10:5: "Whatever house you enter, first say, 'Peace be to this house.'"

Isaiah 26:3: "The steadfast of mind You will keep in perfect peace, because he trusts in You."

Psalm 29:11: "The Lord will give strength to His people; the Lord will bless His people with peace."

Boxes of See's candy covered my dining room table like a 3-D tablecloth. Order forms were flung across my kitchen counters. In spite of my usual diligent avoidance I had somehow wound up in charge of the latest school fund-raising project, and I was drowning. The project was huge. The pressure was on to finalize the profit spreadsheets and to get nine thousand dollars' worth of candy distributed.

My attention diverted, two days' worth of dirty dishes had outgrown my kitchen sink and spilled over the sides like too much water in the bathtub. Scattered across my kitchen table were school notices, unread mail, and piles of paperwork for our next fund-raiser, a cookbook whose deadline was fast approaching (what was I THINKING?!). And, oh yes, in the middle of the muddle were two thermometers, evidence of my boys who were both home sick from school.

As I sprinted from one chaotic room to another, tending feverish boys and throwing logs on the fire that provides our wintertime heat, I kept passing through the kitchen. On maybe my fifth trip I spotted a book I'd been reading over breakfast, spread-eagled on top of the mess: *Making Your Home a Haven.*

I had to laugh. Some haven.

Sometimes life is like that. Sometimes our days are filled with children's Tylenol® and unfolded laundry and it's six o'clock and what am I going to do for dinner? On those days, a peaceful home feels as much like a fantasy as talking lions from Narnia.

But that doesn't keep me from wanting my home to be a haven. And the truth is, despite the inevitable rough days, I still think it's possible.

Isaiah 26:12 says, "Lord, You will establish peace for us." Peace is not the result of a perfectly scheduled day or a perfectly tidy house. Peace is also not something I can will into existence. Peace is a fruit of the Spirit. It's something that God produces when I take my worries and concerns to Him. God is in the business of establishing peace. He can do anything, even in the middle of chaos. My job is to ask.

I love author Claire Cloninger's idea: "When the atmosphere of my home seems unsettled, I sometimes walk from room to room, silently asking the Lord to transform the 'spiritual climate' by the power of His Spirit. It is amazing what a calming effect this can produce, regardless of the circumstances!"[4]

I want to remember to pray over my home today. And then, when I have a minute, I really do need to put away those thermometers and compile the cookbook and wash those dishes and get that candy delivered.

One night when I came home after a full day of doing errands, I thought about how nice it would be if someone were already home and the lights were on, a meal was cooking, and a fire was glowing in the fireplace.

It made me think about home from my husband's point of view. What is the atmosphere as he walks through the door each evening? Are good smells wafting? Is soothing music welcoming? (At least once in a while?)

Later I asked him, and he agreed those would be nice to come home to. "And no one bickering," he added.

Some other ideas for fostering a peaceful home:

◇ Fill your home with good smells—scented candles or fresh flowers, for example. Author Terry Willits suggests starting outside, with a fragrant wreath on your door or potted flowers. (Get a plant for the front only if you'll water it, though; dead plants do not make the jauntiest peace inducers.)

◇ Allow people to use even your "good" furniture—unlike me, who kept my white cotton living room

---

Quotable

There is nothing which has a more abiding influence on the happiness of a family than the preservation of equable and cheerful temper and tones in the housekeeper. A woman who is habitually gentle, sympathizing, forbearing, and cheerful, carries an atmosphere about her which imparts a soothing and sustaining influence. . . .

On the contrary, many a good housekeeper, (good in every respect but this,) by wearing a countenance of anxiety and dissatisfaction, and by indulging in the frequent use of sharp and reprehensible tones, more than destroys all the comfort which otherwise would result from her system, neatness, and economy.[5]

Catharine E. Beecher and Harriet Beecher Stowe,
American Woman's Home

couch pristine for years by the brilliant plan of preventing anyone from actually sitting on it. What I had, in effect, was a very expensive, very large upholstered paperweight.

◇ Remember to strive for balance. We want homes that are orderly enough to be comfortable, not shrines to perfection. Our homes are not museums. Accept that people live there.

◇ Post Scripture verses around your home to remind you that even during the day's mundane tasks, God is present. I write verses I especially like on a whiteboard in my kitchen.

◇ When the week's clutter seems overwhelming, remember that cleats in the middle of the floor represent healthy bodies; half-completed science-fair projects mean creativity; stray books mean active minds are at work. It's all a matter of perspective. ♛

"Peace I leave with you; My peace I give to you; not as the world gives do I give to you. Do not let your heart be troubled, nor let it be fearful." (John 14:27)

prayer

LORD, THANK YOU FOR MY HOME. THANK YOU THAT OUR FAMILY CAN EXPERIENCE PEACE WHEN WE ARE CONNECTED TO YOU. PLEASE PERMEATE OUR HOME WITH YOUR PEACE, AND GIVE ME YOUR PERSPECTIVE AS I GO ABOUT MY WORK.

week 13

Easter, Part 1

My earliest childhood Easter memories are of donning special clothes: a poufy pastel dress, white cotton gloves, an Easter bonnet with ribbons fluttering two feet down my back. Black-and-white photos from that era confirm that my sister and I morphed into angelic (looking) blonde princesses for the day, while my two brothers, also uncharacteristically cherubic, were decked out in their once-a-year sporty little bow ties and plaid seersucker blazers. The whole family piled into the car for Easter Sunday service, sensing the day's uniqueness solely because of our holiday finery. I can only imagine the monumental effort it must have taken my poor mom to get us looking that way; with four of us born in four successive years, there was surely monumental effort in simply getting us up and fed and out the door.

I did not clothe my own boys in Easter bow ties and blazers when they were little, due more to TMS (Tired Mommy Syndrome) than any conscious choice. But as they grew, I realized I wanted to add Easter traditions to our lives—more than just hunting for eggs and heading to church.

When my friend Tracy, who at this writing has six kids from zero to twelve, suggested the following activity, I was excited to try it. It's basically a treasure hunt that's held during the week before Easter. It takes almost no time to set up or execute—an important consideration on heavy homework nights. And the kids loved it. Best of all, it really helped us focus on the meaning of Easter.

Here's what you do: Hide one small item every day beginning with the Saturday before Palm Sunday. (I hid two, so each child could find one.) The hidden items correspond with the story of Easter week. For example, on Palm Sunday, the day Jesus triumphantly entered Jerusalem on a donkey with people spreading palms and garments before Him, hide something that represents a donkey, palm branch, or clothing item. Small toys you already have around the house work fine: stuffed animals, LEGOs®, or doll clothes, for example.

That evening, read aloud the portion of Scripture that correlates with what you've hidden. Then set the kids loose for the hunt. After each evening's search, place the found objects in a basket that sits in the middle of your table. Leave the basket out all week to remind you of the Easter story.

Got it? Here's the week's plan, both for hiding and for reading.[1] You may want to jot the scriptures on the appropriate day on your calendar to help you remember.

Day 1—Saturday before Palm Sunday
Reading: John 12:1–11
Topic: Mary anointing Jesus' feet
Item to hide: bottle of scented oil or perfume
(you may want to hide one per child)

Day 2—Palm Sunday
Reading: Luke 19:28–40; John 12:13
Topic: Jesus' entry into Jerusalem
Items: palm branch, doll clothes, donkey

Day 3—Monday
Reading: Mark 11:11–26
Topic: fig tree and money changers in the temple
Items: coins, fig branch

Day 4—Tuesday
Reading: Matthew 24:36–44; 26:64
Topic: Jesus' teaching on the Second Coming
Items: hourglass, cloud (cut one out from paper or felt)

Day 5—Wednesday
Reading: Matthew 26:1–16
Topic: woman anoints Jesus' head; Judas' plot
Items: scented oil or perfume, silver dollars

Day 6—Thursday
Reading: John 13:1–17; Matthew 26:17–56
Topic: foot washing; Last Supper; Garden of Gethsemane; betrayal
Items: towel, bread, a kiss (wear lipstick and kiss a piece of paper), sword

Day 7—Good Friday
Reading: Luke 22:54–71; 23:13–25, 32–43; Matthew 27:45–56
Topic: the crucifixion
Items: crown of thorns, nail, cross

Day 8—Saturday
Reading: Matthew 27:57–66; Isaiah 53:1–7
Topic: prophecy and guards at the tomb
Items: white cloth, sealing wax, lamb

Day 9—Easter Sunday
Reading: Matthew 28:1–15; Luke 24:1–49
Topic: Resurrection, soldiers paid off, disciples met on the road to Emmaus, breaking bread
Items: empty the basket, line it with white cloth, then put in silver coins, a picture of an angel, and bread. Do this after the kids are in bed Saturday night.

Don't worry about doing this perfectly. If you skip a night or two, simply start where you are. This activity is meant to enhance your Easter celebrations, not add more stress to evenings that are already crazy full.

Enjoy your Scripture reading and your treasure hunt. Especially enjoy the opportunities as a family to dwell on our Lord and Savior Jesus Christ, and the unfathomable gift He gave when He died on the cross for you and for me.

A few years ago I introduced another Easter tradition in our home: making hot cross buns. The buns, which originated in England, are said to have symbolized to early Christians the unleavened bread Jesus ate during the Last Supper. According to *Celebrations* by Becky Stevens Cordello, "Aside from being the traditional breakfast food on Good Friday, a hot cross bun was hung in the home throughout the year to bring good luck to the household. This was a custom followed by seamen as well. The buns supposedly did not become moldy."[2]

I've never tested the no-mold theory, but I can definitely tell you these buns are delicious. If you don't have time to bake them for Good Friday, don't worry; they are wonderful anytime. The recipe makes twenty-four, so you'll have plenty to share with friends or neighbors.

Though it contains yeast, the dough requires no kneading, so don't bother using your bread machine if you have one. (Also, if you leave it on the "dough" setting and forget it's in there, it will overflow.)

If you're really short on time, you could buy premade sweet-ish buns and make only the frosting (recipe below). Pipe a cross on each bun and you're done. But if you're home for about four hours and have the chance, make the whole recipe. They're so good they may become an annual tradition at your house. They certainly have at mine.

FUN FACT

Did you know Easter can occur anywhere from March 22 to April 25? It's the first Sunday after the first full moon on or after March 21. Got that?

HOT CROSS BUNS

This recipe comes from a wonderful homemaking book by Beverly K. Nye entitled *A Family Raised on Rainbows*.[3]

Dissolve:

1 package dry yeast (2 ¼ t.)

in ¼ cup warm water

Set aside. In large saucepan, heat until almost boiling (small bubbles will appear on sides of pan):

1 cup milk

Remove from heat. Add:

1 stick butter or margarine (can cut in pieces) and stir till it melts.

Add:

½ cup sugar

1 ½ t. salt

Combine yeast mixture with milk mixture once the milk has cooled. Add:

3 beaten eggs

Stir in:

4 ¾ cups flour

1 t. cinnamon

1 t. grated lemon peel

Stir until dough is smooth. (Note: dough will be very sticky; no need to add extra flour.) Add:

1 cup raisins, if desired (I omit because unless they're covered with chocolate, raisins frighten my children.)

Cover pan with damp towel and let rise in a warm place until double. When double, stir down. Turn dough onto a floured board. Shape into balls the size of eggs. Place on greased cookie sheet, two to three inches apart, and let rise until almost double again.

Brush tops with:

1 beaten egg white

Bake at 375 degrees twelve to fifteen minutes, until nicely browned. When cool, pipe frosting across the top in shape of a cross. Makes twenty-four.

FROSTING

In medium bowl, stir together:

1 cup powdered sugar

1 T. melted butter or margarine

½ t. lemon or orange extract

enough hot water to make

desired consistency

(probably 1–2 T.)

Pipe a cross on each bun; with leftover icing, pipe a circle or two around each cross. Use all the frosting, especially if you've omitted raisins, because the buns benefit from the added sweetness. (If you don't own a pastry bag, plop the frosting into your sturdiest plastic storage bag, then place the bag into another sturdy plastic storage bag; snip off the corner and pipe away. If you don't double the bag and it ends up bursting and oozing frosting all over your hand, don't say I didn't warn you. Though you may enjoy eating the evidence.)

John the Baptist called Jesus the "Lamb of God who takes away the sin of the world" (John 1:29). Serving lamb for Easter dinner can be one more reminder of Christ our redeemer, the Passover Lamb who was willing to be slain so our sins would be passed over. (To read about the original Passover lamb, see Exodus 12:21–27.)

Easter has historically been a time of great feasting and celebration. Christ is risen! We have something wonderful to celebrate. Make your Easter dinner extra special, with fresh rolls from the bakery, spring vegetables, and a lamb roast. Lamb-shaped cakes are said to be a traditional Easter dessert, so if you happen to find a lamb-shaped cake pan, go for it.

Every roast lamb recipe I've ever seen recommends inserting slivers of garlic into the roast, including this one. This tasty recipe comes from *The Silver Palate Good Times Cookbook* by Julee Rosso and Sheila Lukins, with Sarah Leah Chase.[4] It's ready to pop in the oven in no time. ♛

ROAST LAMB

Preheat oven to 400 degrees.

Peel: **3 cloves garlic** and slice into thin slivers.

Make small slits all around: **1 leg of lamb, 4–6 pounds**, and poke the garlic slivers into the holes.

Rub the lamb all over with: **½ cup fresh lemon juice.**

Then pat the lamb all over with: **1 ½ t. dried rosemary**.

Sprinkle with: **salt and pepper, as desired.**

Insert meat thermometer. Place the lamb in a roasting pan, place it in the oven, then immediately reduce heat to 350 degrees. Roast for 1½ hours for medium-rare, until meat thermometer reads about 150 degrees. Let stand ten minutes before carving. Serves six to eight.

"You were not redeemed with perishable things like silver or gold from your futile way of life inherited from your forefathers, but with precious blood, as of a lamb unblemished and spotless, the blood of Christ." (1 Peter 1:18–19)

prayer LORD GOD, HOW CAN I THANK YOU FOR PAYING THE SUPREME PRICE, CHRIST'S SHED BLOOD THAT IS PRECIOUS, TO TAKE AWAY MY SIN? I DON'T DESERVE YOUR MERCY, BUT I AM SO THANKFUL THAT YOU'VE GIVEN IT TO ME ABUNDANTLY. HELP ME TO FOCUS THIS EASTER WEEK ON WHO YOU ARE AND ALL YOU'VE DONE FOR ME.

stop! ● CHOCOLATE BREAK!
CHOCOLATE TRUFFLES

Turns out the average American gobbles close to twelve pounds of chocolate a year.[5] In an effort to do my part, I give you this: a quick, easy recipe that can be shaped into little balls or into small eggs for Easter. This is based on a recipe from Susan Branch's book, *Girlfriends Forever*.[6]

CHOCOLATE TRUFFLES

Over very low heat, melt: **5 oz. unsweetened chocolate.**

Remove from heat. Stir in, small pieces at a time:
1 stick butter, at room temperature until butter is melted.

Add: **2 cups powdered sugar** and stir well. Roll into small balls
   (or egg shapes) and place on wax paper.
If desired, roll truffles in: **toasted coconut, chopped walnuts, or
   pecans** (optional).

Serve at room temperature. Makes about twenty-six.

week 14

Easter, Part 2

As I considered how to make Easter more meaningful for my family, my thoughts turned to music. I knew some famous composers had written beautiful Christmas music, and I also knew that some of those composers had been Christians. Was it possible there was some wonderful Easter music out there, more than just the few Easter hymns I already knew?

I headed to my library to find out. To my delight, a search turned up three CDs: one by George Frideric Handel, one by Pierre de la Rue, and one by Johann Sebastian Bach.

I checked them all out and spent the next couple of weeks enjoying the beautiful pieces written about our Lord and His resurrection. They were different from the kind of music I usually listen to (the words weren't in English, for one thing!), but as I read some of the English translations, I was moved at how God can use composers of three hundred years ago (or, in the case of de la Rue, five hundred years ago), from countries far away, to reach one woman in her kitchen in California in the twenty-first century. He is an amazing God who uses people across time to bring us His message of hope and reconciliation.

Psalm 150 encourages us to use music in our worship: "Praise the LORD! Praise God in His sanctuary; Praise

new word
for the week:

Accretion (ə-krē′ shən).
A growth or increase in size by gradual addition. As in, *"If I don't watch it, eating too many chocolate bunnies will lead to an accretion in my waistline."*

alternate
new word:

Nimiety (nĭ-mī′ ə-tē).
Excess; overabundance. As in, *"If I start folding a fifty-piece origami Easter scene, perhaps I am exhibiting an unhealthy nimiety of interest in clever holiday crafts."*

THESE ARE THE LYRICS
FROM THE CD
La Resurrezione BY
GEORGE FRIDERIC HANDEL.[1]
MARY MAGDALENE
IS SINGING:

CLEOPHAS, JOHN, HEAR ME,
HEAR WHAT NEW WONDER
HATH BEFALLEN ME!
I HAVE SEEN MY LORD
IN THE GARDEN,
AND THOUGH HE
APPEARED IN THE
GUISE OF ONE OF
THE KEEPERS,
FROM THE ROUGH
GARMENTS
RADIATED A LIGHT SO
PURE, SO INTENSE,
I KNEW 'TWAS HE ERE MY
EYES HAD SEEN HIM.
THEN I RECOGNIZED
THAT FACE,
UPON WHICH PARADISE
DOTH GAZE
TO BEAUTIFY HERSELF.
I SAW THE HANDS, I SAW
THE FEET AS WELL,
AND BEHELD IN THEM,
SHINING AND BEAUTIFUL
AND SPARKLING LIKE STARS,
MARKS OF THE ERSTWHILE
DEADLY WOUNDS.
THEN DID I APPROACH TO
KISS THEM,
BUT JESUS FORBADE ME,
SAYING:
"TOUCH ME NOT!" AND
THEN HE VANISHED.

Him in His mighty expanse. Praise Him for His mighty deeds; Praise Him according to His excellent greatness. Praise Him with trumpet sound; Praise Him with harp and lyre. Praise Him with timbrel and dancing; Praise Him with stringed instruments and pipe. Praise Him with loud cymbals; Praise Him with resounding cymbals. Let everything that has breath praise the LORD. Praise the LORD!"

Follow the psalmist's direction and pull out hymnbooks and any instruments the family plays and make music together. (Combs and wax paper after dinner work.) Sing "Christ the Lord Is Risen Today." And sing with joy! No one said it had to be pretty, just joyful (see 1 Chronicles 15:16; Psalm 66:1).

If you're interested in learning more about Christian music and composers, look for Patrick Kavanaugh's book *The Music of Angels: A Listener's Guide to Sacred Music from Chant to Christian Rock.*[2]

It was with high hopes one recent Easter that I whipped together a batch of homemade salt play dough, ready for the hours of family fun that would result. I imagined my family gathered around the kitchen table, relishing each other's company as we talked of spiritual things and crafted a beautiful Easter centerpiece, just like the one in the magazine.

But I hadn't counted on boys who would rather play video games than join Mom in making spiritually significant art projects. In the end, my fantasy family had to make way for the real one; I ended up making the craft by myself. Nonetheless, I was pleased with the results that night when I went to bed. Pleased, that is, until I woke up the next morning to discover our dog had chosen my salt dough masterpiece as her midnight snack. Salty dog had gotten so thirsty from said snack that she'd drunk buckets of water, then relieved her water-saturated bladder all over the living room carpet.

One emergency trip to Carpet Cleanerville later, I was ready to concede. We were not a crafty, creative family. And we might never be.

On to the next scene, later that afternoon, where I sat dejectedly at the kitchen table with my leftover salt dough, unmolested only because the dog doesn't know how to open the refrigerator.

"Whatcha doing?" asked my son on his way through the kitchen.

"Oh, just trying to figure out what to do with this dough," I said, voice dull. He picked up some clay and began squishing it through his fingers. To my surprise, he began to craft shapes, suggesting new ideas as he went. Together we sat for more than an hour, shaping the dough into a fine new centerpiece, one that included three crosses on a hill, an empty tomb, and a stone that was rolled away. We talked as we worked, and we laughed a lot. It was all I could have hoped for.

Afterward, as we stood gazing at our Easter scene, my arm around my son's shoulder, he said quietly, "This is really neat."

"Yeah," I agreed, meaning more than just the new centerpiece. That day I was struck anew with God's glorious grace, how He cared enough to take the efforts of an overzealous mom, an apathetic family, and a gluttonous dog and somehow turn them into something wonderful.

Turns out I got my family-bonding time after all.

If you want to make an Easter centerpiece of your own, here's the recipe for:

THE BEST, SQUISHIEST SALT DOUGH EVER

Combine in saucepan:

1 cup flour	**½ cup salt**
1 T. salad oil	**2 t. cream of tartar**
1 cup water	**food coloring**

Cook, stirring over low heat until mixture thickens. Remove from heat. Knead on floured counter. Add food coloring as desired. When finished, projects can be air-dried.

Dough will keep in an airtight container in the refrigerator or freezer.

FUN FACT

↰

Did you know that the beautiful composition *Messiah* by George Frideric Handel, which we typically listen to at Christmastime, was played in Handel's day most often around Easter? If you have it on a tape or CD, listen to it in these pre-Easter weeks.

Feel free to create whatever centerpiece you can dream up. We made an igloo-shaped cave, added a blob of dough next to it representing the stone that was rolled away, then filled three hollowed-out eggshells (with two-inch long openings on the side) with carefully squished in crosses, to represent the three men who were crucified: Jesus and the two thieves. We twisted different colors of dough together and put the little rope around the eggshell openings. Then we made a rectangular block of dough which we used for a base (our "hill"), and placed the three eggshells on top.

In one recent year, the two weeks before Easter found our family in the midst of manic activity. We'd hosted my son's birthday/slumber party for eight, held another birthday celebration for the family, gone to a professional ice hockey game, finished two book reports and two science-fair projects, attended four Bible studies (two women's, two men's), two ballet classes, twenty or so baseball practices and games, one doctor's appointment, two dental appointments, and a baby shower. Needless to say, we did not find the time to do many of the Easter projects I had so zealously clipped from luring magazines.

I learned something that year (aside from "avoid luring magazines"). I learned that while I plan way ahead for Christmas celebrations, knowing that my agenda takes up the whole month of December (and then some), I wasn't giving Easter the same consideration. I wasn't setting aside a block of time to celebrate. I had somehow assumed that by thinking about Easter on, say, the Wednesday before, I'd still have enough time to weave the clever Easter basket centerpiece, decorate the wax-painted, hand-dyed Polish Easter eggs, and concoct those luscious-looking chocolate-covered peanut butter eggs.

Based on experience, I know that spring is one of the busiest times of the year for our family. Because of birthdays, anniversaries, science-fair projects, and that most crucial of seasonal activities, baseball, if I am to have any hope of finding quality family togetherness moments, I need to start way ahead.

Start early this year with Easter celebrations. The holiday can be much more meaningful for you and your family if you give yourself more time.

Christ is risen. He is risen, indeed!

Look up the Easter story in the Gospels, and start reading. Even if you have only little bits of time, keep a Bible open and snatch a verse whenever you can. Don't fall into the trap that I did when my kids were little, thinking, *If I don't have time to read it all, I might as well not read any.* Some is better than none. And you will have more time as your kids get older. I promise.

Matthew 26–28   Luke 22–24
Mark 14–16   John 13, 18–20

A great picture book to read as a family—no matter *how* old your kids—is *Peter's First Easter* by Walter Wangerin Jr., and illustrated by Timothy Ladwig.[3]

The Easter Egg
. . . .

Dyed Easter eggs may have originally signified joy, the bright colors of the coming spring, or the blood of Christ, according to *Celebrations* by Becky Stevens Cordello.[4] Whatever their origin, creating festive decorated eggs is a big tradition in many homes.

Before dyeing your eggs, you can draw on a cross or write a message such as "Jesus is Lord" with a crayon. Since wax resists dye, what you've scribbled will stand out like a chocolate bunny in a field of jelly beans. Other ideas for dyed eggs include wrapping them in rubber bands or masking tape before dyeing to make stripes and plaids, and covering eggs with stickers such as hearts, stars, or rings before dyeing.

If your kids are old enough, try blowing out eggs as a family some Sunday afternoon, then make omelets or quiche for dinner. (Alternatively, make chocolate pudding; see "CHOCOLATE BREAK!" after Week 35.) Make sure to rinse the blown shells under running water to clear them of any goo.

When finished decorating, nestle your eggs in a basket or on a pedestal cake plate lined with crumpled green tissue paper, bunches of parsley, tinted-green coconut, or "Easter grass" from the drugstore.

EASY EASTER SALAD

Got a nimiety of hard-boiled eggs? This will use two:

Hard boil: **2 eggs**. When cooked, peel and chop into quarter-inch pieces. Set aside.

In bowl, place: torn up **Romaine, or other lettuce**.

Chop: a couple **green onions**.

If you have picky eaters, place the onions in a small bowl to accompany salad. Otherwise, add onions to the lettuce. Sprinkle the chopped eggs over top of salad. Pour vinaigrette over top.

Vinaigrette

Combine:

3 T. fresh lemon juice
(about one lemon's worth)

¼ cup olive oil

½ t. salt

April Fool's Day Pranks

◇ Make ice cubes with tiny plastic bugs in the center. Plunk them into a family member's morning orange juice.[5]

◇ Serve poppy seed muffins or cake and pretend the seeds are bugs.[6]

◇ Serve breakfast for dinner; greet diners with "Good morning."

"Many other signs Jesus also performed in the presence of the disciples, which are not written in this book; but these have been written so that you may believe that Jesus is the Christ, the Son of God; and that believing you may have life in His name." (John 20:30–31)

prayer THANK YOU, LORD JESUS, THAT I CAN HAVE LIFE IN YOUR NAME, NOT JUST HERE ON EARTH BUT FOREVER IN HEAVEN. THANK YOU FOR LOVING ME SO MUCH YOU WERE WILLING TO GO TO THE CROSS.

week 15

Adventures in Gardening

"Spring has sprung; the grass is riz. I wonder where the birdies is." This eloquent quote is courtesy of my great-uncle Ellis, a "great uncle" if ever there was one.

Spring *has* sprung. The happy daffodils have popped, pulling me to the garden with the same sense of wonder as the arrival of an unexpected package. I am just discovering the joys of growing flowers, for years having thought it was too much trouble. Now this time of year finds me filled with hope. *This* year, my plants will flourish. *This* year, the little seedlings I start by the kitchen sink in the pots my sons have painted for various Mother's Days will grow tall and strong and bear fruit when I transplant them into the yard. *This* year, the dog won't trample the flowers—even the three-foot-high gladiolas—and the deer won't nibble the ranunculus before they bloom. *This* year, I will have basil to make pesto and the glory of homegrown tomatoes for pasta sauce.

It is hope I buy when I study zinnia and marigold seeds on the store's rack of seeds as carefully as though I were choosing a friend. This will be the year . . .

Edith Schaeffer, in her excellent book *The Hidden Art of Homemaking*, lays out her philosophy that as God's children we should seek to reflect our Creator with artistic, creative expression in our everyday lives. Schaeffer has some inspiring words to say about gardening:

> Almost anyone can have enough soil, light and seeds to become involved in the magic of growing things . . . one does not need to have a degree, nor even a tremendous talent, to enjoy and bring enjoyment to others through the medium of gardening. . . . You may have 300 acres to work with, or three; a large and fertile garden surrounding a suburban home, or a tiny square space in the back of your city home; you may have a large balcony with space for . . . containers of some sort, or only a windowsill or two. . . . The day the first tips of green are seen, if they are *your* seeds, planted by your own fingers, there is a thrill that is surely similar to producing an art work.[1]

Schaeffer talks of transforming a dingy downtown Philadelphia apartment into a patch of calm and beauty just by filling a wooden butter tub with blue morning glories, purple and white petunias, blue ageratum, ivy, and leafy vines that cascaded over the sides. She learned that in planting and nurturing a tub of beautiful flowers, she, too, was nurtured.

It doesn't have to take a lot of time or effort to grow something beautiful. God has already done the design work, and He does most of the execution too. Our job is simply to provide the right soil, choose plants that grow in our climate, and give them the water they need.

Have you planted any seeds yet? ("To plant a seed is a hopeful deed.") Or bought any bright flowering plants and placed them where they'll cheer you each time you pass? Give it a try. Start small, with just a pot or a small plot in the yard. You never know what miracles might grow.

While waiting with my friend Pam outside the video parlor for our sons to emerge, I leafed through a gardening book, *Cooking from the Garden* by Rosalind Creasy.[3]

"Listen to this!" I said, and proceeded to read aloud: "'There is a concept I love to contemplate because it is simple, beautiful, and true: that growing, harvesting, preparing, presenting, and eating foods from the garden are all phases of the same activity.'" I looked at her, excited. "Isn't that neat?"

She peered at me over her glasses. "I'll buy that," she deadpanned, "when they come up with a chocolate cake plant."

OK. So let's not go overboard.

But I do think that viewing gardening as a precursor to eating makes the whole endeavor that much more exciting. And I'm sure my family would eat better if we spent more time wandering down rows of homegrown produce than rows of Haagen-Dazs ice cream at the grocery store.

There has been a garden/food connection right from the very beginning. Genesis 1:29 tells us that God gave Adam and Eve "every seed-bearing plant on the face of the whole earth and every tree that has fruit with seed in it . . . for food" (NIV).

About one hundred specific plants are mentioned in the Bible, according to *Reader's Digest Atlas of the Bible*, including such edible varieties as cucumbers (Isaiah 1:8), mint (Matthew 23:23), coriander (Exodus 16:31), and dill (Isaiah 28:25). Bible gardens included onions, leeks, garlic, and melons (Numbers 11:5). Also found in Bible times were sweet-scented herbs, which you just might want to notify your husband his cheeks are remarkably similar to (see Song of Solomon 5:13).[5]

If you look carefully, you will find encouragement in the Bible to try gardening. Genesis 2:15 shows God giving Adam the job of cultivating and keeping the garden. This was before sin entered the world, so it must have been a satisfying, joyful task.

Quotable

Too many people believe that cooking from the garden involves plowing the back forty, but even growing a few basil and tarragon plants or some fancy lettuces among the petunias or some lemon thyme on a windowsill will add immeasurably to your cooking.[4]

Rosalind Creasy,
Cooking from the Garden

The garden was also a place God walked (Genesis 3:8). We can still find God in the garden today—in the sunlight resting on our faces, the small breezes wafting past our ears, the cheerful birds twittering in the trees and the yellow tulips performing for heaven.

Spend a few minutes outside today, in your own garden or someone else's. Imagine your little patch bursting with fresh herbs and vegetables. Be still. Breathe deep, and enjoy God's presence.

And don't even think about chocolate cake.

As I stopped by the library's gardening section (section 635, in case you're interested), I was amazed at the variety of titles: *The Low-Water Flower Gardener*; *The Art of Gardening with Roses*; *Wildflower Perennials for Your Garden*; *The Herbal Tea Garden*; *The Salad Garden*.

Many of the titles suggested theme gardens: the all-white garden, for example, or the edible flower garden. It was inspiring.

Even more inspiring, though, were the resplendent close-up photographs inside the books. You may have no intention of tending six acres à la *Martha Stewart's Gardening*,[7] but the color photographs of glorious blossom after blossom, bouquet after bouquet, will get your heart quickening. With just a bit of effort, your yard, too, could look like that! Leaving the books out and open on your living room table will have you hankering for your dibble.

I must admit I was cheered to read in Martha's book a journal entry from May: "Sweet peas eaten by rabbits; replanted."[8] Even Martha has experienced the occasional gardening disaster. I, too, am plagued by plant-eating critters but don't have the fight to replant. Each spring I give up after round one, conceding victory to the bunnies until next year. My friend Bettye fights the deer at her house, and finally, with a six-foot-high fence, appears to have won. Another friend is at war with a family of moles.

She is not giving up either, and seems to be on the verge of victory with her smoke bombs. Successful gardeners do seem to share the important trait of tenacity.

Since I am no expert at gardening, I pass along some hints from those who

- ◇ Start small. One gardener recommends a four-foot-by-four-foot plot at first; you can add to it each year.
- ◇ Soil preparation is key. Break up the hard ground to about twelve inches (easier if it's just rained), spread four to six inches of organic amendments such as peat moss or manure on top, and then mix it in.
- ◇ Choose sunny gardening sites, but think about the view from inside your house, too, so you can enjoy the garden from the window.
- ◇ Plant at intervals to minimize your risk. (Plant some this week, for example, then wait a week or two to plant the next batch.) That way, one gardening disaster won't wipe out your entire fortune.
- ◇ If you're new to gardening, try planting the same flower in several locations to see where it does best. Next year, you'll know.
- ◇ By planting in pots, you can move them around to find where they grow best and to determine which color combinations look best where.
- ◇ White plants are most easily seen in the dark, so use them along walkways or in dark corners of your yard to make that area "pop out."
- ◇ In deciding what to plant, think back to the plants you loved when you were six, says a friend with a landscape design business. Plant those.
- ◇ And finally, from the Master Gardener Himself: water your garden if you want it to flourish (see Isaiah 1:30; 58:11; Jeremiah 31:12).

I like this quote from *The American Gardener: A Sampler*, originally written by Charles Dudley Warner in 1870 in *My Summer in a Garden*: "Hoe while it is spring, and enjoy the best anticipations. It is not much matter if things do not turn out well."[9]

Good. I will dream and I will hoe and I will hope that the bunnies leave me at least a few blooms to enjoy. After all, it is not much matter if things do not turn out well. ♛

"Out of the ground the LORD God caused to grow every tree that is pleasing to the sight and good for food." (Genesis 2:9)

pra**y**er LORD, THANK YOU FOR THE GLORY OF GROWTH. THANK YOU THAT YOU PROVIDE BEAUTY IN NATURE FOR OUR PLEASURE AND OUR SUSTENANCE, AND THAT SOMEDAY IN HEAVEN WE WILL BE SURROUNDED BY NOTHING BUT BEAUTY. HELP ME TO FIND TIME TODAY TO SPEND WITH YOU, ENJOYING YOUR AMAZING CREATION.

week 16

The Simple Secret to Omitting Stress from Your Life

OK. There is no simple secret to omitting stress from your life. If you are a homemaker, stress comes with the job. In fact, if you are a human being, stress comes with the job.

But sometimes just recognizing the things in life that cause stress can be a huge help. When you look at what makes for a stressful job and match those characteristics against the duties of homemaking, the overlap will astonish you. In her wonderful and informative book *Motherhood Stress,* Deborah Shaw Lewis says a stressful job is one that, among other things, is complex (made up of a number of very different tasks), is characterized by lack of control (the job is largely determined by the schedules of others), and gives the worker no sense of completion.[1]

Does that sound like a day in the life of a homemaker or what?

Think about it. We are responsible for dozens of jobs demanding wildly divergent skills, from helping a child write a book report to efficiently zapping out grass stains, from remembering birthdays and choosing appropriate gifts to knowing what to do with a pound of ground round. We are expected to nurse a baby while corralling a rampant

new word
for the week:

Splenetic (splĭ-nĕt′ ĭk).
Ill-humored; irritable. As in, *"Seven days a week of chauffeuring the family in nine different directions can leave me feeling exceedingly splenetic."*

alternate
now word:

Swivet (swĭv′ ĭt).
A state of nervous excitement, haste, or anxiety. As in, *"Maybe if I spend a few minutes talking to God I won't be in such a swivet."*

toddler—sometimes while we're at the shopping mall!—or fix company dinner while our eight-year-old lies feverish in the next room. Our house that we battled like Hercules to get clean yesterday is today strewn with drinking glasses that never quite made it to the dishwasher, baseball cleats that never quite made it to the closet, and mail that never quite made it to the trash can.

Is it any wonder we're stressed?

Recognizing the inherent stress of our jobs won't make the pressure go away. But it can make us go easier on ourselves.

We can also consider the possibility that our housekeeping standards are too high. As Lewis points out, "Where our grandmothers would brush dried mud off overalls to make them 'wearable' for another few days, if my daughter dribbles milk on her blouse during breakfast, I toss it into the dirty clothes basket and find her a clean top to wear to school. So, while washing a load of clothes is certainly easier today than it used to be, mothers today wash many more clothes, much more often."[3]

If you have a hard time believing your standards are all that high, think about your definition of an acceptable dirt level when your family goes camping. Don't you overlook a lot? Don't you require your children to change into a fresh set of clothes far less frequently? Yet somehow when we return home, it's back to the high bar. I can; therefore I wash.

We need to go easy on ourselves, especially if we're going through a particularly demanding phase of life: babies or toddlers in the house, homeschooling responsibilities, health challenges, unusually heavy chauffeuring or homework assistance duties. We're not trying to win cleanest home of the year award. We're trying to care for our family's basic needs, and to get them, and us, through a stressful period with as much grace as possible.

Ponder the wisdom of this saying, from FlyLady.net, a Web site aimed at helping women become more organized in their homes: "Housework done incorrectly still blesses your family."

Thankfully.

In his famous autobiography, Benjamin Franklin details an interesting experiment he conceived, to accomplish "the bold and arduous project of arriving at moral perfection. I wish'd to live without committing any fault at any time. . . . As I knew, or thought I knew, what was right and wrong, I did not see why I might not always do the one and avoid the other."

Franklin made a list of thirteen virtues, "all that at that time occur'd to me as necessary or desirable." Included in his list were temperance ("Eat not to dullness; drink not to elevation"); silence ("Speak not but what may benefit others or yourself; avoid trifling conversation"); and order ("Let all your things have their places; let each part of your business have its time").

Then he made a chart listing the days of the week. Each week he concentrated on one virtue, marking on his chart in the evening those faults he committed. His hope was to master a virtue each week, then be ready to move on to the next.

After years, really, of experimenting, he discovered his method didn't work. Franklin found "I had undertaken a task of more difficulty than I had imagined. While my care was employ'd in guarding against one fault, I was often surprised by another. . . . I concluded, at length, that the mere speculative conviction that it was our interest to be completely virtuous, was not sufficient to prevent our slipping."

As a mom and homemaker, I, too, would like to attain perfection on this job, eradicating my faults simply by keeping a chart. I'd like my menus to always be balanced, my holiday celebrations memorable, my temper long and my list of undone chores short. But like Benjamin Franklin,

I am sometimes "surpris'd to find myself so much fuller of faults than I had imagined."

In my work at home I fall far, far short of perfection. That realization can lead to stress and feelings of failure if I let it. But just as God loves us regardless of our faults, so does our family, regardless of our homemaking skills.

My home may never live up to that picture in my head of magazine perfection: gleaming oiled wood tables, crystal vases filled with fresh peonies (not a hint of green in the water), pristine countertops, carpeting with those newly vacuumed swoops. Let's face it: even at Thanksgiving when I've spent weeks trying to orchestrate this fantasy, I'm lucky if everything comes together in a perfect crescendo for just one brief moment in time.

And that is precisely the point. The picture *is* a fantasy. A nice one, to be sure, and one I can manage occasionally, with a huge amount of effort, when I'm not experiencing PMS, there's no science fair looming, the kids' sports schedules are at an uncharacteristic lull, and all the planets have aligned. But in reality, it's out of everyday reach as long as the people I live with are audacious enough to actually *use* the bathroom I just cleaned.

We need to let go of the perfect home fantasy, to gently loosen our pinkies then ring fingers from that tenacious grip that if only we tried harder, if only we kept a chart like dear old Mr. Franklin, we, too, could reach perfection. Let's just be thankful for our homes, our families, and our many blessings. And let's remember that even when our countertops sport mounds of papers and catalogs full of things we can't afford, God loves us and accepts us. 'Tis a good thing.

Sometimes stress comes from a particularly wild week that's somehow gotten out of control, like an infection gone mad. One particularly stressful week from springtime past found me in the middle of Little League baseball season, with two boys on two teams at two locations. On top of my regular mothering and chauffeuring duties, I was also contending with a husband who'd just had knee surgery. The kids needed to be in four places at once. (Did I mention the spring music concert?) Now, not only was my husband unavailable as emergency backup driver, but with the knee situation I'd had to become *his* driver, as well.

I didn't know how I was going to cope.

In truth, I didn't cope very well. Fortunately, my parents were able to bail me out one day by driving one son to his ball game while I worked the snack shack at my other son's game (my husband's cell phone in my purse, should he need me).

Somehow I got through the week, tense and ready to bite, not fully able to meet all my commitments but not sure I could have done anything differently under the circumstances.

Later, as I thought back to the crushing load I'd felt, I realized that there had been one thing in my swivet I had forgotten to do. I'd forgotten to come to Jesus.

In Matthew 11:28–30, Jesus says, "Come to Me, all who are weary and heavy-laden, and I will give you rest. Take My yoke upon you, and learn from Me, for I am gentle and humble in heart, and you will find rest for your souls. For My yoke is easy and My load is light."

I looked up *come* in some Bible reference books and discovered that in this instance, it means "come hither and follow." It's an invitation to a group of people, like saying, "Come on, everybody, let's go to my house!" Jesus used the same "come" in Mark 1:17 when He said, "Come, follow me, and I will make you fishers of men" (NIV).

In my anxiety during that tension-filled week, I had forgotten to come. It was as though my wallet were completely empty and I kept trying to spend money that wasn't there, yet the automatic bank teller with plenty of cash in my account was just down the block. How shortsighted, to live as though I have no resources when, in truth, as a child of God all the resources of the world are at my disposal.

I don't always remember during times of stress to come to Jesus, to get rest from Him, to exchange my heavy load for His light one. I like to think I am self-reliant, that I can handle all my problems myself. I often don't ask for help until I'm feeling totally depleted and crushed.

I don't think God wants me to wait that long. I think He wants me to come to Him for help as soon as I realize I'm in deep waters.

And I think He wants me to be willing to ask for help from others too.

The definition of *yoke*, I discovered, is a harness that was never intended to be worn by just one. It was designed for *two* creatures to share the workload. That helps me see how important it is for me to bring my troubles to Jesus when I'm feeling stressed and overburdened. I don't need to walk alone, lugging hundreds of pounds more than I can carry. My shoulders are weak, and He knows that. As soon as I ask Him to, Christ will walk with me, sharing my life and my burdens, taking nearly all the weight from my back so all that's left is an amount I can bear. It is heavy enough, to be sure, but as I walk with Christ, sharing the yoke designed for two, I know it can be carried.

And who knows, He may provide some earthly "fellow oxen" to share my burdens, too, like my parents during that postsurgery week.

Only don't tell my mom I called her an ox.

Next time you're stressed, spend five minutes doing one of the following:

- ◇ Sitting quietly with God
- ◇ Swinging on swings
- ◇ Listening to praise music
- ◇ Enjoying a scented candle
- ◇ Blowing bubbles
- ◇ Squishing play dough through your fingers
- ◇ Coloring

- ◇ Walking outside
- ◇ Gathering the clan for a family hug
- ◇ Taking extra vitamin C
- ◇ Reading *Motherhood Stress* by Deborah Shaw Lewis
- ◇ Reading the book of Psalms (Psalm 107 is a great one)

"For the good that I want, I do not do, but I practice the very evil that I do not want. . . . Wretched man that I am! Who will set me free from the body of this death? Thanks be to God through Jesus Christ our Lord!" (Romans 7:19, 24–25)

prayer LORD, THANK YOU THAT NEITHER DEATH NOR LIFE NOR DIRTY LAUNDRY NOR STICKY FLOORS NOR GROCERY SHOPPING NOR CARPOOLING NOR HOMEWORK NOR SCIENCE-FAIR PROJECTS CAN SEPARATE US FROM YOUR LOVE. WHETHER I HANDLE LIFE WELL OR POORLY, THANK YOU THAT NOTHING I DO WILL MAKE YOU LOVE ME ANY MORE, OR LESS. HELP ME NOT TO BE STRESSED OVER MY IMPERFECTIONS, BUT TO REST IN THE COMFORTING KNOWLEDGE THAT THROUGH CHRIST, I AM ACCEPTABLE TO YOU.

week 17

So You're a Sidetracked Home Executive™?

It wasn't until we had children that my husband's and my organizational shortcomings became problematic. What had seemed like minor messiness was, once the kids came, revealed as the beast it truly was, with the house quickly overrun not only by our own belongings but now a plethora of baby paraphernalia—enough swings and strollers and high chairs and cribs to sink the ark, or to sink our little tract house anyway.

Soon enough we moved to a larger home, but there the original problem persisted. In fact, the larger house simply meant I could never hope to get it all clean at the same time, and now there was that much more space to stash magazines I didn't have time to read and pants that no longer fit. All items that were unsafe for little ones or liable to be gummed and maimed (photos, books, important papers) took a hurried trip to high bookshelves. During those exhausting days that started before dawn and ended after midnight, I was consumed with the demands of keeping my babies alive, fed, relatively clean, and relatively happy. Let's face it: when I had spare minutes, I didn't choose to clear out clutter but rather danced my cherubs around the kitchen, held them in my lap and read picture books, and endlessly rolled tennis balls back and forth with them across the kitchen floor.

new word
for the week:

Fusty (fŭs' tē).
Smelling of mildew or decay; musty. As in *"The laundry must have overstayed its welcome in the washing machine; these shorts smell fusty."*

alternate
new word:

Welter (wĕl' tər).
A confused mass; a jumble. As in, *"Let me move this welter of magazines so you can sit down."*

Once my children reached school age and I had more free time at my disposal, I morphed into frenzied volunteer mom. Room mom, Little League mom, Sunday school mom, field trip mom—you name it, I raised my hand for it. Meanwhile, the diaper rash ointment and six different treatments for cuts and scrapes continued to live on my tippy-top shelves, celebrating each new decade with confetti of dust.

For men, being sidetracked isn't such a big deal; most men have wives to make sure they have clean underwear and food in the refrigerator. But if you're the wife, you're the one expected to provide the underwear and the food, and if you're way more temperamentally suited to creating a spectacular raspberry bombe than to decoding insurance papers and getting them mailed out on time—well, you may be in for a bit of trouble. Which I was.

It was at this point I came to recognize fellow domestic strugglers from my weekly women's Bible study group. Not because they were disheveled (they weren't; in fact, people are always surprised to learn we are "messies," as if we should have a tooth missing or be sporting mismatched socks). But through heartfelt conversations snuck between questions two and three, we learned of our common housekeeping travails. Once we identified one another, it was a short step to agree to meet occasionally to spur each other on in our organizing efforts.

Born-organized friends who hear about our "messies" meetings (named after books such as *The Messies Manual* and *Messie No More* by Sandra Felton) seem baffled and slightly amused. They don't need support groups to urge them to throw out old catalogs and outdated coupons. They already know what to do with scads of children's school papers and stacks of vacation photographs.

But we don't. For whatever reason—a high level of distractibility, too hyper-focused to see the big picture, more right-brained than left—some of us seem destined to be sidetracked, no matter how hard we try. We have no household "systems." Or maybe we had one once, for a few minutes, but the phone rang and it was someone asking us to go to the park, or the children were hungry and it was time to make dinner, or the dryer with our husband's shirts buzzed and we left our half-done system on the kitchen counter where it got pushed into the corner until it gradually became part of the permanent landscape. We may be incredibly organized in some areas—maintaining a killer file system or running Girl Scout fund-raisers with our eyes shut—but when it comes to coping with the myriad tasks that contribute to a smooth-running home, we may be completely overwhelmed, flattened by the tank that just keeps coming.

If you've ever bought a book on housekeeping only to lose it under a pile of clutter; if you've ever failed to notice the dog hair on the couch until a houseguest got up, covered in fur; if you've ever found a toddler-sized sleeper in the mending pile when all household members are taller than you are—you might benefit from a messies support group. Ask God to lead.

Don't despair. Change can happen.

And about that mending pile? Pitch it. No one will ever miss the sleeper.

For our group's first few meetings, we listened to the "Messies Anonymous™ Self Help" cassette tape, which gave us pep talks and instruction in our quest to become better organized. "There are many good things in the world," we learned. "They do not all have to reside in our home."[2]

Once we finished the four-part tape, we kept meeting, even without an official curriculum. We shared reading materials, tapes, and videos we'd found helpful. We challenged one another to write down specific decluttering goals ("I'll work on my messy desk for ten minutes a day"). The next meeting, we tried to remember to ask about progress (being sidetracked, we sometimes, ahem, forgot to ask). One meeting we brought our junk drawers and sorted. Often we'd just talk about housekeeping struggles, sharing tea and empathy. Just knowing that other women faced the same problem seemed to help. It kept us accountable, the same way dieting groups help people who know they'll eventually have to meet up and weigh in.

Some of our group's favorite resources were books and tapes by the Sidetracked Home Executives™ sisters Pam Young and Peggy Jones. The two women, who believe they have attention deficit disorder but have never gotten around to getting diagnosed, have battled disorganization in their own lives and have worked since 1977 to help others.

The system that took them "from pigpen to paradise," as they put it, is based on index cards. You begin with a stack of colored three-by-five cards; dividers on which you write Sunday, Monday, Tuesday, etc.; and a file card box to house them all. You fill out each card with a household chore that needs to be done (color-coded for daily, weekly, and occasional jobs). Then you file each job behind the day of the week you plan to do it.

To use the cards, check your box each day to see what jobs await. When you complete a job, refile the card under the next time the job will need to be done. (For a more detailed account of the system, read Young and Jones's highly entertaining book, *Sidetracked Home Executives*.[2]) The idea is that the card system keeps you on track. With each chore written down and in front of you, you have a concrete plan for the day. Without such a plan, those of us who are sidetracked will simply let the day take over, intending to spend half an hour cleaning out the study but winding up spending three hours reading old love letters instead.

Getting the whole house clean at once may still be a distant dream. But if you've identified a job and done it, give yourself full credit. You're on your way. The box and I applaud you.

A couple of summers ago, a friend from my "messies" group and I traveled to Portland, Oregon, for a Sidetracked Home Executives™ conference. While there, we heard stories from women who've all but drowned in the never-ending responsibilities of running a home. There was the woman whose twelve-hundred-square-foot home had been so filled with clutter her family had been forced to squish into four hundred square feet. As she pondered the monthly expense of those "lost" eight hundred square feet, she asked herself, "Why am I spending all this money storing things that aren't worth fifty bucks a month for me to store in a rental unit?" She decided to hold a huge garage sale and in the process reclaimed her house.

Another woman faced a turning point one day when unexpected company dropped in. "I looked behind me at the inside of the house and was horrified. For the first time I realized, 'This isn't good enough for my family.'" From that point on, she's worked hard to keep her house under control.

Keeping up with housework and down with clutter will never be easy for some of us. But these stories of courage, determination, and hard work give me hope.

If you're trying to recover from a lifetime of collecting too much stuff, be patient with yourself. You didn't get into this mess overnight, and you're not going to get out of it overnight. Just a little bit at a time and you will make progress. Like the motto on the back of my son's football T-shirt says: "I may not be the man I want to be; I may not be the man I ought to be; I may not be the man I could be; but, I refuse to be the man I was."

Getting rid of clutter can be painful. You have to face tough choices about those perfectly good magazines with perfectly good recipes you always meant to cut out and try. Or even harder, Junior's precious first-grade alphabets with the backward D's. (One friend allows herself one trunk of mementoes for each child, and once it's filled, no more.) You don't have to get rid of everything. But you do have to get rid of some things. Taking pictures of your more-beloved clutter makes it easier to say good-bye. You're not compelled to keep the fourth-grade mission project if you have a clear photo of your son holding it.

If you're ready to get started, here are several methods for clutter clear out:

- ◇ The three-bag method, where you work room by room, sorting what you find into bags (or boxes) marked "throw away," "give away," and "put away." Set the timer and work for thirty minutes at a time. When the timer goes off, the throw-aways go straight into the garbage, the give-aways go straight to the car for delivery to the nearest Goodwill (no saving them for the perfect recipient; eject them now!), and the put-aways go back where they belong—i.e., books in the bookshelf, toys in the toy cabinet, etc.
- ◇ The Mount Vernon Method, as practiced by the cleaning staff of George Washington's estate in Virginia and described in Sandra Felton's books. Start at your home's front door and proceed around each room's perimeter, cleaning and clearing out clutter as you go. Eventually you'll make it around the entire house, whereupon it'll be time to start over. "The most important thing about the Mount Vernon Method is that you pace yourself and not overdo," says Felton in *The Messies Manual*. "Don't start out too fast. You will not be able to accomplish the Method in a single day (it took me three and a half months to 'Mount Vernonize' my home)."[4]
- ◇ The "27 fling boogie," as described on the Web site FlyLady.net and also in the book *Sink Reflections* by Marla Cilley,[5] where you grab a bag and as quickly as possible fill it with twenty-seven items to be thrown away. Next time you have a spare fifteen minutes, set the timer, grab another bag, and fill it with twenty-seven items to be given away.

Whatever the method, once you discard extra stuff, you'll be amazed at how much easier it is to keep the house looking decent, even if it's not perfectly polished. Promise. ♛

"There is an appointed time for everything. And there is a time for every event under heaven. . . . A time to keep and a time to throw away." (Ecclesiastes 3:1, 6)

Quotable

What helped me was a realization of how much time and energy I was wasting on clutter. I didn't have the time to dust it, the space to store it, or the inclination to insure it, so I got rid of it. [6]

Pam McClellan,
Don't Be a Slave to Housework

prayer LORD, SOMETIMES I FEEL OVERWHELMED IN MY WORK AT HOME; THERE IS SO MUCH TO DO! THANK YOU THAT MY WORTH DOES NOT DEPEND ON HOW TIDY MY HOUSE IS. PLEASE HELP ME TO CONCENTRATE AND STAY FOCUSED ON THE TASKS YOU WANT ME TO DO TODAY.

CHOCOLATE BREAK! Stop!

EUROPEAN HOT CHOCOLATE

When my mom and dad took a trip to Italy in honor of their fiftieth wedding anniversary, Mom came back raving not about the art or the culture but about the hot chocolate. (That's my mom!)

The Italian hot chocolate, she says, was so thick it was almost a dessert, and she dedicated her next few months to searching for a way to replicate it. She finally found this recipe, thus saving my dad thousands of dollars for a return trip. Now we all get to savor the taste of Italy without leaving our very own kitchens (darn). This recipe has quickly become an indispensable family favorite, replacing the instant packets we used to consider hot chocolate.

Be forewarned, this does take a bit of patience—about fifteen to twenty minutes stirring time. But it's worth every minute, and the perfect reward when you need one. As this recipe contains four cups of milk, award yourself bonus calcium points.

EUROPEAN HOT CHOCOLATE

In small bowl, mix together:

½ cup cocoa powder

1 cup sugar

Set aside. In large saucepan, stir together:

3 T. cornstarch

½ cup water

Add the cocoa/sugar mixture to the water and cornstarch, and stir with a whisk. Cook the mixture over medium-high heat, stirring constantly, as you gradually add: **4 cups milk**.

Bring hot chocolate mixture to a simmer, stirring often for about fifteen minutes, until the mixture thickens.

Drink up. And if you folded laundry and scrubbed the toilet and swept your kitchen floor today, you've earned seconds.

Note: Any leftovers are delicious cold too.

week 18

new word
for the week:

Evanescent

(ĕv′ə-nĕs′ ənt).

Vanishing or likely to vanish; fleeting. As in, *"I'm going to enjoy my shiny sink; the sparkle and clean smell are surely evanescent."*

alternate
new word:

Moony (moo′ nē).

Dreamy in mood or nature; absent-minded. As in, *"Excuse my mooniness; I was distracted by the brilliance of my shiny sink."*

Housework, Done Correctly, Can Kill You

My house is in no danger of being featured in some sleek magazine unless the topic is "How to save wear and tear on your kitchen counters by covering them with unread mail." My family thinks it's hilarious that I'm even writing a chapter about housework. But though I'll never win an award for tidiest home of the year, I have learned through hard experience that I do myself no favors by putting off chores. Sooner or later, I do have to open the drapes and deal with the speckled windows and cobwebs. What could have been a two-minute job if regularly maintained becomes a monstrous task when seriously neglected.

I have learned that keeping up with chores is not a sentence to lifetime membership in the household drudge club, but rather a path to freedom: the freedom to reach into your drawer and be greeted by clean underwear and socks, the freedom to find a pencil with a point when you need it, the freedom to find your kitchen table and be able to eat off it.

Here are a few other housekeeping lessons I've learned along the way:

- ❖ Wash your dishes after the meal, not the next morning when the melted cheese has become superglued to the fork tines.

- ❖ Use a timer for short bursts of cleaning, especially if you're overwhelmed by a task's enormity. Even in two minutes, you can make progress.

- ❖ You can't clean surfaces if you don't have surfaces, say authors Pam Young and Peggy Jones. Work steadily, a little at a time, ridding your tables of newspapers, coupons, and school newsletters that propagate on all available flat spots. At the very least, try to consolidate papers to one pile per room.

- ❖ Have people over often, preferably once a week. That way you'll get the house presentable on a regular basis, stopping the entropy before it multiplies into full-blown chaos.

- ❖ Find cleaning products with scents you like.

- ❖ Hide a treat for yourself by the stain remover or toilet bowl cleaner.

- ❖ "Make sure you stop frequently to admire your work and if your children are helping you, theirs," advises Cindy Tolliver, author of *At-Home Motherhood: Making It Work for You.* "Stand back and take a long look at a beautiful stack of laundered towels, a clean window, a pretty table setting."[2]

- ❖ Accept that keeping up with housework takes time—an estimated fifteen to twenty-five hours a week. If your house is in serious disarray, consider cutting back on outside activities for a while. It's unrealistic to expect you can attend every scrapbooking class and school boosters meeting and still get all your homework done.

- ❖ Lemon oil on wood furniture makes it look pretty.

Author Sandra Felton, in *The Messies Manual*, says, "Our first responsibility is our home, not for the sake of the house, but for the sake of ourselves and our families. The home is the base from which we reach out into the world. When our base is in order and we have a schedule of maintenance, then we can begin to add a little at a time until we see how much we can handle."[4] Once you can find your kitchen table and eat off it, you're on your way.

More Housework Tips

◊ You are not responsible for keeping every grocery bag (or rubber band, or twist-tie) that comes your way. According to Stephanie Culp, author of *How to Conquer Clutter*, ten to twelve bags is plenty. So part with some of your stash.[5]

◊ In the same way that library due dates motivate you to return those books, setting due dates of your own can help you discard household excess. For example, gather stray socks that emerge from the washing machine into a plastic bag, label "Throw away if no mate by _____," and give yourself three months for the missing in action to show up. Try the same tactic with three-year-old magazines or ancient food in the freezer. ("Throw out if unread/uneaten by _____"; give yourself two weeks.)

◊ Did you know that cows reportedly give more milk when they listen to music? Turn up that radio and clean like a madwoman for two songs' worth.

◊ Just because we're doing housework doesn't mean we have to put away our brains. Homemaker Kathryn Donovan Wiegand, a Harvard-Radcliffe graduate and mother of six, says, "Much of the rhythmic routines of laundry, dishes, and toy-sorting keep my hands busy but leave my mind free to ponder Tolstoy's musings on the inevitability of history. I am enjoying *War and Peace* in ten-page bites, sandwiched between dicing carrots and figuring out how our new whizbang electric juicer works. I memorize music from a hymnal propped open on the kitchen counter while doing dishes."[6] Your feet may be planted in front of the kitchen sink, but your mind is free to travel the world.

One woman who has discovered the joy of freedom from clutter is Marla Cilley, a.k.a. the FlyLady. In her book *Sink Reflections*, and on her Web site FlyLady.net, Cilley encourages those of us who are in CHAOS (Can't Have Anyone Over Syndrome) to work on our homes a little at a time, starting with creating housekeeping routines that will become habits. Cilley breaks housework down into manageable pieces that keep you from being overwhelmed. For example, she advises to start with shining your sink. That's it. Once you've mastered that, the next step is to get dressed every morning, all the way to your shoes. Follow that with other "BabySteps," including checking to see where your laundry is, making your bed, and on from there.

Her method takes the complex job of running a home and breaks it into simple steps that work, even for those of us who get sidetracked by the arrival of the mailman. Like the fashion-impaired reaching for her basic black dress, we can reach for FlyLady's routines and begin to get our homes under control. A formula! Routines! They really work.

Along with starting small and developing good habits, Cilley advises short, timed sessions for clearing out clutter spots. A few minutes of attention every day can, over time, reduce that heap of unanswered mail into merely a memory.

The goal, as she reminds us, isn't to end up with a perfect house. Perfectionism, in fact, can do you in, as you will either give up on the impossible task you've set for yourself or, at the opposite extreme, pursue pristine linoleum at the expense of enjoying your family. (No, no, no!)

The goal is a home that looks presentable and functions well. You have permission to haphazardly pull up covers when you make your bed; it's OK to just spritz the toothpaste off the bathroom mirror and leave the tub scouring for another time. Three minutes spent vacuuming high-traffic areas is acceptable. The house will look better than it did.

My friend Kris, who's learning to knit, was told by the lady at the yarn store not to worry about making mistakes in the sweater she's knitting. Those small imperfections prove her sweater was knit not on a machine but by hand, with love.

Just like our homes.

When author Sue Bender (*Plain and Simple: A Woman's Journey to the Amish*) spent some weeks living with the Amish in an effort to better understand and absorb their ways, she was surprised at the attitude these hard-working women held toward housework. With the simplicity of their lifestyle—no electricity, no cars, no soccer leagues to hustle the kids to at three o'clock—the Amish women did their daily chores with contentment. They didn't see the perpetual cycle of cleaning, gardening, canning, and laundry as tedium, something to be hurried through in order to get to something more important. In their minds, the housework was important.[8]

The Amish showed a satisfaction in their work at home in a way that I often do not. There is something to be said for contentment, for being unhurried, for doing what you're doing with serenity and calm. You are doing your job in caring for your home and family. You are confident and fulfilled. The work is necessary; the work is important; the work is good.

To encourage younger women to be "workers at home" is one of the instructions Paul gives older women in Titus 2:3–5. Just what exactly is a "worker at home"?

The King James Version translates the phrase as "keepers at home." Coming from root words for a *dwelling*, *home*, or *household*, plus the word for *guard*, it's the picture of one who watches or keeps guard over the home and family.

The NIV says we are to be "busy at home." Other versions say "domestic," "diligent in home work," "keepers of (their own) houses," "care for their homes," and "home-

Quotable

If you wish to have cleanliness as proof of your efforts, you will find yourself overcome and defeated at every turn. Your best bet is to set a goal, accomplish it, and leave it at that. You vacuumed the carpet. It is now cleaner than it was before, and no matter what you do it is going to get dirty again. The time and energy that you expend trying to delay the next vacuuming will probably cost you more in irritation and anxiety than it would to repeat the task.[9]

Pamela Piljac,
You Can Go Home Again

makers." My favorite is from the J. B. Phillips translation: we are to be "home-lovers." ♥

"Do all things without grumbling or disputing."
(Philippians 2:14)

prayer LORD, HELP ME TO REMEMBER THAT AS I AM A "WORKER AT HOME," I AM BEING OBEDIENT TO YOU. I AM ALSO BEING A BLESSING TO MY FAMILY. WHAT A GIFT YOU'VE GIVEN ME IN THIS FAMILY TO TAKE CARE OF! THANK YOU.

may

week 19

new word

for the week:

Quotidian (kwō-tĭd′ ē-ən).
Recurring daily. As in, *"In between
my quotidian chores of cooking,
scrubbing, shopping, driving,
straightening, and washing, I will try
to find time to enjoy a cup of homemade hot chocolate."*

alternate

new word:

Moil (moil).
Toil; drudgery. As in, *"All moil and
no play makes for a very grumpy
queen."*

Drudgery, Schmudgery

Some women love to make beautiful gardens but hate grocery shopping. Some prize an immaculate home but hate
cooking (those nasty, dirty dishes and splattered stove).
Some, like me, enjoy baking cookies and making jam but
have to force themselves to sort through stray papers or
vacuum.

In our job as homemakers, there will always be some
tasks we greet with the same enthusiasm as the unidentifiable furry objects we find in the back of our refrigerators.
Didn't I just scrub that out last decade?

While our job gives us the freedom to make our homes
in all kinds of ways, let's face it: eventually the house has
to get vacuumed, the kitchen must be scrubbed, and the
need for Honey Toasty-Os will drive us to the grocery. How
we handle doing things we know we should but don't really
want to comes down to a little thing called character.

God appears to value hard work and our willingness to
do it. We are told a godly woman should be busy at home
(Titus 2:5), should work with her hands in delight (Proverbs 31:13), and should look well to the ways of her household and not eat the bread of idleness (Proverbs 31:27).
Many proverbs warn of the danger of sloth: the sluggard
who won't plow will have nothing during the harvest and

will have to resort to begging (Proverbs 20:4); a slothful man has no prey to roast (Proverbs 12:27); one who follows empty pursuits instead of tilling his land will have poverty (Proverbs 28:19); if you till your land you'll have plenty of bread, but if you pursue vain things you lack sense (Proverbs 12:11). It's enough to make you want to rush outside and start tilling.

When I make choices that don't reflect diligence, my family pays a price. If I'm home but choose to put off starting dinner preparations until it's actually time to eat, for example, the result will be a late dinner and cranky, hungry kids who've probably snuck in too many snacks. And who could blame them?

In her book *Still Cove Journal*, Gladys Taber reminds us to appreciate our options:

> When housework suddenly seems unbearable . . . the homemaker has a freedom of choice seldom possible in an office routine. . . . Let the washing go—it will keep. Or go out to cut juniper branches for the ironstone jug. Take an extra pan of bird food out and watch the quail come bobbing along. Or if your conscience will not let you put off the chores entirely, at least pick a job you really enjoy. Instead of running the vacuum, polish the copper (this always gives a sense of accomplishment).
>
> The main thing about housework is that you can change the routine and make your own choices.[1]

Some parts of homemaking will always be a struggle for me. But even though I don't like certain chores and would much rather be baking, I still need to face them. And so do you.

Proverbs 31:13 says an excellent wife "works with her hands in delight." The word *delight* says to me that she does

Quotable

How can you make a boring task that must be done more enjoyable? . . . This is where combining positives with negatives can help you. Make a list of things that appeal to your right brain: freshly baked chocolate-chip cookies; Broadway show tunes; Casablanca; brightly colored envelopes for sorting receipts; breaking up work periods with playful activities; translucent envelopes; jumbo colored clips.

Then combine something from this list with part of your boring task. For example, you might listen to the musical score from Les Miserables *while you are cleaning the bathroom or work on your mileage record while watching* The Big Chill.[2]

Ann McGee-Cooper with Duane Trammell,
Time Management for Unmanageable People

her work with a good attitude—something I admit is often lacking when company's coming and I find myself on hands and knees scrubbing around the base of the toilet and wondering just when, exactly, I signed on for this marvelous task.

A few thoughts to nurture delight in our work:

- *Think of all the women around the world who don't have access to clean running water or electricity or a grocery store filled with more food items than we can identify. Realize how blessed we are with resources as we do our work at home.*

- *Be grateful for your health and the strong body that enables you to work. Many people would love to be up and doing the work we take for granted we can do every day, but they're not physically able. Tell yourself, "I can work. It's a good thing."*

- *Turn chore time into a time of connecting with God. As you work, pray for family or friends; memorize a favorite Bible verse; think of ten things you're thankful for.*

- *Consider that the apostle Paul wrote the book of Philippians while he was arrested and chained to a guard. In this letter, he was bursting with confidence that no matter what his situation, Christ was being exalted. If he could have joy while being chained to a guard, I can have joy as I spritz the dog saliva off the sliding glass door for the hundredth time.*

- *Rejoice that at the same time your floors are getting scrubbed or your kids are making it to swim practice, God is doing something even greater: He is building in you the qualities of diligence and faithfulness.*

- *As you work, remember what you're working for. You are doing this to support the family you love. What could be more important than taking care of your family?*

As well as looking at chores in a different light, a few other strategies can be helpful as you work. Playing music can be a good motivator, either praise music or loud, energetic songs to clean by. One woman swears that wearing bright colors as she cleans gives her more energy.

Listening to a book on tape from the library can make the most tedious chores more bearable. I've learned how Frederick Douglass escaped slavery as I scrubbed my kitchen floor. I've discovered that Benjamin Franklin invented libraries and volunteer fire departments as I matched gold-toed, gray-heeled, long and short white socks. I've learned about motherhood stress (from the book of the same name by Deborah Shaw Lewis with Gregg Lewis) as I erased Christmas "snow" from my window.

You might also try timing yourself as you do your most dreaded drudge work. In their excellent book *Organizing for the Creative Person*, Dorothy Lehmkuhl and Dolores Cotter Lamping point out that "People tend to overestimate the time it takes to do work they dislike, and underestimate the time to do things they enjoy. . . . You can look at a pile of clothes on your bedroom floor and perceive that it will take an hour to clean up. This, of course, would be an overload on your schedule, but in reality it might not take more than five or ten minutes."[3]

Finally, don't forget that "Where no oxen are, the manger is clean" (Proverbs 14:4). As long as we have oxen in our home, we will have cleaning to do.

Also, "But much revenue comes by the strength of the ox" (Proverbs 14:4).

Whatever that means.

Before Laura Ingalls Wilder became known for writing the *Little House* books, she wrote a newspaper column for farm wives. Though most women today have quite a different list of chores than Wilder's—it's been ages since I've milked a cow—nonetheless what Wilder says about the importance of our jobs at home is timeless.

Here's what she wrote in 1923:

Putting up the school lunch for the children or cooking a good meal for the family may seem very insignificant tasks as compared with giving a lecture, writing a book, or doing other things that have a larger audience; but I doubt very much if, in the ultimate reckoning, they will count for as much.

If when cooking you will think of yourselves as the chemist that you are, combining different ingredients into a food that will properly nourish human bodies, then the work takes on a dignity and an interest. And surely a family well nourished with healthful food so that the boys and girls grow up strong and beautiful, while their elders reach a hale old age, is no small thing.

It belittles us to think of our daily tasks as small things, and if we continue to do so, it will in time make us small. It will narrow our horizon and make of our work just drudgery.

There are so many little things that are really very great, and when we learn to look beyond the insignificant appearing acts themselves to their far-reaching consequences, we will, "despise not the day of small things." We will feel an added dignity and poise from the fact that our everyday round of duties is as important as any other part of the work of the world.[4]

"You're doing great. You're achieving your goals. Will you ever look terrific at the beach!"

A few years back, a California company developed a small handheld computer whose sole purpose was to encourage dieters. Throughout the day, as the dieter recorded her food eaten and calories expended, the machine beeped encouraging messages to spur her on.

Wouldn't it be wonderful if, as homemakers, we had a similar device? If, as we diligently performed the most tedious parts of our job, we received that kind of steady, way-to-go encouragement? "Great job on spot cleaning the carpet! That bathroom floor has never looked so sparkly! I love it when the garbage cans are emptied!"

On the bold assumption that no such encouraging voice is following you throughout your day, you're going to have to become your own cheerleader. I once tried some magazine advice and mailed myself a letter of appreciation; when I received it a couple of days later, it made me smile as though it had come from an extremely thoughtful friend.

Don't be shy about rewarding yourself as you do your housework, especially if you've tackled a job you really dislike. The world may not notice you pumiced away the ring around the toilet, but you can promise yourself a twenty-minute break with your favorite magazine once you're done. You might be surprised at how your attitude takes an immediate upturn.

A few possibilities for diligence rewards: Buy some colorful new stickers and, after you've completed a particularly odious task, post one on your calendar (or five). Play the piano for ten minutes or belt out your favorite tune while dancing around the room. (If you have a teenager, ignore the grumbly, "Mom, you're embarrassing me in my own kitchen!") One woman gives herself a pedicure before vacuuming, telling herself that she's "simply vacuuming to pass the time needed for my nails to dry; a facemask would have the same effect."[6] Prop up your feet and savor a cup of tea served in your prettiest mug. Better yet, if you have any energy left after your chores, try making some European Hot Chocolate (see CHOCOLATE BREAK! after week 17).

And remember: You're doing great. You're achieving your goals. Will you ever look terrific at the beach! ♛

"His master replied, 'Well done, good and faithful servant! You have been faithful with a few things; I will put you in charge of many things. Come and share your master's happiness!'" (Matthew 25:21 NIV)

---

praуer LORD, THANK YOU FOR GIVING ME MANY OPPORTUNITIES IN MY HOME TO BE FAITHFUL. HELP ME TO BE PLEASING TO YOU AS I DO THE TASKS YOU'VE GIVEN ME AND TO SEE THE BIGGER PICTURE—THAT YOU'RE BUILDING IN ME THE QUALITIES OF FAITHFULNESS AND DILIGENCE.

week 20

new word

for the week:

Puissance (pwĭs′ əns).
Power; might. As in, *"Kids, don't forget that I have the puissance to decide whether or not you get dessert. Please eat your dinner."*

alternate

new word:

Perspicacity

(pûr′ spĭ-kăs′ ə-tē).
Acuteness of perception, discernment, or understanding. As in, *"I applaud your perspicacity in finishing up those carrot sticks."*

Mother's Day

In the early years of motherhood, I struggled mightily with my new responsibilities. Being home all day, every day, tending my two treasured bundles who were less than sixteen months apart left me feeling profoundly overextended. If one didn't need to be fed, burped, rocked, or changed, the other one did. Routine events like buying groceries, getting a haircut, or going to the dentist seemed like hazy events from the past, nothing I could conceivably ever do again, at least not for a long, long time. Lack of sleep left me, for the first time in my life, unable to balance a checkbook. ("Do I add these numbers, or subtract?") I drove off with my purse on top of the car. I took food from the oven and left the mitts inside. It took four days to make my husband's birthday cake. I was not doing well. Much as I adored my children, I found the intensity of my new job staggering.

It was not an easy time for me, and added to my depletion was the nagging question: why aren't you enjoying this more?

During those difficult, lonely days, I clung to the words of Jeremiah 29:11 like a half-drowned swimmer clings to a buoy: "'For I know the plans that I have for you,' declares the LORD, 'plans for welfare and not for calamity to give you a future and a hope.'" With a one-year-old and a two-year-old, it certainly didn't feel like I had a future and a hope. (The only future and hope I could see was the approach of naptime and my desperate wish that my two cherubs would sleep at the same time.) But I posted Jeremiah 29:11 in my house, some days carrying it with me as I moved exhausted from room to room. Somehow God saw me through.

What I didn't see at the time, with the lack of perspective inherent in any new endeavor, was that this, too, would pass. Which, of course, it did. Now, as the mom of a thirteen- and fourteen-year-old, I am out of those waters that threatened to overwhelm me. I possess a clearer vision of just what the Master Life Preserver was doing. I can see that, though the job has not been easy, nothing I've accomplished in my life has been half so worthwhile as loving and raising my boys.

In the stage of motherhood where I now find myself, with two sons whose lives apart from me do, and should, expand daily, I can see the riches of having been home all these years. When you're home, you know your kids' friends, because you've worked in the classroom, hosted the slumber parties, driven the field trips, and overheard the jokes in the backseat.

You know the parents of your children's friends, because you've cheered with them in the bleachers, chatted while picking up from playdates, discussed the merits of potential birthday gifts, and compared notes on school projects.

Best of all, you know your children, as well as it's possible to know another human being, because you've been there for the first steps, the spelling tests, the Michigan reports. You've driven to the soccer, football, and baseball practices. You've heard the trumpet performances, waited during the orthodontist appointments, administered the antibiotics, and prayed together about bullies. You've given the job your all, the best you had to give. You will never look back at how fast they grew up and regret that

Quotable

"As a father, I happily recognize that the most profound influence on my children is their mother. That's as it should be. My job skills are transferable anywhere, but hers aren't: to our kids she is unique, completely irreplaceable."[1]

James Bemis

you missed it. Because you didn't.

God says in Psalm 37:4, "Delight yourself in the LORD; and He will give you the desires of your heart." Back in the toddler days, my fantasy heart's desire included a part-time job, a nanny on call, and grown-up conversation. But God didn't give me those things.

Instead, He gave me the true desires of my heart, the ones I didn't even know I possessed: the chance to love and nurture my children, to experience every moment possible of this job of motherhood, for as many days as my children and I have together.

If you are home with your children, thank the Lord for these days. Thank Him for the incredible gift of being a mom. And in those moments when you find yourself in waters that threaten to overwhelm you, remember that God's plans for you include welfare and not calamity. "Then you will call upon Me and come and pray to Me, and I will listen to you. You will seek Me and find Me when you search for Me with all your heart" (Jeremiah 29:12–13).

Seems like the kids get trophies or certificates every time they sneeze: for participating in peewee soccer; for entering their Popsicle-stick project in the science fair; for being an outstanding third-grade reader.

They get them because someone, somewhere, decided awards build self-esteem. They encourage effort. Whether the team wins the league championship or goes 0 and 13, whether the child is most valuable player or spends most of his time on the field chasing butterflies, it makes no difference. In recognition for his effort, he wins something tangible.

As I sit at ceremonies, glowing and sparkling as my child receives the latest hardware that will crowd our shelves at home, a niggling little voice in my brain wants to know: Where is *my* trophy? Where's my trophy for getting him to every practice, for finding shin guards that fit and remem-

---

Quotable

God gives us the strength as mothers to do what is "unnatural." It is against our nature to get up three or four times a night, yet we do it. It is against our nature to wipe dirty bottoms, clean up vomit, wipe runny noses, wash piles of dirty laundry, yet we do it. It is against the natural to be unselfish, yet, as mothers, we have to be.[2]

Ruth Bell Graham and Gigi Graham Tchividjian,
Mothers Together

bering to bring after-game snacks when it was my turn? Where's my trophy for keeping those big red socks clean? Where's my trophy for typing the list of parent names and numbers, for practicing math facts in the car on the way to scrimmage, and for getting dinner (such as it is) on the table in ten minutes on practice nights?

If the purpose of trophies is to build self-esteem, don't moms need trophies? Don't we need to be encouraged that what we do matters, that even if we don't produce the brightest, whitest uniform on the field but we manage to get the thing washed and dried in time for its next appearance, our efforts are worthy of praise? And likewise, whether we've produced an offspring who is the fastest one out there or simply a miscast poet with a mouth guard, couldn't we benefit from a little praise?

And since we're at it, when those Olympians stand on the podiums getting their gold medals, where are their mothers? The ones who schlepped them back and forth to those 5 a.m. practices the commentators are always talking about?

So here's my idea: trophies for moms. Not just for moms of Olympians. Not just for heroics like most miles logged on weekday afternoons, or most time killed while waiting for practice to end.

But trophies for all of us. For participation. For effort.

I picture a gold minivan atop a marble base. Our names could be engraved (spelled correctly) on a little brass plate. The activity, the year.

The kids could host a team party, where it would be their turn to do the applauding and glowing.

I'll even volunteer my kids to make the brownies.

Quotable

How quickly the years fly by and will never come again. The best advice we ever received as parents was "take the time." How trite this can seem when you can hardly wait until they are out of diapers, starting school, or graduating. But I believe there is probably nothing in this life that will benefit you more, bring more happiness and peace of mind, or have as far-reaching effects as being a good parent. Take time for open arms, talking, reading, family prayer, building memories, teaching, and just plain caring. . . . No one can take the place of mom and dad.[3]

Beverly Nye,
Everyone's a Homemaker

For a good cry, get a copy of the children's book *Love You Forever* by Robert Munsch, about a mother's love for her child. Have a tissue handy. You will need it. (This also makes a great Mother's Day gift for your own mom or mother-in-law.)

Someone once said if you want to make God laugh, tell Him your plans.

How true that is about motherhood! You may have planned to be the mother of a daughter who loves ruffles and tea parties. You may have wound up with a muddy roller skater who wouldn't be caught dead in a room with chintz.

You may have ordered polite, athletic, intelligent, beautiful children. (Who didn't?) You may have wound up with kids who have physical ailments you've never heard of, a stubborn streak a mile wide, a revulsion to music you love, and Great-Grandpa's nose.

You may have longed for a large, boisterous family. You may have wound up with one child and a hurting heart.

When we take on the job of motherhood, we have no idea what's coming.

As I read from 1 Samuel recently, I was struck by the story of Hannah. Barren for years, she had prayed for a son, promising God if He granted her petition, she would dedicate that son to the Lord.

God gave her that son, and, true to her word, she released the boy back to God. She was so wholehearted in her relinquishment, in fact, that she brought Samuel to the priest Eli while he was still very young and left him there. How hard that must have been as a mother! Yet the Bible shows clearly that she rejoiced as she did it (see 1 Samuel 2:1–10). She completely trusted God for whatever was ahead.

The word used in the Bible as Hannah dedicated her son to God can

---

On June 1, 1990, Barbara Bush, wife of then-president George Bush, gave the commencement speech at Wellesley College. I have always loved her speech, both true and courageous, which gave the wonderful (and not always politically correct) message that nurturing your family is indeed a worthwhile pursuit. Here is an excerpt, as printed in *Barbara Bush: A Memoir*, by Barbara Bush:

For several years, you've had impressed upon you the importance to your career of dedication and hard work. This is true, but as important as your obligations as a doctor, lawyer, or business leader will be, you are a human being first, and those human connections—with spouses, with children, with friends—are the most important investments you will ever make.

At the end of your life, you will never regret not having passed one more test, not winning one more verdict, or not closing one more deal. You will regret time not spent with a husband, a friend, a child, or a parent. . . .

One thing will never change: fathers and mothers, if you have children . . . they must come first. Your success as a family . . . our success as a society . . . depends not on what happens at the White House, but on what happens inside your house.[4]

also be translated as *lent*. She lent her son to God, with full confidence that God would take care of him. What an example to me as a mother—that I need to "lend" my children back to God. In a sense I am not their true parent anyway, only a surrogate whom God has put in charge for a time. I can open my grip with confidence, knowing they rest in the hands of their heavenly Father, who loves them even more than I do.

I hope I remember that in the years to come. ♦

"And He was saying to them all, 'If anyone wishes to come after Me, he must deny himself, and take up his cross daily and follow Me. For whoever wishes to save his life will lose it, but whoever loses his life for My sake, he is the one who will save it.'" (Luke 9:23–24)

prayer THANK YOU, LORD, THAT YOU ARE WATCHING OVER MY FAMILY. HELP ME TO LOVE MY CHILDREN YET HOLD THEM LOOSELY WITH FULL CONFIDENCE THAT THEY ARE IN YOUR HANDS. THANK YOU FOR GIVING ME CLEAR DIRECTION AS A MOM, THAT IT IS ONLY WHEN I DIE TO MYSELF THAT YOU CAN BRING ABOUT TRUE LIFE. STRENGTHEN ME FOR THIS INCREDIBLY DIFFICULT YET IMMENSELY GRATIFYING TASK OF MOTHERHOOD.

FUN FACT

Mother's Day originated in 1907 when Anna Jarvis of Philadelphia wanted to honor her mother and arranged for a special church service to be held. By 1914, Congress declared the second Sunday in May as Mother's Day. You can wear a white carnation to remember a mom who has died or a colored one (usually red) to honor a mom who is still living.

week 21

new word

for the week:

Soporific (sŏp′ ə-rĭf′ ĭk).
Tending to induce sleep. As in, *"Lying in a lawn chair with the sun on my face has a deliciously **soporific** effect."*

alternate

new word:

Sybarite (sĭb′ ər-īt).
Anyone very fond of luxury and pleasure. As in, *"If I'm not careful I could easily sit in the backyard all spring and become a complete **sybarite**."*

Here Comes the Sun: Warm-Weather Homemaking

You wake up in the morning planning to catch up on laundry, change the sheets, and make a fancy dinner. But when you look out the window, you find it's a gorgeous, sun-filled day. What do you do?

a) Doggedly stick to your plan. After all, failing to plan is planning to fail.
b) Shelve the laundry and time-consuming dinner for another day, grab the kids, and head outside to soak in the sun.

Gee, let me think a minute.

One of the joys of being home with your family is the ability to be flexible with your time. While you can't put off chores forever without eventually facing no-more-clean-underwear syndrome, you can certainly afford to take off an occasional morning. If sunlight's raining down on your back deck, calling you, by all means go. Take some time to wander among the flowerbeds or push your children on the swings. Sit in the grass and paint your toenails or spread out a blanket and read to the kids.

You can be productive outdoors, too, if you choose to be.

You could sit at the picnic table and sort through mail that's piled up.

You could bring out bills and pay them accompanied by bird twitters.

You could take your basket of clean laundry to your favorite part of the yard and fold away.

If you're making a craft as a gift, you could bring it outside and spend fifteen minutes on it.

If you have notes of encouragement or thanks that need writing, you could bring those outside.

Invite your kids to come out, too, to enjoy a snack with you while you work. It's a great way to reconnect after school —assuming, of course, they're not off at baseball or soccer or music lessons.

While you're outside, meditate on scriptures you've wanted to memorize, or ponder Proverbs 3:5–8: "Trust in the LORD with all your heart and do not lean on your own understanding. In all your ways acknowledge Him, and He

Warm-weather snack ideas:

◊ green grapes, washed and frozen

◊ lemonade frozen in plastic cups. Though it takes some hacking with spoons to actually eat this, it's one of my kids' favorites. (My son suggests telling your kids, "You can't have this unless you come outside.")

◊ smoothies, which is just a fancy way of saying any combination you happen to have of sliced fruit, yogurt, juice, and ice, tossed into the blender and whirled. (You can also freeze ripe bananas, peel and all; next time you make smoothies, remove the peel and toss frozen banana into blender with rest of ingredients.) For fun, finish off with one of those bendy straws or a small paper umbrella on a toothpick.

For more kid-friendly yet healthy snack ideas, check out Vicki Lansky's book, *The Taming of the C.A.N.D.Y. Monster*.[1]

will make your paths straight. Do not be wise in your own eyes; fear the LORD and turn away from evil. It will be healing to your body and refreshment to your bones."

Lean back and look for the cloud pictures God has painted as you think about His tremendous love for you. Breathe deeply. Say a prayer of thanks. Enjoy being a homemaker outdoors.

FUN FACT

↻

According to the *Encyclopedia Britannica Intermediate,* "Sunlight is the oldest known bleaching agent. The ancient Hebrews and Egyptians dipped their fabrics in water and set them out in the sun to bleach." [3]

In her book *A Family Raised on Rainbows*, Beverly Nye says, "I love to go out on a fresh spring morning and hang my sheets on the line. I know it takes me longer than it should but the smell of the air and all the magic sounds keep me spellbound, and I hate to go back into the house. After the sheets have basked in the sun and fresh air all day, I make up the beds again. And let me tell you, you don't need any pills to help you fall asleep. There's nothing quite like those fresh sheets." [2]

I can't personally vouch for the soporific effect of sunny-smelling sheets, having resorted to line drying only occasionally over the years, usually when my dryer's on the blink.

But though my own experience with line drying is scant, my mom does remember her mom hanging clothes outside. They ended up "stiff," as she recalls, and there was always the danger of leaky birds passing overhead. But she does remember the clothes' fresh smell, something almost everyone who's ever line dried mentions.

In fact, that smell is one of the main reasons my friend Kathi still line dries. "When people say fresh from the dryer, they mean the smell of perfumes and detergents," she says. "Line fresh smells like clouds and fresh-cut grass."

People who line dry swear by it. Along with the chance to get outdoors, they appreciate the energy savings. They also tout the benefits of the sun gently bleaching their "whites," and the way the sunlight freshens linens and banishes germs.

In fact, a woman named Helen Mather wrote an entire book about line drying. She traveled across the country twice, photographing clotheslines and talking with their owners. Committed line dryers would ask her to pass them some clothespins, then "proceed to deliver commercials for a product that is absolutely free."[4]

I wonder if, like bread baking, line drying is a task we homemakers gave up on too soon, not realizing that along with our clothespins we'd also be surrendering the sun on our faces, the breeze in our hair, the sight of butterflies darting through the yard as children play under floating sheets and pretend to be royalty.

Or is it all just misplaced nostalgia?

I'm not sure. All I know is I'm heading off to look for a line and some clothespins. It's a nice, sunny day, and I'm hoping to capture some of those clouds in my sheets.

If you want to give line drying a try, here are a few tips:

1. Whites and sheets are perfect candidates for line drying (sunlight bleaches and also kills germs). Hang shirts upside down to avoid clothespin shoulders.
2. Dark and bright colors should be hung out of direct sunlight to prevent fading, or else turned inside out.
3. Towels are reportedly not the best line-drying candidates—that old "stiffness" thing—but if you want to try anyway, shake well to fluff up before hanging. ("Make them snap," stresses author Cheryl Mendelson in her book *Home Comforts*. "This loosens up the pile very effectively."[5]) Or partially dry in the dryer then hang outside to finish.
4. If you don't have a clothesline, you can do what my great aunt used to do: lay wet clothes over the bushes and wait for the sun to work. (Don't lay clothes over wood, such as a railing or a fence, however; the wood can leave a stain.)

May is National Salad Month. (Don't tell me you haven't marked it on your calendar!) What better way to celebrate the arrival of warm weather than to include an inventive salad in your dinner plans?

Think broader than your usual bag of salad greens and sliced tomato. Next time you're walking the supermarket aisles, take a moment to marvel at all the lettuces.

Why doesn't anyone ever write about how beautiful vegetables are? Isn't produce the most appealing aisle in any supermarket? Isn't a salad the prettiest part of any meal? [6]

Ann Hodgman,
Beat That!

Red or green, frilly or smooth, bouffant or delicate, a caterpillar of lettuce heads snaking along the produce bins may include all kinds of lettuces you've never noticed before. Pick one that's new to you and bring it home for dinner. It's OK to mix your new find with an old favorite. (I was in my thirties before I learned that lettuce mixing was not a misdemeanor.)

Add something different: orange or grapefruit slices, dried apricots, sliced strawberries; leftover green beans, steak strips, grilled zucchini; dried cranberries, kidney beans, diced avocado; cashews, pine nuts, sprouts. Cookbooks can be a great inspiration. (When was the last time you made Caesar salad, or spinach with hot bacon dressing?) Or look in your fridge or pantry for new ideas.

Some unusual combinations you may want to try:

◊ Salad greens with diced papaya or mango, baby shrimp, pecans, and a sesame oil dressing

◊ Romaine with crumbled feta cheese and quartered strawberries

◊ Spinach or romaine with toasted pecans or pine nuts, blue cheese, and pomegranate seeds in a light vinaigrette

◊ Leafy greens, mandarin oranges, green onions, bacon bits, and walnuts, topped with an Asian dressing with sesame oil

Even if some in your family like "normal" food and others live for octopus with roasted goat cheese, you can still satisfy everyone by setting out each ingredient in its own bowl and serving the dressing on the side.

And speaking of dressing—if you have time, it's not hard to make a basic vinaigrette. Conventional wisdom says use three parts oil to one part vinegar (so ¾ cup oil, ¼ cup vinegar, for example), but if you want a lighter version, try less oil. Experiment to see how little you can get away with. For variety, substitute lemon juice or orange juice for the vinegar. You can also add small amounts of flavorings, such as:

- Dijon mustard
- honey
- soy sauce
- minced garlic
- minced ginger
- minced green onions
- chopped anchovies
- chopped fresh basil or other herbs (such as tarragon, dill, or rosemary)

For salads that keep a couple of days, consider skipping the greens and marinating other bite-sized vegetables, such as cut-up carrots, cauliflower, green beans, mushrooms, tomatoes, and cucumbers. Refrigerate, and pull out when ready to serve.

MOM'S YUMMY CHINESE CHICKEN SALAD DRESSING

My mom didn't invent this, but she's the one who gave me the recipe, so I get to name it after her if I want. Mom uses this for all kinds of salads, not just chicken salad. But if you're making the Chinese chicken variety, toss together **thinly chopped lettuce, shredded cooked chicken, three diced green onions, a couple of tablespoons of slivered almonds,** and a **couple more tablespoons of sesame seeds toasted in the oven until brown** (watch carefully, as they brown quickly). Then

Combine:

½ cup salad oil	2 t. salt
¼ cup rice vinegar	2 t. Accent
2 T. sugar	1 t. pepper
2 T. sesame oil	

Shake well and pour over salad.

Serve your salad alfresco, in the prettiest part of your yard, where you can truly appreciate National Salad Month. And be thankful we're not celebrating another special May holiday: Fungal Infection Awareness Month.

More warm-weather homemaking ideas:

◇ Get rid of fuzzy bathroom rugs for summer.

◇ If picking up kids from school, surprise them with a cold drink in the car (ice water's good if spills are likely).

◇ Dust off your tennis racquet, grab a child, and head for the courts.

◇ Ditto with your bike. Head to your local park.

◇ Dig up some golf shoes or your teenager's cleats and aerate your lawn as you amble across, enjoying the day. If you're feeling especially energetic, push your lawn mower at the same time.[7]

◇ Pull weeds for ten minutes.

◇ Make a pitcher of sun tea. Fill a clear glass pitcher (or jar) with water, drop in a few tea bags, cover with plastic, and place in full sun for an hour or two. When it's strong enough, take inside and pour over ice.

◇ Wash your kitchen windows and let the sun shine in. While you're at it, open them up and enjoy the smells and sounds.

"Rejoice always; pray without ceasing; in everything give thanks; for this is God's will for you in Christ Jesus." (1 Thessalonians 5:16–18)

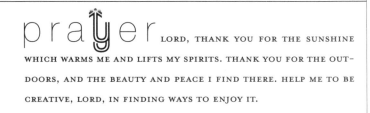

prayer LORD, THANK YOU FOR THE SUNSHINE WHICH WARMS ME AND LIFTS MY SPIRITS. THANK YOU FOR THE OUT-DOORS, AND THE BEAUTY AND PEACE I FIND THERE. HELP ME TO BE CREATIVE, LORD, IN FINDING WAYS TO ENJOY IT.

CHOCOLATE BREAK! stop!

CHOCOLATE FONDUE

This wonderful recipe comes from a 1979 cookbook that was produced by the Junior League of Dayton, Ohio, and is credited to Mrs. Bruce A. Triplett. It is scrumptious when served with fresh strawberries, chunks of banana, and wedges of apple. If you have any zucchini bread or banana bread on hand, these also make good "dippers," cut into cubes.

When you're done fonduing, you'll have plenty of sauce left over to use on ice cream. Sorry to stuff you with calories so close to bathing-suit season, but considering even the *smell* of chocolate "can have a calming effect on the brain"[8] I think you'll agree the medicinal benefits alone provide reason enough to proceed.

CHOCOLATE FONDUE

In saucepan over low heat, combine:

4 T. butter

8 oz. unsweetened chocolate

Stir until melted. Add:

1 ¾ cups sugar

2 T. cornstarch

pinch salt

¼ cup light corn syrup

13 oz. can evaporated milk

1 t. vanilla

Continue cooking over low heat, stirring until sauce is smooth and thick. Pass the fondue forks, dip in strawberries, banana chunks, apple wedges, marshmallows, angel food cake, and whatever else sounds good, and enjoy.

week 22

new word

for the week:

new word

for the week:

Plethora (plĕth′ ər-ə).

Superabundance; excess. As in, *"After the **plethora** of school awards ceremonies, music recitals, and class parties these last weeks, our family is eager for some unscheduled time."*

alternate

new word:

Clamant (klā′mənt).

Urgent; compelling. As in, *"I have a **clamant** desire to stay in my jammies till 10 a.m. for a week or two."*

Dream On:
Planning for Summer

When my children were younger, my summertime goal was to keep them busy with low- or no-cost recreational activities. To keep us from getting sucked in to TV land, I planned weekly picnic and park days with other moms, signed the kids up for summer-reading programs at the library, and headed to the crafts store for supplies.

Now that my kids are teenagers and their school-year sports, music, and academic commitments leave us gasping, we look forward to a quiet, unscheduled summer the way a marathoner eyes the finish line. For these summer months, our family calendar, normally crammed full of hieroglyphic commitments, is as close to blank as we can make it. We've scheduled dentist, optometrist, and sports physical appointments, but that's about it. We don't want a plethora of planned activities to get us out of the house. We want downtime. Rest. Restoration.

My kids, in fact, were the ones who made this clear when they informed me that what they were most looking forward to one summer was "just staying home." Which makes it all the more evident how important it is to ask.

As you think ahead to summer, give some thought to the school year just behind. Are you exhausted from the previous nine-month blur? Is your family starved for plain, old-fashioned togetherness time, where you actually spend an evening at home participating in that ancient ritual once known as a sit-down dinner? (And no, I don't mean sitting in the van with a mittful of french fries.) Do you dream of hang-out, sleep-in, do-nothing days punctuated by occasional outings to the library or movie theater or pool?

Conversely, if your school year has been pretty low-key, your fantasy summer may include a schedule brimming with soccer league, swimming lessons, Cinderella theater camp, and five-day Vacation Bible School, topped off with a week at Grandma's—in other words, a summer so packed with activity that there's no room for pathetic wails of, "M-o-o-o-m! There's nothing to do-o-o-o!"

Whichever philosophy fits your family best this year, now is the time to start making plans, whether you hope to catch the free museum days, make the deadline for tennis camp, or drive off to that beautiful campsite in the redwoods secure in the knowledge there will be a genuine campsite waiting for you once you arrive.

Don't assume that what worked last summer will work again this year. The water slides that enthralled just months ago may now be viewed like a piece of meat that's been in the refrigerator too long. Kids make quantum jumps in the span of a year, so an autopilot repeat of last summer's successes may not work.

Ask God to show you how much activity your family needs, which summer programs to sign up for, or whether He wants you to simply lay low and leave lots of white space on the calendar.

Some statistics from American Demographics *magazine:*

◊ "According to the 2000 Roper Youth Report, one-quarter of 6- to 17-year-olds feel they don't have enough free time. Surveys by Teenage Research Unlimited in Northbrook, Ill. have found that the biggest complaint among U.S. teens is anxiety from their overbooked lives."

◊ "Kids are three times as likely to feel time-deprived as their parents believe."

◊ "Kids who used to complain of ennui during drowsy summer afternoons now identify stress as their biggest concern, according to several survey firms."

◊ "When Simmons Market Research Bureau recently surveyed 6- to 11-year-olds as part of its annual Youth Poll, the kids named soccer, Rollerblading and bowling among their favorite leisure activities."

> ◇   "Of the 12- to 17-year-old respondents, volleyball and weight training increased by double-digit rates in the past two years and now rank higher than camping and hiking. Only swimming, a hot weather essential, attracts a majority of teens and children."
>
> ◇   "The top five sports for children, according to an online survey by research company Element, are swimming, bicycling, basketball, in-line skating, and baseball."[1]

As He matured from child to man, "Jesus kept increasing in wisdom and stature, and in favor with God and men" (Luke 2:52). Those four areas of growth—intellectual, physical, spiritual, and social—are helpful to keep in mind as we raise our own children. "What would you like to see happen in your children's lives? How do you want to see them develop? Ninety days of progress toward these objectives lie ahead, but only if you have a clear picture of your plan," say Kathy Peel and Joy Mahaffey, authors of *A Mother's Manual for Summer Survival*.[2]

Peel and Mahaffey suggest you hold a family meeting before summer starts and talk about goals for each child. Get the kids' input. "Ask yourself, 'Where do I want this child to be in each of these areas by the time school starts?'"[3]

Take time to pray for God's guidance. He knows your children's strengths and weaknesses; He knows in which areas they most need to grow. Ask Him to show you the summer goals He would like you, as their mom, to help them reach.

Maybe your goals include wanting your child to be well prepared for the next school year (intellectual), learn to be a better friend (social), study the book of Psalms (spiritual), and become more diligent at picking up after himself (physical). So how do you get there?

Goals that are meaningful should be both measurable and attainable. Better than, "I want my child to be well prepared for school," would be, "I want him to be able to type twenty-five words per minute by September so he can type his papers." To reach that objective, you may decide to buy a computer-typing program and have him practice twenty minutes a day on Mondays, Wednesdays, and Fridays, immediately before lunch.

My son's goals this summer include, among other things, to get in shape for high school baseball. To work toward this goal, he plans to take a two-hour daily strength and conditioning class offered at school, go to the local batting cages at least four times a week during July, and get out to the field to practice flagging down ground balls ten times. It's a concrete, measurable plan that's challenging but attainable.

Start thinking and praying now about summertime goals for your kids, and be prepared to see them grow in wisdom and stature, in favor with God and men.

Some wonderful Bible studies for youth, from preschoolers up to teens, are published by Joy of Living in Oak View, California (1-800-999-2703, or www.joyofliving.org). They'll help your family stay focused this summer on God's Word, which is "perfect, restoring the soul" (Psalm 19:7).

Are you worried your kids will become television zombies this summer? Wondering if too much TV will deaden their brains, make them more aggressive, encourage them to be sedentary, feed a craving for junky toys and food, and expose them to all kinds of values that you don't share?

You're probably right. Research has documented for years the harmful effects of too much television. And let's face it: unless the TV is in a closet somewhere, it's likely that our homes, too, are casualties of too much television.

So what can we do about it?

Develop a TV-watching plan, before the summer even starts. Make kids earn television time by doing educational or physically active things. For every thirty minutes spent working crossword puzzles or practicing the trumpet, for example, they earn thirty minutes of TV privileges. You could give them one half-hour show per day for "free" (that's grace) and have them earn the rest. This encourages them to be thoughtful consumers, actively considering the shows being offered rather than passively breathing in show after show.

Make a list of shows you and your husband find acceptable, and let the kids pick from that.

If your family balks at the idea of TV limits, have everyone keep a viewing log. They'll probably be shocked to see just how much they watch. (According to the Department

> ## Quotable
>
> *Summertime is also the year's best opportunity to encourage a child's daily time with the Lord alone. Be sure to allow a block of time for this in every day's schedule, preferably in the morning. (It certainly beats cartoons and game shows.) Let them sometimes observe you sitting down with your Bible as a healthy model; don't always do this before they're out of bed.*[4]
>
> **Dean and Grace Merrill,**
> *Together at Home*

Television is the bane of the modern home, but only because it is so often abused. People who cannot find time to cook, see their children, entertain, read, visit, listen to music, exercise, talk, clean, or do their laundry nonetheless spend many hours—around twenty hours on average—watching television every week.[5]

Cheryl Mendelson,
Home Comforts

FUN FACT

⅃

Memorial Day, the last Monday in May, honors everyone who's ever died serving our country in war. To celebrate, bring out the flags and say a prayer of thanks for these heroes' courage, which makes our freedom possible.

of Education, kids in the U.S. watch an average of three to five hours per day.)

Try a TV-free evening or a TV-free week. Plan fun family activities instead: a board-game tournament, a flurry of Christmas gift making, an after-dinner stroll around the neighborhood, or a game of tennis. You could start a Friday-night tradition of roller-rink excursions or jigsaw puzzle marathons.

At my sister-in-law's house, they have put the television in the closet and bring it out only on special occasions. Life without television can work.

Proverbs 16:16 says, "How much better it is to get wisdom than gold!" Let's help our families gain wisdom about their TV habits by setting limits and by being good examples ourselves. This summer, no television zombies!

If you plan it, it will happen:

. . . .

- ◇ A weekly field trip to local sites of interest your family doesn't usually have time for
- ◇ A patriotic party, on the Fourth of July or any summer day, with red, white, and blue food, paper plates, candles, miniature flags on toothpicks, noisemakers, a backyard parade, and tapes of marching songs. Check your grocery store for patriotic doodads such as stars-and-stripes cupcake papers, sparkling grape juice wrapped in red, white, and blue foil, and a pot of puffy white chrysanthemums wrapped in patriotic paper.
- ◇ A summer garage sale to unload clutter
- ◇ One-on-one time with each of your kids—maybe a mother-and-child weekend trip, if finances allow
- ◇ Those summer-reading requirements assigned by school
- ◇ Volunteer opportunities. Many high schools require community-service hours (we've packed produce at the local food bank and helped with church projects), but younger kids can make crafts or cookies and deliver to hospitals or

convalescent homes. One mom made this a once-a-week project throughout the summer.

◇ More chores. With lighter schedules, summer may be just the time to teach your son to make bacon and french toast or teach your daughter to sew.

◇ A media "fast" week, where the entire family turns off all TVs, radios, CD players, and video games for seven days. A seminary professor who assigns this exercise reports that his students "become less restless," "value conversation and silence more highly," and learn "how aspects of our lives we take for granted can crowd out God and replace what is sacred with what is trivial or even profane."[7]

"But to this one I will look, to him who is humble and contrite of spirit, and who trembles at My word." (Isaiah 66:2)

prayer LORD, HELP US AS A FAMILY TO ESTEEM YOUR WORD AS HIGHLY AS IT DESERVES, AND TO MAKE READING IT AND STUDYING IT A HIGH PRIORITY THIS SUMMER. THANK YOU THAT YOU ARE SO FAITHFUL TO MEET US AND TEACH US WHEN WE COME TO YOU, SEEKING.

week 23

new word

for the week:

Muzzy (mŭz′ ē).

Muddled, confused. As in, *"Please excuse me for sounding muzzy; I just assisted thirty fifth graders in making intricate beaded frogs at the end-of-the-year party."*

alternate

new word:

Gaminerie (gə′ mēn-ə-rē).

An impudent or wisecracking outlook. As in, *"After enduring my sons' gaminerie throughout the year, their teachers deserve a hearty June thank you."*

School's Out!

How do you spell relief? S-U-M-M-E-R V-A-C-A-T-I-O-N!

Whew! We made it through another school year. Another nine months of spelling tests, book reports, and science-fair projects. ("What Makes Photographs Fade," anyhow?)

After thirty-six weeks of school, times two kids, I figure I made 360 turkey sandwiches, participated in twenty-three field trips, class parties, and bake sales, patched or replaced ten pairs of school pants, doctored seventy-two scabs (a modest estimate of two per week), made thirty-six trips to the library, and helped study for seventy-two Bible-memory-verse tests.

I bought (and sold) wrapping paper, magazines, raffle tickets, and jog-a-thon laps. Signed 108 permission slips and forked over ninety-seven dollars for incidentals.

Helped complete one state notebook (Michigan state song: "Michigan, My Michigan"), one state float, one report on the Nile, one static electricity/balloon experiment. Car-pooled seventy-two hundred miles, not counting practices for football, basketball, wrestling, baseball, and band.

"What I don't get," said my brand-new fifth-grade graduate, "is why you're relieved, Mom. You didn't even do any of the work."

Sigh.

Celebrate! It might be a tangible gift (our friends who love baseball give their son catcher's gear); a special dinner out; or simple, heartfelt words of praise. However you do it, make sure you let your kids know how proud of them you are for all their hard work this school year.

I like to dig out my children's big stuffed teddy bears for special occasions. A few days before school's out, I dress them in sunglasses, a Hawaiian lei, a straw hat, with paws wrapped around fans or sand buckets. I prop Brown Bear and Grey Bear in the front window, ready to greet whoever drives up with their signs: "Congratulations!" and "Just two more days!"

Some moms take a picture on the last day of school, to mark the year's changes (especially notable if you have kids wear the same clothes they wore on the first day of school).

Don't underestimate the power of tradition either. My fifteen-year-old sophomore, who towers over me and shaves, recently asked, "Mom, are we gonna get baseball cards? It's tradition!" I'd forgotten I'd bought them cards in past years to commemorate school's end. (If you're not sure if you have end-of-the-year traditions, ask your kids; they'll remember! Something you thought you'd done once or twice may, in their minds, be a cherished annual event.)

GROCERY REMINDER: Quit buying the snack-sized chips or cookies you've been sliding into brown bags and start stocking up on fresh fruit, frozen treats, lemonade mix, and ice cream cones.

As our kids reach their teen years and are taught by seven or eight teachers apiece, it's tempting to give up on the end-of-the-year teacher thank-you gifts. It can be daunting to come up with seven gifts, times however many kids you have.

But when you consider what teachers have endured over the last nine months—the testing and correcting, the amusement and frustration, the continuing to show up each day to teach our angels whether they felt like it or not—the conclusion I reach is that now that my kids are teenagers, their teachers deserve my thanks more than ever. Teaching, like mothering, seems to me one of those professions where it takes every sweat bead of patience and creativity and good humor to keep at it each day and not give up. Progress can be hard to detect. Teachers must wonder, many days, if they are getting anywhere.

I love the Bible verses that promise that God's Word, once planted, will not return void: "It will not return to Me empty, without accomplishing what I desire, and without succeeding in the matter for which I sent it" (Isaiah 55:11; also see verses 8–10). Those verses make me think of teachers, and how the seeds of knowledge and compassion that good teachers plant in their students will most assuredly bear fruit. It might take years. But the seeds my sons' teachers have planted in them will, I believe, one day germinate. My boys will read *frijoles* on a Mexican restaurant's menu and, thanks to their Spanish teacher, know that they're being offered beans. They'll see a painting in a museum and, thanks to their European-history teacher, recognize it as impressionistic. They'll tour our nation's capital—maybe with their own children someday—and thanks to a government teacher's diligence, be able to explain how a bill becomes a law.

So we still make a point to give each teacher a special thank you at the end of the school year, even if it's small. Maybe it's a note of thanks from me or, even better, my child. Maybe we include a bookmark, or a five-dollar gift certificate for coffee, or a small box of truffles purchased at a nearby import/export store.

It's not the monetary value of the gift that matters. It's the acknowledgment that these teachers have poured their lives into our children.

And for that, we are exceedingly grateful.

Teacher Gift Ideas

I've heard from more than one teacher that they're in no need of any more coffee mugs, even ones with "Best Teacher" sentiments on them. What they do appreciate, however, are prepackaged gourmet foods (though dieters may prefer something nonfattening), gift certificates (to bookstores, restaurants), trays of cookies delivered to the teacher lunch room for the staff to share, or a book or video for the staff to enjoy.

Other inexpensive ideas include a plastic bottle of bubbles with a card thanking them for a fun year, a candle with a card thanking them for lighting up your child's year, or a personalized stamp with the teacher's name on it.

Deliver your gifts the week before school's out, if possible. It's easier for the teacher to get them home if they're not juggling thirty of them. I like to think the gift's early arrival makes it a little more special, too, like the one present you get to open on Christmas Eve before the deluge.

I miss having time with my kids during the busy school months. The hectic schedule of homework and after-school sports leaves me hungry for unscheduled hours to just be together and enjoy one another. Now that school's out, I'm relishing the idea of lazy mornings in our pajamas, snuggling together on the couch to read, and afternoons at the library or in the pool. I'm looking forward to 9 p.m. barbecues and to staying up way past our bedtimes watching movies.

As soon as the school year is over, make a point to do something fun with your kids. Play cards, hit the tennis ball back and forth, ride bikes. Take them to the local farmer's market or maybe a nearby park or historical landmark you've always wanted to visit. Escape the scorching heat by going to a matinee in an air-conditioned theater, or to the bowling alley or the ice rink.

One of my very favorite warm-weather outings is taking my children berry picking. Each year we go to a farm about an hour away and spend a couple of hours in the sun with our red wagon and purple-stained fingers and mouths, our long flat cardboard boxes slowly filling with ripe, juicy olallieberries. It's about as close as our family will get to a Norman Rockwell painting (especially if you ignore the little grumbling voice, "I don't even like olallieberry jam"). The boxes fill slowly, but time goes by quickly for me as I imagine the twenty pounds of berries we pick transformed into jewel-toned jars of jam. (See

Quotable

The fruits do not yield their true flavor to the purchaser of them, nor to him who raises them for the market. There is but one way to obtain it, yet few take that way. If you would know the flavor of huckleberries, ask the cow-boy or the partridge. It is a vulgar error to suppose that you have tasted huckleberries who never plucked them.[1]

Henry David Thoreau,
Walden

week 29 for more on making jam.) I love the whole process, start to finish. (My mom, at sixty-eight, picked berries with us for the very first time a couple of years ago and enjoyed it so much it's now become a tradition for her too.)

So find something fun to do with your family this week. Plan an easy dinner: fruit salad, cheese and crackers, sparkling apple juice served in wine goblets.

Enjoy these first days of summer vacation. You've earned it!

Give your car a thorough cleaning, inside and out. Run it through the car wash, get out the whiskbroom, and flick away the remnants of a year's worth of McCrumbs.

Fun Family Ideas for Summer

Pick at least one idea to try this week and get your family's summer off to a fun start.

- ◊ Let your kids teach you to play chess (or teach them).
- ◊ Head to a nearby park with a lake. Feed the ducks, skim stones, play Frisbee®. See if your husband can join you for a picnic lunch or dinner.
- ◊ Check out some kids' cookbooks from the library and teach your kids to cook. If they're reluctant, let them choose a chocolate concoction and watch them perk up.
- ◊ Find a nifty craft and make it together. (Candle making? Soap carving?) Have the kids help select the project to improve the odds you won't be piecing together those mosaics all by yourself.
- ◊ Go miniature golfing.
- ◊ Pick flowers, ferns, or leaves and flatten between pages of a big phone book topped with something heavy—books or a brick. A couple of days later, extract your treasures and glue with white glue onto heavier-than-normal paper. Use as stationery, make into a bookmark, or mat and hang as a picture; add a Bible verse, if you like.
- ◊ Consider designating one night a week during summer as special family fun night. Find something you all enjoy—jigsaw puzzles, movies, board games—and commit every Tuesday evening, say, to doing it together. One summer our family instituted family tennis night and was delighted at how much we looked forward to it each week. (Our serves and volleys improved too.)
- ◊ Crank up the music and jitterbug barefoot across the kitchen. Try anything by the Beach Boys or the soundtrack to the movie *Grease*.

◊ Make a great breakfast. It's probably been months since you had a leisurely morning to spoil your family.

◊ Start a prayer journal with the kids. Write down requests and note the answers. At the end of summer, you'll have a tangible record of God's faithfulness. ♥

"Behold, children are a gift of the LORD, the fruit of the womb is a reward." (Psalm 127:3)

---

prayer LORD, THANK YOU SO MUCH FOR THE IN-
CREDIBLE GIFT OF MY CHILDREN. HELP ME NOT TO TAKE MY TIME WITH
THEM FOR GRANTED AND TO SEIZE EVERY DAY'S OPPORTUNITY TO LOVE
THEM AND TO BUILD GOOD MEMORIES.

week 24

Father's Day

Clunk. The plastic ball bounces off the hood of the car. My husband grins and says, "I'll bet you can't hit my knuckleball!"

Most families view their cars as an expensive investment, if not covering them with car covers, at least attempting to park them out of harm's way. My husband, as relaxed and Type B as a person can get, deliberately parks the car to be used as a backstop when he and our sons play whiffleball in the driveway.

He is a child at heart. At birthday parties, other kids announce to mine, "You guys are lucky. You have a fun dad." He offers our youngest a dollar to jump in the frigid swimming pool. He drives us around unfamiliar neighborhoods at Christmastime and declares we are to vote for the best-decorated home "in the entire free world." At his urging, we hold Monopoly champion-of-the-week ceremonies, chanting the victor's name in unison with our fists raised.

My kids have a fun dad. He loves them with his whole heart, and they know it.

I asked my husband how we as moms can help promote that bond between father and children. He had two answers.

First, he said, we need to spend lots of time together as a family, including some of it without Mom there.

Second, we wives need to honor our husbands as the head of the home (see Ephesians 5:22–24 and 5:33). When the kids see us respect our husbands and look to them as leaders, they'll do the same.

As Ephesians 6:1–3 says, "Children, obey your parents in the Lord, for this is right. Honor your father and mother (which is the first commandment with a promise), so that it may be well with you, and that you may live long on the earth." (The word *honor* can also be translated "value" or "revere.")

So let's honor our husbands and teach our children to do the same. Start with giving him a warm greeting when he gets home from work: a family hug, a smile, some special attention. Let him know how much you appreciate him and all he does for your family. See if you can't make him feel like the most loved dad in the entire free world.

> ## Quotable
>
> *This moment of homecoming is often an accurate thermometer that gauges what we truly feel about those who share our roof. In fact, I suspect the quality of our front-door reception can greatly determine the atmosphere of that afternoon and evening's life together.*[1]
>
> **Karen Burton Mains,**
> *Open Heart, Open Home*

If you've been married for a while, it may be hard to think of creative new ways to show love to your husband. You've already tried the lipstick on the mirror, and he never even found the steamy note in his underwear drawer. Besides, your family's schedule is too crammed and you're too broke for any outrageous show of affection. Right?

Wrong. Believe it or not, there are lots of fun, creative ideas for making your husband feel special that don't take scads of time or money. Best of all, someone else has already thought of them.

Dating Your Mate: Creative Dating Ideas for Those Who Are Married or Those Who Would Like to Be by Rick Bundschuh and Dave Gilbert is filled with enough suggestions to keep you going for months.[2] Though the ideas are directed at husbands and wives, you can tailor many of them to include the kids too.

One idea is to play checkers and, on the bottom of your

By profession I am a soldier and take pride in that fact. But I am prouder, infinitely prouder, to be a father.[3]

General Douglas MacArthur

Childrearing advice: "Try to get one that doesn't spit up. Otherwise, you're on your own."[4]

Calvin Trillin,
Family Man

husband's pieces, tape small notes that must be read (and obeyed) when he loses that piece. Examples are "Stop! You get a two-minute back rub" or "I will get your slippers for you." They can also include promises for future favors ("I will bring you a cup of coffee tomorrow morning").

Another suggestion is to make three cutouts of animals from cardboard. On the back of each, write an item your husband has needed to buy. Put the cutouts around the house, then give your husband a dart gun with only one dart. He gets to fire at the animal of choice. If he hits it, the family will go on a "safari" to purchase the item. (Our family modified this by making the prizes not items to purchase but family outings, such as breakfast out for the four of us. He got to shoot at all the animals and choose his favorite prize from all he knocked down.)

A third idea is to unroll the toilet paper a ways and write a message, then roll it back up and wait for the discovery. Be careful to use a nonsmear pen, suggests my practical son—just in case.

There are all kinds of fun ideas in this book (and in other, similar books too). So if you suspect your creative brain cells have died, get thee to a bookstore or library for new inspiration on showing love to the man in your home.

To show love to your husband, you and your children can do one or more of the following:

- Pray for him, especially if he has a rough day ahead.
- Pick flowers from the yard and put them on his nightstand.
- Make him king for a day, complete with paper crown and hokey cape (a towel or blanket with safety pins works fine). The king decides on the day's activities and meals; family members are his faithful servants.
- Run him a warm bath. The kids can add bubbles and scout around for a cold drink, a snack, a favorite book or magazine.

After fifteen minutes, put a towel in the dryer so he can fluff in luxury.

◇ Together, make him his favorite cookies.

As Dr. James Dobson says in his book *Complete Marriage and Family Home Reference Guide*, "When you stand where I am today, the relationship with those you love will outweigh every other good thing in your life."[5]

My kids' opinions of the top five characteristics that make for a good dad:

1. Someone to look up to, who sets a good example ("so you'll know how to live")
2. Someone who spends time with you, sharing unique experiences ("building a deck, using a log splitter, going fishing—it doesn't matter what it is"), so you know who he is
3. Someone who's understanding ("not quick to get angry; that's in the Bible")
4. Someone who's caring ("he loves you")
5. Someone who sets something aside just to spend time with you ("even if it's not something that important, like going to dinner with people he doesn't like")

Don't forget this Father's Day to let the dad(s) in your life know he is special.

A simple gift we made for my husband one year was a "job jar." We took an old canning jar, decorated it with stickers, and filled it with ten promises from each family member, each on a separate slip of paper. (An example from our then six-year-old son: "Thank you, Dad, for doing all this hard work for us and thank you for being our dad. I will climb one tree for you.") Every household job my husband completed, he got to choose one slip of paper from the jar.

My husband loved his jar so much that every Father's Day for the next couple of years he requested a refill. It was with great fanfare we gathered 'round the table at the completion of yet another chore to see what praise and reward awaited.

Try making a job jar of your own. Because you can never have too many six-year-olds climbing a tree in your honor.

Want to make breakfast in bed for Dad? Try this special toast-egg creation. It's easiest if you have a heart-shaped cookie cutter, but if you don't, improvise with a knife.

FUN FACT

Father's Day originated after a Spokane, Washington, woman named Sonora Louise Smart Dodd heard a sermon on Mother's Day in 1909 and wanted to honor her father, who had raised six children on his own after his wife died. It wasn't signed into law until President Richard M. Nixon did so in 1972. According to *Family Traditions* by Elizabeth Berg, "The rose is the official flower for Father's Day—red roses as a tribute to a living father, white ones for remembrance" of those who've died.[6]

Step 1: With cookie cutter, cut out heart from middle of one or two pieces of bread.

Step 2: Butter each side of bread (the part of the bread with the crust, not the heart shape).

Step 3: Place bread in skillet; cook over medium heat until golden. Flip bread.

Step 4: Break egg in heart-shaped hole and cook until done—about five minutes.

Step 5: With beamish face, serve to Dad.

Note: To make these for the whole family, use a griddle; you can make up to six at a time.

"Older women likewise are to be reverent in their behavior, not malicious gossips nor enslaved to much wine, teaching what is good, so that they may encourage the young women to love their husbands, to love their children." (Titus 2:3–4)

prayer

LORD, THANK YOU FOR MY HUSBAND. THANK YOU THAT HE SO FAITHFULLY TAKES CARE OF OUR FAMILY. HELP ME TO HONOR HIM AS THE HEAD OF OUR FAMILY, AND TO TEACH OUR CHILDREN TO DO THE SAME. OPEN MY EYES THIS WEEK TO CREATIVE WAYS OUR FAMILY CAN SHOW HIM LOVE.

week 25

Let the Games Begin: Summer Fun

Eager to plant summer memories, I made my kids a proposal: "Let's go to San Francisco!" A few days later we were off to the big city, just an hour and a half away—me, my two boys, my friend Kris, and her daughter Sydni.

An hour and twenty-five minutes into our trip, a small but distinct voice came from the back seat. "Eeew!" One of our passengers had thrown up.

After a quick blotting with a roll of paper towels I'd fortuitously thrown into the van that very morning, and reassurance that in spite of the evidence the child in question didn't feel all that bad, we were off to explore the city with our slightly fragrant but still remarkably cheerful crew. Our first stop was Ye Expensive Touristy Clothes Shoppe where, price irrelevant, we urgently needed to replace one wilted pair of hole-in-the-knee sweatpants and hand-me-down sweatshirt with odorless garments. Mission accomplished, we marched out of the shop holding the original ensemble at arm's length as if it were a chicken gone bad. Relieved at the prospect of breathing through our noses again, we plunked it straight into the nearest trash can.

Next stop, ferry terminal. We had planned to take a boat ride to a nearby island where we'd rent bikes, but by the time we reached the terminal we were too late; the last ferry to Angel Island had departed. Deciding any ferry would do, off we floated to another destination, one with no bikes but plenty of gift shops and trinkets for every allowance.

Our day in San Francisco was filled with fascinating sights, smells, and tastes. Some we'd expected to find, such as cable cars, crab cocktails, and huge vats of chocolate at Ghirardelli Square. But many, we hadn't: a docked World War II submarine open for inspection, the surprise of a performing parrot in the middle of a bustling shopping district, a street artist who created in minutes intricate paintings of the solar system using only spray paint and a blow torch. As we walked back to our car at day's end, past reggae bands playing by the ocean, we made one final shopping detour to purchase some "essence of tangerine" oil which, considering the morning's start, hardly seemed a luxury. It had indeed been a memorable day.

I am thankful for days like that, days that are filled with vibrant images wedged firmly in my mind, ready to be pulled out and fingered like a familiar necklace. But as my husband pointed out later that evening, it's the day-in, day-out ordinary moments of a childhood summer—the movie excursions, the Yahtzee® games, the friends over for barbecued burgers—that likely seep into our children even more permanently, etching themselves into their hearts and becoming, by sheer repetition, simply part of who they are.

The next time I get a hankering to go on an adventure and make memories with my kids, I'll probably go. But I won't discount those other, more ordinary days either, the ones that find us home, reading on the couch, making cookies, or building sofa cushion forts.

Anyone for a game of checkers?

For summer fun at home:

. . . .

◇ Make blue Jell-O® and float gummy fish in it. Use a glass container for the full fishbowl effect.

◇ Pull out family videos from your child's first trip to the zoo or last year's Christmas pageant, gather round with popcorn, and relive the memories.

◇ Give the family pet some extra TLC—brush him, take him for a walk, give him a summer bath.

◇ Check out astronomy books from the library's children's section, or just lie back on your deck one night and see which constellations you can identify. If you're so inclined, cocoon yourselves outside in sleeping bags and talk long into the night. By the way, meteors, or "shooting stars," typically appear every fifteen to twenty minutes, and you can see more of them after midnight than before. For the most spectacular showers, with anywhere from 10 to 150 meteors per hour, check out the sky each year on January 3; April 21; May 4; July 28; August 11; October 21; November 3; November 17; December 13; and December 22. Mark some of these dates on your calendar; the August 11–12 shower is supposed to be especially easy to see (something to do with meteors appearing to radiate from a constellation named Perseus).[1]

◇ Pull out your dusty sewing machine and teach the kids to sew. Start by having them practice stitching without thread along the lines of notebook paper, and soon they'll be adept enough to make festive fabric pillowcases for Christmas gifts.

◇ Experiment with holiday recipes you don't have time for the rest of the year. Fashioning Easter egg truffles or extra-fancy Christmas cookies can be a grand midsummer activity.

◇ Spend a day with your kids snapping pictures of life's everyday moments. For photos with a completely different fool, try a roll of black-and-white film. (Camera stores should carry this.)

◇ If midsummer boredom hovers like a swarm of mosquitoes, check out *Family Fun* magazine, which contains scads of ideas from crafts to recipes to homemade toys to kid-friendly vacation spots.

You may have tangible wealth untold;
Caskets of jewels and coffers of gold.
Richer than I you can never be—
I had a mother who read to me.[2]

Summer is an ideal time for reading, for both you and your children. What nicer way to while away a lazy afternoon than to sit beneath a shady tree and page through an absorbing story?

My son's second-grade teacher once advised me to keep

reading out loud to my children even after they could read for themselves. Evidence supports that wisdom. According to a report issued by a national Commission on Reading, "The single most important activity for building the knowledge required for eventual success in reading is reading aloud to children." The same report says, "It is a practice that should continue throughout the grades."[3] (See Jim Trelease's excellent book, *The Read-Aloud Handbook*, for more on the benefits of reading aloud.)

As your child grows older, time for reading together may become as rare as a weeknight with no homework. Don't give up. You can still listen to books on tape in the car. On long family vacations, you can still bring a book and read out loud. Don't forget about picture books, too, and occasionally bring a couple home from the library even once your kids have outgrown your lap and you're beginning to wonder if you'd fit in theirs. You never know when you can convince a warm body to share the couch and a poignant picture book.

Jim Trelease's *Read-Aloud Handbook* is a great resource for finding age-appropriate books your kids will like. They are grouped by type of book (wordless books, picture books, short novels, etc.), and Trelease tells you what age they're appropriate for, number of pages, and a short synopsis of the plot. Another terrific author who writes about reading is Gladys Hunt, who wrote *Honey for a Child's Heart: The Imaginative Use of Books in Family Life*,[4] which contains lists of best-loved children's books for kids aged zero to fourteen, and *Honey for a Teen's Heart*.[5]

To encourage kids' reading, see if your local library or bookstore sponsors a summer reading program, where kids who read a certain number of books by summer's end can earn a free book. You might also consider starting a neighborhood book club, where the kids meet during summer to discuss a book they've read, or a mother-daughter book club.

Moms with grown kids can read the same books as their kids and discuss them via e-mail or over the phone or at the next family gathering.

And remember what Mark Twain said: "The man who does not read good books has no advantage over the man who can't read them."[6]

Does seeing your half-empty photo albums give you that same sense of guilt you get when you think of your (broken) New Year's resolutions? Do your album pages leapfrog from your child's one-year-old birthday party, complete with chocolate cake smeared on his adorable apple cheeks, straight to the pomp and circumstance of fifth-grade graduation? Well—nervous throat clearing here—me too. And just as years of household neglect creates a jumble of clutter we cannot dig ourselves out of overnight, so with the photos. It took me years to get to where I am now (a huge moving box full of most of my kids' childhood photos). And while there's no way I can possibly get caught up in a single season, summer does seem an ideal time to at least make a stab at getting a few more pictures into the books.

I have become enamored these last few years with the Creative Memories® photo albums, which look like works of art complete with colorful background paper, stickers, and journaling to help you remember who, what, when, and where. These albums are gorgeous to look at, partly because you get to crop out the more boring parts of your photos—a delight for the serial snappers among us who don't realize that right behind our child's beamish face skulks an unmade bed. With cropping, you can also squeeze lots of pictures onto one page. And you learn quickly you don't have to include all ten pictures of your daughter in her adorable bumblebee costume. The compulsive yet very bad photographer can give herself a limit of one page per activity (one for each child's basketball season, for example), and manage to compile a very nice album despite lack of photography skills.

Also—and this may be the best reason for busy homemakers to consider—photo consultants often host "crop nights," where you bring your album, photos, and supplies to someone else's home and spend several devoted hours without the distraction of, "Mom, can I have some ice cream, and can you move all your stuff off the table so I can eat it?" If the phone rings, you don't need to answer it. If the dog needs to be let out, you don't need to let him out. It is not your dog.

My friend Karen lives more than an hour away, and we don't get to see each other often.

If your photos are hopelessly disorganized—whether residing all over the house or hiding on high shelves away from the "baby" who is now fourteen—here are a few tips to help you get started:

- ◇ Look high, look low, check drawers, boxes, closets, and piles, and locate all those envelopes stuffed with photos. Take a week or so to gather them all in one spot. Buy large lidded plastic bins at the drugstore to collect your finds.

- ◇ Sort them by year, as close as you can tell. Use large manila envelopes, marked 2000, 2001, etc.

- ◇ Begin your current album with your most recent photos, say the authors of *The Creative Memories Way*.[7] This gives you a place to start and keeps you from getting bogged down at the huge task ahead. As you get caught up with current photos, you can work backward as time allows.

- ◇ Check out *The Creative Memories Way* for album ideas to inspire you.

Photo crop nights give us a perfect excuse to get together. For about the same as it would cost for popcorn and a movie, we get a whole evening to gab (and to make some nifty albums too).

Though these albums do take time—up to an entire evening for one finished page if you're my speed—you have at least accomplished something. And as my son's track coach says, a little running is better than none. I think the same applies here. ♛

"Let your speech always be with grace, as though seasoned with salt, so that you will know how you should respond to each person." (Colossians 4:6)

prayer THANK YOU, FATHER, FOR SUMMER AND THE EXTRA TIME I CAN SPEND WITH MY CHILDREN. I PRAY THAT MY WORDS WOULD BE FILTERED, LORD; THAT YOU WOULD HELP SEASON THEM WITH GRACE AS I SPEND MORE HOURS WITH MY FAMILY.

week 26

Chore Time: Training the Children

new word
for the week:

Desultory (děs′ əl-tôr′ ē).
Occurring haphazardly; random.
As in, *"I hope I can teach my kids
enough household skills so they
won't be disheartened by **desultory**
housekeeping habits."*

alternate
new word:

Snarky (snär′ kē).
Testy or irritable; short (chiefly Brit-
ish). As in, *"I'll try not to be **snarky**,
kids, as I learn to be a better delega-
tor of household chores."*

Given a spare hour, I am far more likely to call out to my kids, "Who wants to make chocolate pudding?" than "C'mon, kids, let's sort through the baseball cards on your floor!" So who can fault them for being, um, rather easy-going when it comes to keeping their belongings tidy? If I'm not good at doing chores myself, how can I coach my children to be? How can you teach what you don't know?

As Sandra Felton says in *The Messies Manual*, while we may have contributed to the bad habits our kids have developed, it's never too late for any of us to develop new ones. Felton encourages, "Habits are not broken in a day, or in a week. It takes patience and determination within ourselves to overcome these obstacles. . . . Change is always hard, but it is worth it."[1]

Don't think that because you're not perfect at keeping house you have nothing to teach. I'm no great pianist, but I can still show my kids where middle C is and help them learn to follow simple sheet music and use proper fingering. Likewise, while no one will ever mistake my home for the Institute of Order and Beauty, I can still share what I know with my children. As I work at getting better at running a smooth household, I can take the opportunity to pull them aside and watch as they sort and start a load of laundry. I can talk to them as I cook, explaining why I'm using one particular pan instead of another. I can work next to them after dinner, putting away leftovers as they load the dishwasher and see just how much is involved in "doing the dishes" (unloading clean dishes, washing out pots, clearing and sponging down the table).

As I clarify in my own mind the skills I'd like my sons to know by the time they're on their own, asking them to help around the house has morphed from my need for help to their need to know. These are basic life skills they're going to need—and soon! My friend Pam helped each of her teenagers plan, cook, and clean up after one dinner a week so they'd not only know how to make a few basic dishes but also appreciate the effort that goes into making a meal.

A speaker I once heard advised the audience that if they felt the need to train their kids in almost every area, ask the Lord, "Where do I start?" It may be cleaning out the car once you get home from excursions; it may be picking up toys before lunch. Whatever it is, be open to God's leading. Just as in beginning an exercise program or trying to change the way we eat, start small. Dramatic speeches about how "Things are gonna be different around here from now on!" are likely to lose all impact once the heat of the moment is past. A better approach is that chores are a part of life; training our children to help with the home's upkeep is simply part of their education, like teaching them to brush their teeth.

As Tim Kimmel says in his book *Little House on the Freeway: Help for the Hurried Home*, "Anything you do to prepare them for the future is a way of saying 'I love you.'"[4]

Let the lovin' begin.

In the last dozen years, I've tried all kinds of ideas to motivate my kids to help with household chores. There was the paper "clock" we made, the boys' names on each of the two hands and chores to be done written on the clock's face; each week the hands rotated so chores could be swapped. There was the maze I drew with different tasks on each square; when the child reached his finish line, he earned a prize. There was the coupon book I stapled together of construction paper, with prizes such as "rent movie of your choice" or "Mom takes you for one breakfast at McDonald's" redeemable for every five chores completed from my master list.

Each of the schemes worked—for a while. But reminiscent of those finger-painting days when it took me longer to set up the project than it did for the kids to whip off a quick masterpiece and commence sword fighting with sticks, sometimes my charts' success lasted not much longer than the time it took to draw up the thing in the first place.

While I have enjoyed the creativity of devising new systems with charts and stickers, and while I believe trying different techniques has helped me stay interested in training my kids, I have finally given up on the idea that there is a magic plan somewhere that, at the suggestion of dusting, will make my cherubs tap dance with joy. (Chores don't exactly inspire me to tap dance either.) I'm beginning to see that I don't always need to make chores fun. As adults, we work because there's work to be done. My children need to learn this too.

One spring, I suggested to my husband we hold a family meeting to discuss how to manage the mountains of laundry that arrive each spring along with the first cry of "Batter up!" Before the vague pleas for help had even left my lips, a hopeless wave came over me. Why did I think this would work? The jock straps, sliding shorts, baseball pants, white socks, stirrup socks, undershirts, overshirts, and entirely different sets for home games versus away games versus practices had every spring been dumped into a nightly heap on the laundry room floor, a huge compost pile of sweat. Why did I think this year would be any different? My husband, who is much better than I at breaking

> ## Quotable
>
> *Trying to get others to participate does not happen overnight. I wish I could tell you some magic phrase that would make everyone want to pitch in right now. Of course, there is none. You probably already know two approaches that do not work: complaining and acting like a martyr.[5]*
>
> **Kathleen A. Kendall-Tackett,**
> *The Hidden Feelings of Motherhood*

a problem into parts and spotting a solution, called the kids over. "Hey guys, when you take off your baseball clothes every night, stick them into the washing machine, OK? And the last one to do it, start the machine."

No pleading, no charts with stickers, no rewards. Just a simple, specific request. It worked (at least for a while). Imagine that.

I read an article that stated it wasn't worth delegating tasks that are done rarely (filing income taxes, say) because it would cost more time to teach someone than the time it would save you. What is worth delegating is any task done routinely and often. Which is to say most household chores.

I don't know about you, but I'm not so good at delegating. I tend to ask for help rarely, typically waiting until I'm really stressed before asking (think Thanksgiving). By that time I'm in no mood to handle a family member who's less cooperative than the family cat or one who doesn't complete the job the way I'd envisioned it.

I need to practice delegating during times of calm so I can count on my family's help during times of stress.

I also need to remember that asking for help is not a sign of failure. It's a sign of humility, being able to acknowledge you're not superhuman and you can't fit twenty-four hours' worth of work into twelve. I love what James Thornton, author of *Chore Wars*, says: "Don't be ambivalent about asking other family members to do their share. Maybe you feel on some level that these jobs really are your responsibility alone. This is crazy. Sharing work is good for everyone."[6]

In *The Family Manager*, author Kathy Peel recommends delegating organizational chores, such as putting the pantry in order, to your more left-brained, organized children. More creative jobs, such as designing the flowerbed, can go to the right-brained, artistic members of the family. "Discover what family members are good at, and put them to work in that area. When they're working at something they're gifted at, they'll usually work harder and faster, and you'll have less griping."[7]

If you're not sure of each child's preferences, ask. They can probably tell you if they'd rather concoct a salad or help with after-dinner cleanup.

Don't forget to express appreciation for the help you do get. If anyone's ever awarded you with a "Thank you so much for the delicious dinner!" you know how good it feels.

A few suggestions for motivating your children to help with chores:

. . . .

◇ *Chore Wars* author James Thornton advises, "Rather than launching on a dissertation any time you want something picked up, keep it simple. . . . Say: 'Books!' or 'Games!' or 'Wet towels!' The pithy approach communicates without criticizing or expressing all the anger and annoyance you might be feeling."[8]

◇ Write down chores you expect your kids to do rather than making verbal requests; somehow, it seems less like nagging. Leave a list by their spot at the table, or post little notes by the messes. (On a pile of clean clothes: "Please put us away. We are cold out here!") Says author of *The Messies Manual*, Sandra Felton, "Writing, especially typing, is much more official than Mom. Mom's voice fades quickly and can be forgotten. Writing stays there until it is dealt with."[10]

◇ For prereaders, draw pictures of the task you'd like them to accomplish.

◇ Be clear about when you'd like the work completed.

◇ You may get help faster by saying no TV, computer time, or going outside until chores are finished.

◇ Bribes work. "Once we finish our chores, I'll take you for ice cream / to the park / to the library."

◇ For some families a regular fifteen-minute cleanup before lunchtime (or dinnertime or bedtime) works.

◇ Clean with your kids so no one feels like they're being "punished."

◇ An idea that's worked well for our family—especially when company's on the way and it's blitzkrieg-cleaning time—is to list each specific chore ("clean

> ### Quotable
>
> *Sometimes, it might seem easier to just do a given job yourself. . . . Perhaps short term this might actually be correct—but you have to think long term. Remember: Your loved ones will never become competent self-starters if they aren't given ample opportunities to practice.*[9]
>
> **James Thornton,**
> *Chore Wars*

kids' bathroom toilet"; "clean kids' bathroom mirror"; "wipe down kids' bathroom countertop and sink"; etc.) and set the list on the kitchen table. With timer ticking, we run to accomplish our task of choice, run back to cross it off the list, then proceed to our next chosen task, seeing how far we can get in the allotted time. The beauty is that while you're doing your "favorite" chores, someone else is likely to do your least favorite ones. With several people playing, you'd be surprised at how much you get done in a short time.

For more ideas and inspiration, check out the terrific book *Chore Wars* by James Thornton. ♛

"She watches over the affairs of her household and does not eat the bread of idleness." (Proverbs 31:27 NIV)

prayer LORD, THANK YOU FOR ENTRUSTING ME WITH MY KIDS, TO LOVE AND TO TRAIN. PLEASE GUIDE ME AND SHOW ME WHERE TO START. GIVE ME A VISION FOR THE CHARACTER QUALITIES YOU DESIRE FOR MY FAMILY (DILIGENCE? PRODUCTIVITY?), SO I CAN HELP ACCOMPLISH YOUR PURPOSES.

CHOCOLATE BREAK! Stop!

BROWN BOTTOM CUPCAKES

These delicious cupcakes first entered my life on a visit to my in-laws that fortuitously coincided with their church bake sale. After we inhaled these, my wonderful mother-in-law Mary Ann got the recipe from her friend who'd baked them.

These are the cupcakes my children now request for every birthday. They freeze well, too, but many's the scoundrel who nabs them straight from the freezer and microwaves them for immediate ingestion. Pardon the crumbs around my mouth.

One warning: with the cream cheese filling that's plopped on before baking, they may look a bit odd to young, finicky eaters who haven't yet tried them—kind of a cheesecake-like appearance on top. But don't worry; once they take a bite they'll be hooked. Better yet, they may never take a bite and then you'll get to eat them all yourself. It could be worse.

BROWN BOTTOM CUPCAKES

Cream together:

8 oz. package cream cheese
1 egg
1/3 cup sugar
1/8 t. salt

Add: **1 cup chocolate chips**
Set aside. In separate bowl, sift together:

1 ½ cups flour
1 t. baking soda
½ t. salt
1 cup sugar
¼ cup cocoa

Add:

1 cup water
½ cup salad oil
1 T. vinegar
½ t. vanilla

Fill cupcake papers about half full of batter. (Make sure to use papers, by the way; cupcakes will stick to the muffin pan if you plop the batter in directly.) Drop one full tablespoon of the cream cheese mixture into the middle of batter. Bake thirty minutes at 350 degrees. Makes twelve to sixteen.

No frosting needed. Honest.

(Note: Fill any empty muffin cups with water as you bake, to prevent bottom of empty cups from burning.)

week 27

Trippity Doo Dah: The Family Vacation

My husband and I still remember the infamous getaway where we spent hours packing up diapers, wipes, pacifiers, bottles, portable cribs, swimsuits, beach balls—not to mention our two little boys—and filling the car like overstuffed bratwurst, preparing to head out on a three-hour drive to visit relatives for the weekend. It took us an exhausting day and a half of preparations, and we looked at each other more than once and wondered if the monstrous efforts were worth it. But finally, we were ready.

Twenty minutes into our trip, a little voice came from the backseat. "I pooped." A quick look verified our son's claim. In fact, he was guilty of underreporting. The child, indeed, needed a bath, as well as a new set of clothes—possibly even a new car seat—and the sooner the better.

It was the final joker that made our whole house of cards tumble down. What were we thinking, planning a trip to sunshine and poolside with two babies who needed to be kept out of the sun and couldn't yet swim?

We turned the car around and went home.

These days, our vacation challenges are different. We have two teenagers now, who are not so sure bonding with Mom and Dad sounds as enticing as a week in front of video games like Crashman Meets MegaRaider.

new word
for the week:

Peregrination
(pĕr′ ə-grə-nā′ shən).
A traveling, roaming, or wandering about; a journey. As in, *"Let's have a grand time on our family's **peregrinations** this summer!"*

alternate
new word:

Frisson (frē-sōɴ′).
A sudden, passing sensation of excitement; thrill. As in, *"Honey, doesn't it give you a **frisson** to realize there's a bathroom stop in just forty-eight more miles?"*

Their reluctance aside, we've decided it's still important for our family to take the time to reconnect. Busy summer schedules replete with baseball camps, marching band practices, and football conditioning (not to mention Crashman) don't leave as much time for togetherness as I would like. So off we go, this summer like almost all the rest, for a week of memory making that I hope will remind us we're still a family.

I hope you're planning to get away as a family this summer, too, whether it's camping at the beach, visiting sisters and brothers-in-law, or going on some exotic trip to a far-off destination. In spite of my fourteen-year-old's grumbling, "I don't see what's so great about memories, anyway," this time together is important. Memories bind us into a unit like sticky Japanese rice holds together sushi. The years with our kids are short. It's easy to let them slip away, one ordinary twenty-four hours followed by another, if we don't intentionally jolly things up once in a while.

Here's hoping your summer adventures bring you some fresh, out-of-the-ordinary, day-jollying experiences.

And that you get farther than twenty minutes down the road.

Before you go, here are some prevacation suggestions for things I often remember only when it's too late:

◇ If you don't want to come home to bags of cucumber juice in your crisper, make sure you clean out your refrigerator—at least the fruit and vegetable compartments—before you leave.

◇ As you're heading to the post office to have mail delivery stopped, pick up postcard stamps and slip them in your wallet so you'll be ready when the urge strikes to tell Aunt Millie, "Wish you were here!"

◇ Hunt through your junk drawers for unused labels (think "Hello, my name is . . ."). Copy names and addresses of people you want to send postcards to right on the label, so you don't have to bring your address book with you. (And yes, cut off the "My name is" part so the card recipients don't think you're a total dork.)

◇ To avoid greasy surprises, pack travel sizes of moisturizers or foundations you've used before, or take the trouble to dump your regular cosmetics into those eensy little bottles. Do as I say, not as I do.

◇ If you've bought itty-bitty hairspray, test it out before leaving to make sure the spray lands on your actual hair and not in your eye, like a lemon with a perverse sense of humor.

❖ Even if you have a zillion-dollar camera that zooms, pans, and flosses your teeth, consider bringing along disposable cameras. That way (a) everyone has his own camera to document the trip (label whose is whose with masking tape), and (b) when you survive your family's white-water rafting trip, specifically Agony's Nightmare Rapids Revenge, you will have proof.

❖ Stick two large plastic garbage bags in your suitcase, one for dirty clothes (makes doing laundry when you get home a cinch—no sniffing for what's clean and what isn't) and one for bathing suits or other still-damp clothes.

❖ If you have time, change sheets the day before you leave for your trip. Fresh sheets are a wonderful welcome back.

❖ During vacation, keep a family journal. If your kids think this sounds too much like homework, act as the family scribe yourself. Ask family members at the end of each day to describe their highlight. Expect to be surprised. (You thought the kids' highlight would be the breathtaking scenery, but it was really when they leaped over the rock-filled gorge and heard horrified Mom utter a word she doesn't ordinarily say. Not that I have experienced this personally, last summer, in Colorado, or anything.)

❖ As you peruse gift shops for trinkets for the folks back home, make a point to pick up some postcards for yourself too. They can help you remember just where you were when you saw those amazing red rocks in the shape of kissing camels (it was Colorado Springs). Toward the end of a trip, it's also fun to send yourself a postcard, reminding you of all the good memories you're sure to forget the instant you get home and see the liquid cucumber. For those whose photography motto is "quantity, not quality," postcards make good photo album material, too, making a welcome addition to the personally shot pictures of moose herds at the side of the road, which, once you get developed, look remarkably like fuzzy lint in a field.

❖ Also, save brochures so once you get home you can identify where you were.

❖ Most importantly, remember that God is with you on your trip. He doesn't live only in your house or your state. He is everywhere. You may feel lost or disoriented when you're in unfamiliar surroundings. But He will never leave you.

Psalm 139: 7–10 says, "Where can I go from Your Spirit? Or where can I flee from Your presence? If I ascend to heaven, You are there; if I make my bed in Sheol, behold, You are there. If I take the wings of the dawn, if I dwell in the remotest part of the sea, even there Your hand will lead me, and Your right hand will lay hold of me." That's comforting as we embark on new adventures to new places. He is with us in all of our family's peregrinations.

Have fun and build memories!

Getting home from vacation used to mean a too-abrupt switch from a week of rambling relaxation to—boing!—sudden supercharge mode as we rushed to take care of mail, laundry, phone calls, and neglected yard. It took us a few years to realize that returning from a trip didn't have to be such a sudden reentry into the everyday hurricane. Now we make a point to set aside at least a day or two after we're home to still officially be on vacation. For us that means not returning any calls that came in while we were gone and letting the answering machine take any new calls. We don't schedule social events; some years we've even put off picking up mail. I don't feel guilty about going incommunicado. Our family's life, like almost everyone else's I know, is so hectic during most of the year that we need this time to reconnect.

One fun activity to help stretch vacation just a wee bit longer is to take any travel brochures you've collected and use them to make placemats. Get large pieces of cardboard (your local office supply store should sell a package for only a couple of dollars), sit the family down with scissors, glue sticks, and brochures, and have them cut out pictures of favorite places they saw and things they did. Add to the supplies doubles of vacation photographs you've had developed, ticket stubs, menus—any mementoes that bring back special memories.

Once each family member has glued his pictures and created his collage, take them to be laminated. A copy shop charged me a couple of dollars each, but a friend told me a teacher's supply store would do it even cheaper. You've now got a set of personal placemats that should bring a smile to everyone's face every time you sit down to eat.

Take a couple of postvacation days before rejoining the whir of the world's activity. Just a few more moments to play Monopoly, watch movies, and reminisce about the vacation you're still technically on. The world can wait.

Often I find myself with an uncharacteristic urge to clean immediately following a vacation. It might have something to do with marking my territory, or maybe I've just gotten enough distance to actually see the grime. In any case, if you surprise yourself with a postvacation urge to clean, take advantage of it. Sponge off those kitchen counters, spray the front of the dishwasher, scrub that flour canister. You're experiencing a chronic frenzy of cleaning that the Germans would call Putzfimmel.[1]

Which must have been coined by a German woman just back from vacation.

Ideas for celebrating Independence Day:

◇ Read aloud as a family portions of the Declaration of Independence. You can find it in the encyclopedia.

◇ Sing (or hum) "The Star-Spangled Banner."

◇ Make ice cubes with maraschino cherries and serve with blue Kool-Aid® for the classic red, white, and blue look.[2]

◇ Listen to tapes of military marches checked out from the library. *Red, White and Brass* by Canadian Brass is festive and stirring.[3]

◇ Halve a watermelon, scoop out the insides with a melon baller, then fill with red, white, and blue fruit. (Red: watermelon, strawberries, raspberries, cherries, red apples. White: bananas, honeydew melon, pineapple, grapefruit. Blue: blueberries, purple grapes, plums, blackberries.) Sprinkle with shredded coconut.[4]

RED, WHITE, AND BLUEBERRY PIZZA

This is a yummy, very pretty dessert my friend Pam makes for the Fourth of July.

Preheat oven to 350 degrees. Grease and flour an eighteen-inch pizza pan. With floured hands, smush: **18-oz. package refrigerated sugar cookie dough** evenly onto bottom of pan. Bake fourteen to sixteen minutes, until lightly browned. Cool. With electric mixer, beat: **½ cup whipping cream**, to form soft peaks.

Fold in: **8 oz. low-fat vanilla yogurt**, to blend. If making ahead, cover and refrigerate at this point. Before serving, spread whipped cream mixture evenly over cooled cookie crust. Arrange over top:

      1 pint basket (12 oz.) strawberries, stemmed and halved

      1 cup blueberries

Cut into twelve wedges and serve immediately.

"Who shall separate us from the love of Christ? Shall tribulation, or distress, or persecution, or famine, or nakedness, or peril, or sword?" (Romans 8:35 NKJV)

prayer

FATHER, THANK YOU THAT EVEN WHEN WE'RE FAR FROM HOME WE CAN'T BE SEPARATED FROM YOUR LOVE. BE WITH US ON OUR VACATION, LORD. HELP US TO ENJOY ONE ANOTHER'S COMPANY AND BE PATIENT WITH ONE ANOTHER AS WE ATTEMPT TO RECONNECT AFTER THE BUSY SCHOOL YEAR.

week 28

for the week:

Delectation

(dē′ lĕk-tā′ shən).

Pleasure, delight. As in, *"It is hard to hide my delectation at the prospect of a mocha frappuccino on a sunny July afternoon."*

alternate

new word:

Prink (prĭngk).

Primp. As in, *"I believe I will take the opportunity after I've finished my frappuccino to prink for a few minutes; I have some jasmine honeysuckle powder that would be just the thing for prinking."*

Shh! The Queen Is Rejuvenating: Nurturing Ourselves

Some days are like last Monday. A mix-up with a friend meant I had to make an unexpected hour-and-a-half drive. Upon my return home I received a call from my husband who was at the airport about to leave for Europe but who, in a tiny, hopeful voice, asked if I would mind terribly looking for the passport he'd left behind and driving it up to him at the airport—a two-hour round trip. Later that evening as I pulled into the garage with my son, he abruptly remembered he'd left his backpack at the gym and off we went on another hour's drive to retrieve it.

Ahh, life as a homemaker.

Some days are like that. Some weeks are like that.

Sometimes we just need a hug.

When I'm feeling down because of the circumstances of life—"It's not the big things that get me," says a friend, "but the little, everyday stuff"—it helps me immensely to start taking special care of myself. Sometimes I need to wear an outfit that makes me feel pretty, to use both the body powder and the cologne, to reward myself with a lemon scone from the coffee place or a few minutes on the couch with a novel. A real glass with real ice in my car's drink holder instead of my usual dilapidated lukewarm water bottle reminds me I am not the family's hired chauffeur, simply a means for others to get what they want. I am a real person, a person who is valued. I matter.

When we consistently put our family's needs ahead of our own, we can easily forget we even have preferences. A meal out that doesn't include small plastic toys? A car ride that's not accompanied by a peppy rendition of "And Bingo was his name-o"? We have to be careful that in our zeal for our families we don't lose track of ourselves.

In *The Sidetracked Sisters' Happiness File*, authors Pam Young and Peggy Jones suggest starting a list of all the things you love to do, then making sure to incorporate them into your life. Young and Jones's list includes "Sitting in the sun. . . . Long walks in the country. Window-shopping. Christmas music. Cooking. . . . A nap at 2:30. Eating in a restaurant. . . . Playing the piano. . . . Reading a good novel. A crackling fire."[1] Your list might include writing a letter, praying, watching a "girl movie," working on a crafts project, taking a bubble bath.

Choose one thing from your list and ask God to help you find ways to incorporate it into your life this week. If it will help, tell a friend or family member your plan, or ask them to do it with you. For future reminders, jot on your calendar an occasional, "Choose one fun activity from list."

Be kind to yourself. Be good to yourself. You are precious to God!

> ## Quotable
>
> *People say that life is the thing, but I prefer reading.*
>
> **Logan Pearsall Smith**

"I cannot live without books," said Thomas Jefferson (who, incidentally, had to sell off his library of more than 6,000 books in later years to pay off debts).[2]

A life without books would be dreary indeed, especially during summer when looser schedules and long sunny days await. If reading is one of your passions, take time out this summer to read essays by E. B. White and Calvin Trillin, humor by Erma

Bombeck and Dave Barry, great theology by C. S. Lewis and Ray Stedman, and novels by Jan Karon and Margaret Mitchell (don't miss *Gone with the Wind*).

If finding time to read is as elusive as locating a bathing suit that's truly thigh slimming and waist nipping, try one of these strategies:

◇ Listen in the car to books on tape (your local library probably has a slew of them).

◇ Look in the children's section of your library for shortened versions of great literature; read the shorter, kids' version if it's all you have time for.

◇ Sample short stories or essays by various authors. Keep a list of favorites so you can go back to their longer works later, when you have more time.

"For we are His workmanship" (Ephesians 2:10).

"For God so loved the world, that He gave His only begotten Son" (John 3:16).

"Behold, I have inscribed you on the palms of My hands" (Isaiah 49:16).

"Do not fear, for I have redeemed you; I have called you by name; you are Mine!" (Isaiah 43:1).

Throughout the Bible, God has told us over and over how valuable we are to Him. Not because we've done anything to deserve it, but simply because He created us and He loves us. Rather like how we feel about our own children, wouldn't you say?

I am sometimes struck by my own failure to treat myself as a special, loved daughter of the King. What is it about serving the family all day that makes me forget that it's OK to treat myself well too? I'm not talking about buying a new living room set. I'm talking about taking a quiet moment during the day to reflect on the wonder of being crafted by the same God who made the sun and the stars.

God made us unique. In thousands of years, He has created no one else exactly like you. Bask in that thought.

Quotable

To avoid burnout, treat yourself well. You are not only the anchor of your family; you are an important person in your own right. You count, and your needs are important. When you feel irritable, anxious, or depressed, stop and ask yourself an important question: What do I need right now? When you identify the need, plan a way to meet it.[3]

Debbie Barr,
A Season at Home

Ponder the things that make you special—your hobbies, your interests, your strengths. Appreciate who He made you to be. And when you have a few spare moments in your day, spend them playing on the piano the song that only you can play, planting the garden that only you can plant, or knitting the scarf that only you can knit. Remember that you are special. Simply because He made you.

The write-up in the women's magazine promised that all I had to do was sign a check and soon I'd become a new woman, receiving in the mail a one-week supply of pampering goodies: "beauty in a box." Never one to be suckered in by outlandish advertising claims, I immediately mailed in my entire stash of birthday money. Beauty in a box, on top of a box, underneath a box, any way I could get it, I wanted it.

Now, I am well aware that beauty cannot be bought (see I Peter 3:3–4); true beauty comes from the inside, emerging like a brilliant orange monarch butterfly from a life yielded to God. But those expensive eye creams I laughed at just a few years ago are suddenly taking on a new allure with each new "greater than / less than" sign appearing at the corner of my eyes. I was willing to part with a little cash in the hopes of some beauty payback.

What fun when my box arrived! Day one's abundance included a fingernail brush, cuticle cream, an orange stick for pushing back cuticles, hand cream, and thin white cotton gloves to be worn for fifteen minutes while the cream soaked in. Another day piled me high with tools to soak my feet in scented water, scrub away calluses, separate my toes, and paint my toenails bubblegum pink.

As any woman could guess, it was weeks and weeks after the happy box's arrival before I had the chance to actually use all seven days' worth of beauty treatments. (In fact, the hot-oil hair treatment still waits unopened on my bathroom shelf.) But just receiving the box made me feel

Quotable

Arranging a bowl of flowers in the morning can give a sense of quiet in a crowded day—like writing a poem, or saying a prayer. What matters is that one be for a time inwardly attentive.[4]

Anne Morrow Lindbergh,
Gift from the Sea

special and pampered. It was delightfully self-indulgent, a grand experiment in treating myself like a queen.

Most of us will never have months to cream ourselves à la Queen Esther (see the book of Esther, chapter 2, for more on that). But if you can sneak off to the bathroom once in a while for a few minutes to slather, I say do it. See if you can't squeeze in some time before your next meal to actually use some of those lotions, potions, and polishes that are lurking on your bathroom shelves behind the tweezers and thermometers. When we're feeling spent, we really do need to take some time, no matter how brief, to pamper ourselves. Massaging your hands with that exotic honey bee/lotus blossom lotion you got last Christmas may be just the perk you need to help you face the rest of the day with energy and optimism.

I hope you're feeling more beautiful already.

"God created man in His own image." (Genesis 1:27)

prayer LORD, THANK YOU FOR CREATING ME IN YOUR IMAGE, FOR MAKING ME SPECIAL. HELP ME TO VALUE MYSELF THE WAY YOU VALUE ME, AND TO TREAT MYSELF AS A SPECIAL, LOVED CHILD OF THE KING.

week 29

Feasting on Fruit

I stood on the top step of the rickety metal ladder, leaning hard over the blackberry prickles in my yard and willing my arm to grow just an inch longer so I could reach the tempting berry that teased past my fingertips. I was determined to get it. After a few long seconds of teetering, to the strains of squawking blue jays alerting each other to an invader in their midst, I finally had my prize: a beautiful, plump blackberry. Gloating at my success, I pulled myself upright on the ladder, ready to plunk the berry into my container. Just then my head ran smack into an entire clump of perfect purple blackberries; it was hovering so close I could have licked it.

How like me, I thought, to strain for the little jewel out of reach when right under my nose (actually, my eye) was an entire clump of rubies. And how like God to gift me with the very best: no earning necessary, a free gift, mine by virtue of simply looking, reaching, and taking.

July is a wonderful month to thank God for His goodness, in so many areas of our lives. As we walk through the grocery store and see bins overflowing with juicy strawberries, cherries, and peaches, let it remind us of God's abundant provision. In the past He faithfully provided

new word

for the week:

Comestible

(kə-mĕs′tə-bəl).

An eatable; an article of solid food. As in, *"Family, come gawp at these delectable* **comestibles** *I canned with my own two hands!"*

alternate

new word:

Redolent (rĕd′ ə-lənt).

Having or emitting fragrance; pleasantly odorous. As in, *"This kitchen is* **redolent** *of sweet summer berries; an awesome homemaker must live here!"*

Quotable

Summer parties do not need desserts, I think. A bowl of cool fresh fruit topped with mint is a good ending. But my friend Martha glorifies ripe, juicy cut-up fruit by serving the slices in a soft honey-colored custard sauce. Ripe strawberries, savory peaches, dark plump blueberries—almost every kind of fruit is graced by the sauce. It is not a thick, heavy, too-sweet sauce but thin and delicate so that it does not overwhelm the fruit. It is, in short, just right. It reminds me of a time in my life devoted to Floating Island [a dessert of chilled custard, with meringues floating on top], which I loved with the passion my grandchildren feel for chocolate layer cake.[1]

Gladys Taber,
Still Cove Journal

manna in the desert to the Israelites. He faithfully provides for you and me today.

Make sure to fill your grocery cart, and your menus, with a good variety of the fruits in season now. Sliced, sugared, layered with yogurt and granola, dipped in chocolate, pureed into frozen smoothies—try them all. Scan your cookbooks and recipe clippings for ideas. You can never have too much fruit. (OK, so maybe my ten-year-old nephew can, who polishes off three pounds of cherries then holds his stomach for a few hours and groans. But most of us can't.)

You can imagine my ineffable delight when, on a recent vacation, we came upon a "chocolate extravaganza," a dessert buffet made up entirely of chocolate. I was as happy as a puppy who could hardly believe her good fortune at receiving a squeaky new chew toy.

Of all the wonderful cakes, candies, and other goodies, my favorite was the simplest: festive and elegant **chocolate-dipped strawberries**. When we got home I tried making them, and they were, indeed, so easy that kids can do it (or help). We made some for a party but, unfortunately, ate them all before the guests arrived. Oops.

Leaving the hulls on, wash the strawberries and dry well. Line a baking sheet with wax paper. Melt **several squares of semisweet baking chocolate** in the microwave or in a saucepan over low heat; stir till smooth. Dip each berry in the chocolate, then place on wax paper. When the tray is full, refrigerate. These don't keep well, so eat within a few hours.

Note: Baking chocolate works better than chocolate chips, giving you a thinner coating that's easier to bite through. Try to save a few for your guests.

If you've ever bought an entire watermelon, you can't help but notice that no matter how many people you're feeding, you always end up with at least half the beast left. Here are a few ideas on what to do with all that extra fruit, before you reach the "Why'd I ever buy this thing anyway?" stage:

◊ For a delicious fruit punch, puree 3 ½ cups seeded watermelon cubes in small batches in your blender. In a pitcher, combine the watermelon puree with 3½ cups lemonade or limeade and 2 cups orange juice. Stir and enjoy.

◊ Cut several ¾-inch slices from the watermelon, then slice into wedges two inches across at the rind. Dip into fresh-squeezed lime juice spiked with a dash of salt and a dash of Tabasco sauce. Serve as an hors d'oeuvre or snack.

◊ For dessert or a snack, dab a slice of watermelon with sour cream (or plain yogurt) and a sprinkling of brown sugar. This is yummy, easy, and surprisingly addictive.[2]

◊ When you don't think you can face that hunk of fruit one more time, chunk what's left into two-inch cubes, discarding rinds and seeds, and freeze in Ziploc® bags. Later in the summer, when you've given it a rest, use in frozen fruit smoothies (see week 21).

◊ Congratulate yourself. Well done, you thrifty watermelon steward.

I love the smell of bubbling berries and sugar as they cook into jam. The sweet scent lingers in my kitchen for hours like the perfume of a favorite friend long after she's gone home.

I love the rows of glistening jars that line my counter. I leave them there for sometimes as long as a week, reveling in their silent congratulations each time I go by. It's a wonderful feeling, this burst of productivity that leaves behind visible evidence, proof of efforts. The verse keeps circling through my brain: "She looks well to the ways of her household, and does not eat the bread of idleness" (Proverbs 31:27). My arm's starting to hurt from patting myself on the back.

Olallieberry jam is my husband's and my son's absolute favorite. No matter how many pounds of berries we pick each summer, we never have enough to last the whole year.

Quotable

It is a thrill to possess shelves well stocked with home-canned food. In fact, you will find their inspection, often surreptitious, and the pleasure of serving the fruits of your labors comparable only to a clear conscience or a very becoming hat.[3]

Irma S. Rombauer and Marion Rombauer Becker, *The Joy of Cooking*

Every April we're scrounging in the cupboards. "Is this the last jar?"

Because of our inevitable shortfall, my husband blanches when he sees me giving away even one jar as a gift. But jam does make a wonderful gift. People give you enormous credit for a process that's simpler than baking a decent batch of cookies. (Which, in a profession where many of your efforts go unnoticed, is not such a bad thing.) If you can boil and stir for a couple of minutes, you can make jam.

My mom, who first tried it a couple of years ago, had been put off for years thinking jam making involved huge kettles and gallons of boiling water. She remembered her own mother sweating over the wood-stoked stove in the hot, humid Virginia summer and had no desire to repeat that performance.

Mom was delighted, however, to discover that in making jam there were no vats of boiling water in sight. "If you can read, you can do it!" she says with glee. For cooked jam, you simply pour the mixture into hot, sterilized jars (which stay hot thanks to your trusty automatic dishwasher) then invert them on the counter for five minutes to make a good "seal" between the jar rim and the rubber

Equipment Needed for Making Jam

My husband's grandma taught me to make jam years ago, and every time I pull out my supplies it's a sweet reminder of her. You don't need much equipment: a large cooking pot, measuring cups, a couple of bowls, wooden spoons. Fruit, plenty of sugar, pectin. And containers: just about anything that will freeze if you're making freezer jam; for cooked jam, canning jars sold in boxes of a dozen at the grocery store, with flat lids and screw bands to top off the whole shebang.

The smaller jars are perfect for gift giving; buy larger jars if you have a large family or go through lots of jam.

When you buy a box of jars, it generally comes with enough bands and lids for your first batch. The jars and bands are a one-time investment since they're reusable year after year; only the flat lids need to be new each time you make jam, to ensure a good seal.

Also helpful, though not vital, are a colander, a ladle, and a wide-mouth funnel, for pouring the jam into the jars without slopping it all over the rim.

ring on the lid. "But try freezer jam first," suggests Mom, because it sidesteps the whole sterilization issue. When you see how easy that is, you'll be ready to venture on.

All instructions for both freezer and cooked jams are found in little boxes of pectin that you can buy at the grocery store. So get some pectin, some berries, some sugar, and give jam making a try. Before you know it, you'll be admiring the jewel-toned jars lining your own kitchen counter and basking in the praise of friends and family who believe you to be very clever indeed.

"The fruit of the Spirit is love, joy, peace, patience, kindness, goodness, faithfulness, gentleness, self-control" (Galatians 5:22–23).

In the past when I've read this list, I've thought the qualities mentioned were traits I was supposed to try hard to exhibit. Then one day it occurred to me: a fruit tree doesn't struggle to produce fruit. For a fruit tree, fruit comes naturally. Give it water, sunlight, soil with nutrients, and time and—ta da!—it produces fruit.

I believe that's how God works the fruit of the Spirit in us. Producing fruit is what we are made for. With enough water, sunlight, etc. (in other words, time spent reading the Bible, praying, asking Him to help us as we follow Him), God will bring about fruit in us. We don't need to struggle to produce some foreign product, any more than a cherry tree has to struggle to produce tennis balls. All the struggling in the world won't get a cherry tree to grow tennis balls; and all the struggling in the world won't increase its crop of cherries either. All it takes for a good crop of cherries is water and light and good soil and time. Same as us.

As we depend on our Father as our source, reading His Word and letting it transform our thinking, we can have confidence that He will bring about love, joy, peace, and patience in our lives. "For it is God who is at work in you," says Philippians 2:13. Thank heavens!

Spend some time today reflecting on the list of fruit from Galatians. Ask God to show you the one fruit you need more of in your life right now. Pray specifically that God would bring about that fruit in you.

Then watch Him grow. ♛

"Abide in Me, and I in you. As the branch cannot bear fruit of itself unless it abides in the vine, so neither can you unless you abide in Me. I am the vine, you are the branches; he who abides in Me and I in him, he bears much fruit, for apart from Me you can do nothing." (John 15:4–5)

prayer THANK YOU, LORD, FOR BEING SO FAITHFUL TO WORK IN ME. HELP ME TO REMEMBER TO TURN TO YOU IN MY LIFE AS A HOMEMAKER WHEN I AM NOT FEELING VERY FRUITFUL. THANK YOU FOR THE ASSURANCE THAT YOU ARE THE FRUIT PRODUCER; I AM MERELY THE DISTRIBUTOR.

week 30

new word

for the week:

Lucre (lōō′ kər).
Money, profits. As in, *"Just think of all the lucre you'll make, kids, when you sell your old toys."* Not to be confused with sucre, the basic monetary unit of Ecuador.

alternate

new word:

Ersatz (ĕr′ säts).
Substitute; artificial. As in, *"When we shop at the flea market, I hope I don't accidentally buy ersatz 'silver' that's really stainless steel."*

Flea Markets

My kids and I spent several hours in the garage recently, pricing what we hope will become "another man's treasure" at our upcoming church flea market. Small rubber balls, outgrown T-shirts, books that are too "young" for our household—they're all getting sorted and boxed and readied to slide into someone else's van.

My boys, less motivated by sentimentality than I am, are eager to ditch unused science kits and origami paper. They, of course, didn't pay for any of this stuff originally, so earning ten cents on the dollar doesn't bother them much, it being their ten cents and my dollar.

I, seeing the picture in my head of warm, educational family time, not to mention the inevitable school-year lurch for forty-minute emergency science-fair projects, sneak a few of their discards back onto the shelf. I'm not yet ready to ditch the hope that someday we may prove to be an origami family, or a chemistry family, at that.

Maybe in another year I'll be ready to loosen my grip on the croquet set and the remains of the colored pencils (saffron, plum, and nougat, after all, can make mighty fine pictures).

Whenever I do go through the pain and agony of clearing out some belongings, I realize how little most of the cluttery trinkets are worth. It makes it easier, next trip to the amusement park, to turn down the begging pleas for the Orca the whale penny ("Only fifty cents, Mom!"). I already picture the thing on next summer's flea market table, selling for just a nickel, or even less.

The flea market exercise also gives us the perfect opportunity to talk about what's really valuable in life, about how the things of this earth are so easily destroyed by moth and rust, about our true treasures residing in heaven.

It's also fun to talk about the wisdom in buying used. A paperback for a quarter and an action figure for a dime make the benefits of frugality pretty obvious.

Not a bad profit for a few hours' sorting.

Organizational expert Barbara Hemphill, in a July 1999 *Guideposts* article, observes that the key to getting organized is "flow." "The problem isn't that too much material flows into a home or office—it's that too little flows out."

I have often pictured my home as a giant in-box, with piles of mail, magazines, and purchases coming in almost daily and not enough going out. No wonder it's hard to find a place for it all.

A friend who grew up in a military family and moved frequently as a child still combs through her belongings regularly to weed out what her family doesn't use. Twice a year at least, she culls through linens and kitchenware, sweaters and gardening bric-a-brac. Whatever's deemed unneeded goes to friends or charity. I admire her greatly, not possessing the character to so readily let go of belongings I'm afraid I would miss.

Lynda Millner, author of *The Magic Makeover*, advises, "Every time you add something to your wardrobe, get rid of something old or rarely worn. Cluttered, crammed closets waste precious time while you're searching for the right outfit. . . . Closets should not be museums. They should be full of the present and future, not the past."[2]

Her wisdom holds in other areas too. If we get new coffee mugs, we can discard the old mismatched ones. That's flow.

Selling stuff at our church's annual flea market is the perfect antidote to my family's flow problems. The opportunity to earn something for the pain of sorting and releasing is good motivation, especially for those of us whose frugal conscience whispers, "You can't get rid of that; it's still good!" With the lucre earned at the flea market, we can visit other people's booths and come home with a few treasures of our own (as long as it's less than we came with).

So take a good look around your house. If you haven't sat in it, squeezed into it, mailed, watered, or read it in the last year, say *Sidetracked Home Executives*™ authors Pam Young and Peggy Jones, you need to dump it. (See www.shesintouch.com; "How to De-Junk Your Home" video.) Clear your bookshelves and drawers and marvel at the surprise of empty shelf space. And as you work, sing to the tune of the well-known Christmas song: "Let it flow, let it flow, let it flow."

"What are you doing?" I asked my friend Debby at a recent church flea market. Though her kids were junior high and high school age, she was taking home an armload of stuffed animals and plastic toys.

"Shh!" she whispered conspiratorially. "These are for the dog!"

If you've popped into a pet store lately and spotted the $12.95 chew toy, you'll appreciate Debby's idea. For about a quarter, you can pick up an old stuffed bear or bouncy plastic ball and be a hero to your pup. From your pet's perspective, a cracked Frisbee or hard plastic football is equally spectacular. When I think of the squeaky rubber toy I just bought for $6.95, I could kick myself. (Make sure to watch for plastic eyes or other parts that could choke your pet, though; remove any hazards once you get the toys home.)

Flea market shopping, as well as selling, is fun, though you need to be discriminating and not let bargain fever overtake you. The idea is not to replace junk you just cleared out (do you really have time to finish someone else's great-aunt's half-knitted blanket?). But if you shop with a clear idea ahead of time of what you're looking to buy, you can find some treasures.

At one flea market, I looked specifically for small crocks I could fill with chocolate butter I planned to give as Christmas gifts. Though I didn't find any crocks, I did find a small canning jar with an attached hinged lid that was the perfect size and shape. Only a quarter.

Over the years I've also purchased a great selection of exercise videos. One gently used tape gives me a workout for less than the cost of a class at a health club or gym, and I can use the tape over and over again. (And occasionally I can even convince a bored teenager to join me in lunges and squats, at least for a few minutes until he decides it's more fun to offer snide commentary.)

A few more flea market tips:

◇ When you first get there, scan through the booths quickly before purchasing anything to get a feel for prices.

◇ Be aware of the two kinds of booths: those run by people who are cleaning out their garages and want to simply get rid of stuff, and those run by people whose goal is to make real money. Just because you're at a flea market, don't assume everything is bargain-priced.

◇ Bring small change such as quarters or one-dollar bills, in case the person running the booth runs out.

◇ You'll have a better selection earlier in the day, but by day's end prices may be slashed to almost nothing. So shop accordingly. ❦

Quotable

In deciding what to keep, ask yourself (1) How long since I used this item? (2) Can I justify keeping it? (3) What will happen if it's gone? (4) Is it an irritant?[4]

Dorothy Lehmkuhl and Dolores Cotter Lamping, *Organizing for the Creative Person*

"Do not lay up for yourselves treasures on earth, where moth and rust destroy and where thieves break in and steal; but lay up for yourselves treasures in heaven, where neither moth nor rust destroys and where thieves do not break in and steal. For where your treasure is, there your heart will be also." (Matthew 6:19–21 NKJV)

prayer LORD, THANK YOU FOR SHOWING ME SO CLEARLY THAT MY TREASURE IS NOT MY POSSESSIONS. THANK YOU FOR THE REAL TREASURES IN MY LIFE: MY FAMILY, MY FRIENDS, AND MY RELATIONSHIP WITH YOU.

CHOCOLATE BREAK! stop!

CHOCOLATE BUTTER

True chocolate lovers do not limit ourselves to dessert only; we look for any excuse to sneak some in, any time we can manage it. This recipe, from Sharon Tyler Herbst's wonderful *The Food Lover's Guide to Chocolate and Vanilla*, is a marvelous addition to your breakfast menu.[5] Do not eat it straight, as one of my girlfriends did. It is meant to be spread on toast, pancakes, biscuits, or, my very, very favorite, toasted English muffins. You will be hooked.

CHOCOLATE BUTTER

Melt: **1/3 cup chocolate chips**

Set aside to cool. In medium bowl, using electric mixer, beat together cooled chocolate and **½ cup butter, softened**.

Add **2–4 T. powdered sugar**, to taste and **1 t. vanilla**.

Stir to incorporate. Cover and refrigerate. Before serving, let stand at room temperature twenty to thirty minutes, if you can stand it (I never can.). Otherwise, microwave for a few seconds to soften. Spread on toasted English muffins for breakfast bliss.

(You can multiply this recipe, make ahead, and freeze for Christmas gifts.)

week 31

new word

for the week:

Captious (kăp'shəs).
Marked by a disposition to find fault and make petty criticisms. As in, *"Honey, if I keep complaining and being captious, feel free to point to the roof and I'll remember to read Proverbs 25:24."*

alternate

new word:

Sibilance (sĭb' ə-ləns).
A hissing sound. As in, *"If you hear a strange sibilance coming from my lips, you'd better steer clear for a while."*

God's Recipe for Wives

The best marriage advice I ever received came twenty years ago from a friend. It was just a few weeks after my wedding, and Andrea and I had gotten together for a game of tennis on the college campus where I'd recently graduated. After our game, I must have been telling her that marriage was harder than I'd thought. That was when she said something I have never forgotten.

"Have you ever thought about the difference between goals and desires?" she asked me. "Your desire may be to have a happy marriage. But you can't control that; that takes two people. The only thing you can control," she said, "is you. So even though your desire is to have a happy marriage, you have to make it your goal to be a good wife."

As our conversation progressed, this wise and godly friend encouraged me not to worry about whether I thought my new husband was doing a good job. The only job description I should be concerned with was my own. Was I being a good wife?

This was a new way of looking at things. Suddenly I saw that I didn't need to "fix" my husband. If I was to be concerned with anyone's "fixing," it ought to be my own.

I've thought of that conversation dozens of times since. Why is it so easy to see the glaring faults of someone else yet conveniently overlook my own? Why am I so quick to spy my husband's selfishness yet be blinded to the ugly "me" gremlin hiding in my own pup tent?

Our pastor recently preached on 1 Corinthians 13, the "love chapter." In looking back at his notes, he realized he'd last taught on that section some two decades ago, before he was married. How easy that passage was to preach on then! How easy it had seemed, to love with patience, kindness, and unselfishness, before twenty-some years of marriage had shown him that that kind of love, God's kind of love, doesn't come naturally.

That's why God has to remind us. "If I speak with the tongues of men and of angels, but do not have love, I have become a noisy gong or a clanging cymbal" (1 Corinthians 13:1).

I want to love my husband with a love that doesn't seek its own. A love that doesn't act unbecomingly. I want to love him with God's love because my own is fickle. If I've gotten enough sleep, the dog didn't throw up on the carpet, and it's frozen pizza for dinner, I feel loving; if, on the other hand, my feelings were hurt by a captious comment, someone forgot his lunch, and my son's toothpick model of the Eiffel Tower is due tomorrow, I feel not so loving.

Loving my husband, with God's love, is assignment enough for the rest of our days together. Lesson noted. Game on. It's love-love.

> ## Quotable
>
> *The greatest favor we can ever bestow on our spouses is to turn our expectations of them on ourselves. In other words, instead of longing for an ideal mate, become one.*[1]
>
> **Glenda Revell,**
> *With Love from a Mother's Heart*

AN EXCELLENT WIFE IS THE CROWN OF HER HUSBAND, BUT SHE WHO SHAMES HIM IS LIKE ROTTENNESS IN HIS BONES. —PROVERBS 12:4

In the months prior to our wedding, Mark and I met half a dozen times with the couple who performed our wedding ceremony. They employed a unique style of premarital

The apostle Paul didn't say that love bears some things, that love believes only in the best things, that love hopes for a reasonable period of time, or that it endures for a while. No, love is a divine absurdity. It is unreasonable. Paul said, "Love bears all things, believes all things, hopes all things, endures all things." Love is limitless. For-give-ness is to give infinitely, without end. . . .

This is our human predicament: we are able to sin infinitely against one another, but we are able to forgive only finitely. Left to

cont. ⇒

counseling: they'd assign us a passage of Scripture, then tell us to read and reread it as many times as possible until we met again. We were to stew on the verses, look at them from every angle, come up with questions about them. A few weeks down the road, when we reconnected, we'd talk about what we'd discovered.

It was amazing to see how much the Bible had to say about marriage! Sometimes our talks lasted five or six hours.

We started with Genesis 2:18–25. From this passage we learned that woman was made to be man's "helper," his ally, his partner in life. We saw that woman was created differently than man: while Adam had been formed from the dust of the ground (Genesis 2:7), Eve had been made from Adam's rib (Genesis 2:21). So woman, coming from man's side, tended to be more relationship oriented. Man, coming from the ground (the source of his work, keeping the garden), tended to be more work oriented.

All this made sense, and in the years to come it helped us see our differences not as signs that we were mismatched, but as normal and typical of males and females everywhere. (Men aren't from Mars or women from Venus; men are from dust and women are from ribs.)

We saw in Genesis 2:24 the importance of husband and wife leaving their families of origin to put each other first in their new family ("leave and cleave").

Genesis 2:25 taught us the importance of being naked and "not ashamed." This, we concluded, meant not only in the obvious physical sense but in the emotional sense, as well. We should feel free to bare our true selves, even the least attractive parts, to each other in a way we couldn't with anyone else.

What a lot to gain from a short section of Scripture. And what a good lesson at how much wisdom the Bible holds if we will only take the time to look.

More Good Verses to Chew On

You may want to take just one passage at a time and read it over and over. If your husband is willing, have him read it too. After a couple of weeks, set aside an evening to share your insights.

◆ EPHESIANS 6:12. Our enemies are not flesh and blood (each other), but rather the spiritual forces of wickedness in heavenly places. So when we have a conflict, it's not my husband who's my enemy; it's sin that's my enemy. My husband and I are on the same side.

◆ EPHESIANS 5:22–33. We are to submit to our husband's authority, not because he's always right but because God is. Like it or not, wives under their husbands' headship is God's plan. He says that's how things work best. Can we trust Him? Yes!

◆ EPHESIANS 4:15. We are to "speak the truth in love," which means being both completely truthful and completely loving at the same time. So truth without love is out. ("You drive me crazy with that hair in the sink!") And love without truth is out. ("The hair in the sink doesn't bother me a bit, swee-tums.") So try truth and love together. ("I think you have very beautiful hair" [as long as you think that] "and I also love our sink" [if you do] "but I do believe the sink looks prettier when there's no hair in it.") Accompanied by a winning smile.

◆ I PETER 3:1–12. This wonderful section on marriage tells us, among other things, not to return evil for evil but give a blessing instead. So even if I think my husband isn't shining, I am to shine anyway.

◆ I CORINTHIANS 7:2–5. Our bodies are not our own. We belong to each other. It is my job to make

Rules for Admiration

1. Accept him at face value

2. Think about his manliness

3. Observe his manliness

4. Listen to him talk

5. Admire his manliness in words

6. Be sincere

7. Be specific[5]

Helen B. Andelin,
Fascinating Womanhood

Quotable

A tart temper never mellows with age, and a sharp tongue is the only edged tool that grows keener with constant use.[4]

Washington Irving,
"Rip Van Winkle"

sure my husband's sexual needs are satisfied; it is his job to make sure mine are. Your husband will love these verses automatically, but when you put them into action you will be amazed at how much blessing they bring into your life too.

MY BELOVED IS MINE, AND I AM HIS.
—SONG OF SOLOMON 2:16

"Admire him for his masculine characteristics," I read. "His deep voice, his heavy walk, his large hands." I began to snicker.

"What is it?" my husband asked. Mark and I were sitting at a picnic table in a mostly abandoned park, engrossed in our books while our two sons were heaving baseballs against the side of a cinder-block building and running to catch the ricochet.

I laughed. "It's this book. Can you believe this? It says to admire your husband for his manly characteristics." I laughed again. "Isn't that funny?"

Mark was quiet for a moment. "What's so funny about that?" he asked.

My eyes got wide. "You mean it? You mean you'd like it if I commented on your . . ." I looked at the book for direction, "on your manly hands?"

He shrugged. "Yeah. It's kind of nice." He went back to his murder mystery as I sat, stunned for a minute, staring through my sons but not at them. This man who loves pillow fights and pinball and hurling himself into the swimming pool in the biggest, hugest cannonballs, would like to have his hands admired?

The book I was reading, *Fascinating Womanhood* by Helen B. Andelin, which originated from materials first produced in the 1920s, was telling me that men love to be admired by the women in their world. "This admiration is a source of great happiness, and the lack of it one of his most distressing miseries."[5] I do admire my husband for his many wonderful qualities (so many manly ones too!). But in the chaos of the day, I don't always remember to tell him. Our words can have a tremendous impact on our husbands, for good or for ill. Proverbs 12:18 says, "Reckless words pierce like a sword, but the tongue of the wise brings healing" (NIV).

Our husbands desire us to be their cheerleaders, their number one fans. Ephesians 5:33 makes a special point to remind us to give our husbands respect. When we admire them and take the time to tell them so, we are meeting some of their deepest needs.

Pulitzer-Prize-winning author Phyllis McGinley sums it up well in her 1965 book *Sixpence in Her Shoe*: "Praise is better than wheat germ for even the least vain of men, and every wife ought to keep a supply in her pocket ready to scatter like manna."[7] ☙

Quotable

My mother has often said that she believes many marriage tensions would be absolved if each couple would take just five minutes a day and pray uniquely for the other one's needs. [6]

Gigi Graham Tchividjian,
Thank You, Lord, for My Home

"Your adornment must not be merely external—braiding the hair, and wearing gold jewelry, or putting on dresses; but let it be the hidden person of the heart, with the imperishable quality of a gentle and quiet spirit, which is precious in the sight of God." (1 Peter 3:3–4)

---

prayer

LORD, THANK YOU SO MUCH FOR MY HUSBAND. TEACH ME TO BE A GOOD WIFE AS I LOOK TO YOUR WORD FOR GUIDANCE. HELP ME TO BE WILLING TO LIVE MY LIFE YOUR WAY, FATHER, ACCORDING TO YOUR INSTRUCTIONS. THANK YOU FOR THE BLESSINGS THAT WILL BRING.

week 32

new word

for the week:

Gustatory (gŭs′ tə-tôr′ ē).
Of or pertaining to the sense of taste. As in, *"You have got to try this homegrown tomato; it is a gustatory marvel."*

alternate

new word:

Interstices

(ĭn-tûr′ stĭ-sez′).
Narrow or small spaces between things or parts; crevices. As in, *"I am hopeful I won't find any decomposing zucchini bread in the sofa cushion interstices."*

The Bountiful Garden

My husband refused to plant zucchini this year.

"I'm tired of our friends running and hiding whenever they see me coming with a brown paper bag. I'm tired of zucchini muffins, zucchini nut bread, zucchini pancakes. I'm tired of zucchini the size of baseball bats." He sighed heavily. "No more zucchini."

I'm as willing as the next person to admit that an innocent six-pack of seedlings planted in springtime can easily morph into a midsummer zucchini-jungle nightmare capable of swallowing a full-sized dog. But one little, teeny, tiny zucchini plant?

"Absolutely not."

So this year, in spite of a wonderful garden planted and watered by an even more wonderful gardener (that would be my husband), I knew with certainty. No zucchini unless I were to buy zucchini.

I did a little recipe sleuthing to see what delights I might be missing. There was zucchini quiche. Zucchini dip. Fried zucchini sticks.

Zucchini marmalade. Barbecued zucchini. Mexican scrambled eggs with zucchini.

Sea bass with sun-dried tomatoes and zucchini. Zucchini stuffed with cottage cheese and shrimp. Zucchini mushroom loaf. (Some poor sap must have planted a whole flat.)

And more. There were zucchini-enriched meatballs (peel before shredding, warned the recipe writer, so your picky little detectives won't be able to spot telltale green flecks). Zucchini bread with ½ cup mini chocolate chips added. Zucchini cobbler, made with zucchini juice left over after all that chopping.

I've got to admit, these sounded valiantly creative. But meanwhile, a science-fiction scenario played out in my head. While the cook stands innocently dicing her latest garden baseball bat, the large, hairy plants stand behind her, tendrils menacing, conspiring to overtake the family as they sit down obliviously to their dinner of zucchini mushroom loaf.

I have no reason to think this could be occurring at this very moment in your own backyard; all I'm saying is, zucchini growers beware. There may be a conspiracy brewing, and I'd hate for you to be the last to know.

> ## Quotable
>
> *I can't emphasize strongly enough that the average family doesn't need more than one to three [zucchini] plants.*[1]
>
> **Marian Morash,**
> *The Victory Garden Cookbook*

As the country song so aptly puts it, "There're only two things that money can't buy, and that's true love and homegrown tomatoes!"

If I could have only one plant growing in my yard, it would be homegrown tomatoes. "No doubt the taste for these has grown sharper from the fact that we have them all year round in an inauthentic condition of preservation," says an essay by Elizabeth Hardwick.[2]

Author Rosalind Creasy concurs. "Once you have tried a fully ripened fruit, store-bought ones will seem a travesty."[3]

A travesty, indeed. Most of the tomatoes from the store may look like tomatoes, but that's where the similarity ends. There's no getting around it. The only true tomato is a homegrown tomato.

If your garden contains more than a couple of tomato plants and you're wondering how you'll use all those delicious red orbs, here are some suggestions: You can make tomato juice and can it; whip up tomato soup, some to eat and some to share; hollow out tomatoes and stuff them with cooked orzo pasta mixed with store-bought pesto sauce. You can dry tomatoes, sliced in half lengthwise almost all the way through, in your oven at low heat (200 degrees for nine to twelve hours) and store covered with olive oil in jars. If just getting them picked is all the effort you can expend right now, bring your extras to church or to your local fire department and bless others with your surplus. Your local food bank may accept produce from home gardeners too.

My favorite, indescribably delicious homegrown tomato recipe comes from a book called *The Bountiful Kitchen* by Barry Bluestein and Kevin Morrissey, whose authors, in addition to providing wonderful recipes, describe how they manage to grow fruits, vegetables, and herbs in containers on the nineteenth floor of a Chicago apartment.[4] This is a slightly modified version of their fresh tomato sauce, which is out of this world served on spaghetti and sprinkled with grated Parmesan cheese.

OUT OF THIS WORLD FRESH TOMATO SAUCE

In the bowl of a food processor or blender,
Combine:
1–2 garlic cloves, peeled and minced (about 1 t.)
1 bunch arugula, stemmed and roughly chopped (about
    1 cup) (This is optional; if you omit you will have a
    delicious but slightly runny sauce; alternately, substitute
    1 cup of Romaine)
1 t. coarse kosher salt
Process in food processor or blender until lettuce is very finely chopped. Add:
¼ cup olive oil
several large tomatoes, cored and roughly chopped
(about 2 cups)

Process to "a chunky puree." Refrigerate and use over pasta within a few days.

Note: Extra garden tomatoes can be chopped and frozen in Ziploc® bags in 2-cup amounts for fresh tomato sauce later. Come November, you will exult in your industriousness.

If you've got absolutely no time to do anything with your homegrown tomatoes, freeze them whole in a Ziploc® bag, then later this fall, when making a top-of-the-stove recipe like stew, remove them and add to the pot (substituting for a can of tomatoes). The skins will come off on their own and float to the top where you can whisk them away like unwanted phone solicitors.

Check out *The Gardener's Handbook of Edible Plants* by Rosalind Creasy, which gives growing instructions, recipes, and information on preserving various fruits, vegetables, or herbs.[5]

Another great book with ideas for your harvest is *The Victory Garden Cookbook* by Marian Morash.[6]

For information on canning, freezing, or drying, see *Sunset's Home Canning*.[7]

When we moved to our present house years ago, we became the happy inheritors of a number of spearmint plants. As anyone who's ever grown mint can attest, you can neglect it completely and still it flourishes. (In fact, if you're not careful, mint can take over your garden, so if you don't want a whole field of it, grow it in a pot.)

In any case, if you have mint, you probably have a lot of mint. To make good use of it, try these suggestions: immerse it in tea; dice it and add to salad dressings; collect it in bunches for a fragrant bouquet, either on its own or with other flowers or interesting branches from your garden; sprinkle it over fruit salads; microwave it dry, which gives your kitchen a great (albeit brief) aroma; add it to grape juice / citrus punch; chew it for fresh breath; freeze it in ice cubes to add to your tea or lemonade.

KIMBERLY'S KILLER SALSA

My sister-in-law Kimberly makes the best salsa in the world.

Chop up:
3–4 tomatoes
1 medium onion
1 bunch cilantro
Mix together. Add:
1 14 ½-oz. can diced tomatoes with jalapenos
dash of garlic salt (to taste)
dash of lemon pepper (to taste)
1 T. fresh lime juice
Stir together and pour into serving bowl.
Serve with tortilla chips.

When you can't face one more glass of minted iced tea, try:

. . . .

You Deserve a Break Today Mint Facial

Stir **½ cup fresh mint leaves** into a pot of **boiling water**, then remove the pot from heat. Drape a towel over your head like a tent and (carefully! not too close!) lean over the steam. Enjoy five minutes of fragrant, well-deserved pampering.

Other suggestions for an herb abundance:

◇ Play like the seventeenth century and spread fresh herbs across your kitchen table before setting out pewter and wooden ware.[8]
◇ Chop up basil leaves and layer them in a jar alternately with Parmesan cheese. Freeze, then add more basil leaves to the jar whenever they're ready to be pinched off. (If you're like my family, the jar will never get full. You will eat this as fast as you make it.) Sprinkle the mixture on salads, or even better, over halved (homegrown) tomatoes, heated on the barbecue.
◇ Chop up extra herbs and place a tablespoon in individual compartments of an ice-cube tray. Cover with 1 T. of water and freeze, then store in Ziploc® bag. Next time you're making soup, stew, or a sauce, pop in a couple of cubes as your food simmers.

Take a pair of scissors into your yard and look for exuberant, healthy plants to transform into interesting bouquets for your table. God provides plenty of raw materials; we just need to provide the vase.

"Let the peoples praise You, O God; let all the peoples praise You. The earth has yielded its produce; God, our God, blesses us. God blesses us, that all the ends of the earth may fear Him." (Psalm 67:5–7)

prayer LORD, THANK YOU FOR PROVIDING SO MANY GOOD GIFTS IN THE GARDEN. HELP ME TO APPRECIATE THEM TODAY AND TO USE THEM TO BLESS THOSE AROUND ME. THANK YOU FOR YOUR AMAZING CREATIVITY.

week 33

Too Hot to Cook: Summer Food Ideas

A few summers ago, my family sat around the dining room table at my sister's house in Norway and delighted in one of the best when-it's-too-hot-to-cook dinners anywhere: *skive* (pronounced she' va).

Our *skive* dinner started with a long baguette of fresh bread placed on a cutting board at the table. Each of us got a ¾-inch thick slice, which we spread with creamy butter. Over the next several minutes we painstakingly extracted crabmeat from shells or peeled incredibly sweet Norwegian shrimp and laid our treasures on our bread. We worked ardently, trying not to drool, adding more and more seafood for as long as we could stand it. Finally, after agonizing minutes of anticipation, it was time. We cut off the corner of a little packet of mayonnaise and squeezed a thin serpentine rope over the seafood. We pinched a lemon wedge across the sandwich and, balancing our creation so as not to lose even one precious morsel, took a bite of what is surely one of the most exquisite summer meals in existence.

We did this for hours, peeling and eating our way through perfect open-faced sandwich after perfect open-faced sandwich, long into the Norwegian night (which, curiously, looks at midnight as though it were still dusk).

new word
for the week:

Torpid (tôr′ pĭd).
Deprived of the power of motion; dormant. As in, *"Kids, let's not spend our entire summer like **torpid** blobs in front of the TV set."*

alternate
new word:

Cavil (kăv′əl).
To raise unnecessary or trivial objections; to carp. As in, *"No **caviling** about turning off the TV. I'll race you outside for a squirt-gun fight!"*

An indefinable air of festivity hovered at the table as we cut bread together, sharing the knife and passing the lemons.

To this day, *skive* remains one of my family's favorite summertime dinners. Baby shrimp sold already cooked and peeled make for a far less labor-intensive meal (though I suspect we miss something by not having to work so hard). The kids enjoy seafood-free *skive*, which is bread spread with peanut butter and drizzled with honey, or else covered with jam. Other options include thinly sliced salami paired with Swiss cheese, or butter and crumbled blue cheese. You can add thin rounds of cucumber or slivers of raw green pepper, sliced at the table with a cheese slicer that looks like a cake server punched with a horizontal slit.

Paper plates are perfect for a *skive* fest, which can travel from kitchen to patio to family room floor, wherever's coolest. As you toast each other's health, wish each other *skoal*—cheers.

Here are some quick hot-weather dinner options:

- ◇ Tomatoes sliced in wedges almost all the way through, topped with a scoop of chicken or crab salad, made from meat-in-a-can or bought premade at the grocery store
- ◇ Avocado halves stuffed with crab or shrimp salad
- ◇ Niçoise salad, made of canned tuna, hard-boiled eggs, canned new potatoes, canned green beans, wedges of tomato, anchovies, and lettuce. Arrange ingredients in sections on a platter, then drizzle with vinaigrette.
- ◇ One of my favorites: a papaya cut in half, seeds removed and discarded, each half filled with ¼ pound cooked baby shrimp. Serve with lime wedges. To eat, scoop out with spoon, leaving outside of papaya as "bowl."
- ◇ Chilled, canned beef consommé (buy the kind that says "gelatin added"), served with lime or lemon wedges. Add a green salad and breadsticks or rolls.
- ◇ Raw vegetables (such as mushrooms, cherry tomatoes, cauliflower, or broccoli spears), served with a dip. For a complete meal, add chunks of cheese, hard-boiled eggs (cooked early in the morning), and slices of cold ham, rolled.
- ◇ A cheese and fruit tray, served with crackers or slices of french bread. Cherries and Stilton are a delicious combination, as are nectarines and peaches with Parmesan; fresh pineapple with blue cheese; Granny Smith apples and Morbier (kind of a cross between Monterey Jack and blue cheese); and watermelon with smoked mozzarella.[1] If you have time, check your phone book for a nearby deli or grocery store with good cheese selections and take the kids for a field trip.

Barbecuing is one of summer's delights, a wonderful way to enjoy the warm evenings without heating up the kitchen till everyone feels like a melted ice cream bar. I have girlfriends who do the backyard barbecuing all the time—from Kathi, who after eight attempts at barbecuing and "messing it up eight different ways" finally admitted she needed to watch her husband in action to see how it's done; to Sis, whose dad was a fisherman and who can do anything from diagnosing engine troubles to gutting a salmon.

The only time I've ever barbecued was one party when I took over for my husband when he was called away as the burgers were cooking.

"This isn't so hard," I said a few minutes later upon his return.

"Give me that," he answered, grabbing the long-handled spatula. "You're not supposed to know that."

Here, from my husband, an Eagle Scout, are instructions for three ways to start that barbecue going if you have a charcoal, kettle-type grill. Allow thirty to forty-five minutes to heat up the coals:

1. Put thirty to forty briquettes in a pile; squirt five to ten seconds' worth of lighter fluid all over. Let it sit for one minute. Throw a lit match on it.

2. Buy presoaked (automatic light) briquettes. Light.

3. My husband's preferred method, which needs no lighter fluid and heats up quickly: Use a "fire chimney" (a metal tube sold at the hardware store; or, alternatively, a two- or three-pound coffee can with top and bottom removed and holes punched around the bottom edge). Fill ½ to ¾ of the way with briquettes. Crumple up two full sheets of newspaper and put underneath the chimney. Put chimney with paper on kettle grill (not the grill you cook on, but the grate that sits a few inches underneath it). Light the paper, wait twenty minutes or so, then dump the hot coals onto the grate. Set the chimney aside while you cook (but not on a wooden deck, and away from small children since it will be hot).

The coals are ready when they're covered with gray ash, and red and glowing on the inside.

Make sure to leave the vents in the bottom or the lid open, warns my friend Kathi. If the holes are closed and you put the cover on, the fire will go out. You can adjust the vents, closing them partway if the fire is getting too hot. In general, the more open your vent, the hotter the fire.

(For a gas grill, incidentally, you don't need to worry about charcoal, lighter fluid, or matches. You just turn the gas switch on, push the igniter button, and, shazam, the thing is ready to go.)

So if it's too hot to heat up your kitchen, consider grilling something on the barbecue, outside in the shade—maybe a nice, big salmon fillet. My husband, when I quizzed him how long to cook salmon, retained his air of mystery by claiming, "A seasoned barbecuer doesn't time things. He knows by experience and by look and feel when it's right." I did get him to acknowledge that you flip salmon for even cooking, and fish should be flaky when done. Add a little butter and a squeeze of lemon and mmm.

FUN FACT

"The original idea was to feed a large outdoor gathering by roasting an animal, perhaps a whole sheep, goat, or pig, in front of or over a fire on a homemade spit that pierced the animal from *barbe à la queue*—literally, from whiskers to tail. Thus the word *barbecue* came into our language and spread all over the world." [2]

One of our favorite barbecue meals is chicken burgers, which we learned from the best man at our wedding, Jeremy, and his wife, Donna. Now we make these all summer long.

JEREMY'S CHICKEN BURGERS

In large bowl:

Combine: **a couple cups of soy sauce**
about half a cup of honey
Whisk well. Add:

8 chicken thighs, skin and bones removed (most grocery stores carry these already skinned and boned, fresh or frozen)

Cover with plastic wrap and marinate in the refrigerator until time to barbecue—anywhere from thirty minutes to overnight. Cook until done. (Don't you love that? My husband says poke to see if it's ready. Or you can always slice into one and make sure the center is no longer pink.)

Serve in: **8 hamburger buns**, with **lettuce or tomato slices** if desired.

Add a hunk of watermelon to each plate. Dinner.

"The slow-cooking pot does not make your kitchen hot in the summertime," says Mable Hoffman in her book *Crockery Cookery*.[3] Mable hasn't steered me wrong yet, and I have become quite enamored with my trusty Crock-Pot in recent years. What better way to enjoy my family and beat the summer heat than to delegate dinner preparations to an appliance?

Most of the time, Crock-Pot cooking makes life immeasurably easier on the cook. But I still remember one time when a poor recipe choice on my part led to a very long morning in the kitchen.

My first mistake was to select from the freezer a whole chicken as my intended victim. Whole chickens, I should have known, take a while to thaw. Even using the microwave, it took a full sixty minutes to ready my four-pound baby. But resilient homemakers adjust, I told myself cheerily. In an uncharacteristic burst of ambition, I figured I'd use those sixty minutes to start some laundry, rev up my bread machine, and whip up a quick dessert with some aging apples. What a productive morning I'd have! What good smells would reward us that evening! Sometimes I am so clever!

The timer announcing my thawed chicken dinged at the precise moment I was knuckle-deep in excavations with my apple corer. I had been up for hours, we were nearly to lunchtime, and my Fancy Apples and Chicken à la Crock-Pot were still a vague and distant hope. As I pulled the still-raw chicken from the microwave, I accidentally brushed its top against the microwave's interior. Oops. I'd have to disinfect that in a minute.

Since my recipe called for cut-up chicken parts, I pulled out my cutting board and tried to remember just how you butcher a chicken, anyway. My knife wasn't as sharp as I'd remembered. I slipped and skidded, envisioning the blade missing its target and getting my hand instead. Just how significant is a thirty-nine-cents-per-

FUN FACT

↰

"With the exception of hobos and cowboys, Americans didn't really cook over open fires outdoors until after World War II. Charcoal wasn't even invented until the 1920s, when Henry Ford wanted to recycle excess wood from his factories into something productive and called on Thomas Edison to design briquette factories."[4]

pound bargain, I wondered, when you factor in emergency room deductibles?

I hoped the family wouldn't notice the now odd-shaped chicken parts, with random bones poking unexpectedly from peculiar angles. I couldn't help seeing that the pile of carcass and skin I was producing was three times the size of the edible chicken pile. It looked like barely enough for my ravenous thirteen-year-old's afternoon snack.

Later, as I spent a good ten minutes disinfecting kitchen surfaces with bleach, I tried to remember why, exactly, I had thought myself so clever this morning.

I've learned that easy Crock-Pot meals and whole frozen chickens are not necessarily a good pair. The only intact fowl I want to tango with between now and Thanksgiving is the precooked, already-roasted kind sold by my grocery store.

Now there's a way to beat the summer heat.

KRIS'S CROCK POT CHICKEN

Pour bottled **teriyaki sauce with sesame seeds** over your family's favorite **cut-up chicken parts**. Cook in crock pot on low for seven to eight hours.

"Jesus answered and said to her, 'Everyone who drinks of this water will thirst again; but whoever drinks of the water that I will give him shall never thirst; but the water that I will give him will become in him a well of water springing up to eternal life.'" (John 4:13–14)

---

prayer LORD JESUS, THANK YOU THAT YOU ARE THE WATER THAT SATISFIES COMPLETELY. THANK YOU THAT YOU FILL US WITH WHAT WE REALLY NEED AND THAT WHEN WE REST IN YOU WE ARE REFRESHED, FILLED TO OVERFLOWING. HELP ME TO REMEMBER TO COME TO YOU EVERY DAY TO GET REFILLED. GIVE ME A THIRST FOR YOU, JESUS, THAT WILL NOT BE QUENCHED UNTIL I SPEND TIME WITH YOU.

week 34

The Job of Queen: Homemaking As a Profession, Part 1

new word
for the week:

Soupçon (sōōp-sôn′).
A very small amount, a trace, a touch. As in, *"To manage my castle well requires more than a **soupçon** of hard work and good humor."*

alternate
new word:

Fillip (fil′ əp).
Anything that tends to rouse or excite; a stimulus. As in, *"Reading Phyllis McGinley's book* Sixpence in Her Shoe *is an excellent **fillip** when I am feeling discouraged in my queenly duties."*

Not long ago, a woman from our auto insurance company called to confirm which cars we drive and their mileage. She asked my husband's occupation and the number of miles he commutes each day. Then she asked my occupation.

"I'm a homemaker," I answered.

"Thank you. That's all I need to know."

"Don't you want to know how many miles I commute?"

"Nope. That's it," she said, and hung up.

I hung onto the phone for a few moments, mouth agape like an air-deprived carp. I "commute" at least twice as far as my husband each day, bringing kids to and from school, to practices and home again, to eye appointments, dental appointments, music lessons. One busy school week, I clocked myself at 429 miles.

No commute? Remind me of that tomorrow when I wake my son at 5 a.m. for the thirty-five-mile round trip I'll be making to get him to early morning weight training.

Sometimes it feels as though we homemakers are dismissed by the rest of the world. They don't seem to comprehend that we actually have a job. According to authors Darcie Sanders and Martha M. Bullen, who wrote *Staying*

Home: From Full-Time Professional to Full-Time Parent, "Most of the work that mothers do at home is invisible—not because it doesn't happen, but because the culture refuses to acknowledge it as work that requires skills and talents."[1]

Historians can pinpoint the long-ago government decision that brought about the devaluing of a woman's work at home. In U.S. census data prior to 1850, each family's economic activity was reported collectively. In other words, the census did not report on what the father did, the mother did, and the children did; it was assumed that the family worked together as a unit, and as a unit made its income from the family business.

It was only after 1850, as more and more men left their farms or cottage industries and began to work for someone else, that employment began to be tallied individually. Now the census was interested in knowing the "profession, occupation, or trade" of each individual in the household.

Though the great majority of women described their occupation as "housekeeper," according to *The Price of Motherhood* by Ann Crittenden, a decision was made in 1870 that only the women who kept house for someone else, for pay, would be counted. Thus in one fell swoop, the arduous labor of homemakers who cooked, laundered, cared for children, tended the garden, canned, cleaned, raised animals, sewed, and performed other duties for their families, was "dismissed as irrelevant."[3]

No queen appreciates having her arduous, twenty-four-hour-a-day labors dismissed as irrelevant. But I take comfort in one small fact: as long as my insurance company doesn't recognize that I have a job, and one that includes a hefty commute to boot, I'm probably saving a whole lot on insurance premiums. Guess the joke's really on them.

Twice in the last couple of months I've found myself chatting with men whose wives had recently quit their full-time paid jobs to stay home with their families—one, after seven years in the work force, the other after ten. The remarks from both husbands were remarkably similar: that their family life is so much better now that their wives are home. "When I get home from work now," said one husband, "the kids are happy, their homework's been done, and dinner is underway." He noted that everyone is much more relaxed, and that the evening is free of the nonstop chores that once consumed after-work hours. "Our whole evening has opened up."

His wife, standing next to him nodding in agreement, had to laugh. "I'm worth my weight in gold, and I know it." The Bible supports that fact. Proverbs 31:10 tells us the worth of an excellent wife is "far above jewels."

It's hard to quantify that kind of value. Efforts to put a modern-day dollar amount on the jobs we do at home have resulted in some pretty high figures. In 1978, lawyer Michael H. Minton devised a chart listing all the duties a wife performs. He came up with twenty-three different jobs, including food buyer, tutor, waitress, laundress, chauffeur, family counselor, housekeeper, cook, errand runner, bookkeeper, dishwasher, dietitian, and secretary. Figuring how much each job was worth per hour and multiplying that by the hours per week the job was performed, he came up with a total yearly value. Minton's dollar value per year for a homemaker—and this was back in 1978, mind you—was $40,288.04.[5] In 1997, a court case placed the monetary value of wife and mom at just under $65,000 a year.[6] In 2001, author Ann Crittenden estimated the value of a mother's work at an annual $100,000—"at the level of a middle manager, plus the additional occasional services of a psychologist, financial planner, a chauffeur, and so on."[7]

The work we perform each day in our homes is incredibly valuable. "Few women realize what great service they are doing for mankind and for the kingdom of Christ when they pour their energies into maintaining a shelter for the

Quotable

What's missing from so many affluent American households is the one thing you can't buy—the presence of someone who cares deeply and principally about that home and the people who live in it; who is willing to spend a significant portion of each day thinking about what those people are going to eat and what clothes they will need for which occasions; who knows when it's time to turn the mattresses and when the baby needs to be taken out for a bit of fresh air and sunshine.[4]

Caitlin Flanagan,
"Leaving It to the Professionals"

From the raw material of four walls and a roof, a shelter over our heads, we will have made a home by force of our own personalities. We will have warmed, cheered, and sustained the head of that house, turned progeny into a family. We will have learned a dozen skills and enjoyed the fruits of such skills. For us the baby will have taken his first step, repeated his first word. We will have heard the schoolchild call "Mommy" as soon as he puts a foot inside the door, not so much to have a reply as to be assured that he is safe, life is ordinary, and that We are there. . . .

Free choice, importance, the prizes as well as the perils of a career—they are all ours. What more can one ask of a profession? [10]

Phyllis McGinley,
Sixpence in Her Shoe

family and nurturing their children—the foundation on which all else is built," says Dorothy Kelley Patterson in *Where's Mom? The High Calling of Wives and Mothers.* "A mother builds something far more magnificent than any cathedral. . . . No professional pursuit so uniquely combines the most menial tasks with the most meaningful opportunities."[8]

In diligently taking care of our families, we are bringing them innumerable blessings, along with the clean underwear. Next time you pass the mirror, stop and take a moment to look into those eyes shining back at you. Repeat: "I am worth my weight in gold. And I know it."

It was a gorgeous summer day as I browsed through the gift shop I'd wandered into while on vacation in Portland, Oregon. While leafing through a book, I heard the man behind me say, "I applaud you in your endeavors." I looked at him, puzzled. My endeavors? In paging through a book?

"Your shirt," he chuckled.

I'd forgotten. I was wearing my Sidetracked Home Executives™ T-shirt, the one that lists the mother's creed on the back: "I am responsible for creating a climate of love, peace, joy, beauty, abundance, health, and order in my home. I am raising future citizens of the United States of America. What do you do?"[9]

I smiled back at the man, thanked him, and went on browsing. I, too, applaud all of us homemakers, for our arduous endeavors in raising our children, loving our husbands, and taking care of our homes. It is easy to forget as we make yet another peanut-butter-and-jelly sandwich, scour out the sink one more time, and assault the chocolate milk stains on our child's brand-new tan pants, that in making a home we are creating a climate where our families can grow and thrive. We are providing an atmosphere where those we love can gain security and know all the way to their bones that they are deeply treasured. It's a valuable, significant, important job. I will wear my shirt proudly.

"Therefore, do not throw away your confidence, which has a great reward. For you have need of endurance, so that when you have done the will of God, you may receive what was promised." (Hebrews 10:35–36)

prayer LORD, YOU HAVE ENTRUSTED ME WITH A BIG JOB IN CARING FOR MY HOME AND MY FAMILY. SOMETIMES I DON'T FEEL UP TO THE TASK. PLEASE GIVE ME YOUR FAVOR AND YOUR HELP WHEN I AM FEELING OVERWHELMED.

FUN FACT

According to *The Price of Motherhood* by Ann Crittenden, "Homemaking, the fundamental task associated with raising the young, is still the largest single occupation in the United States." [11]

week 35

The Job of Queen: Homemaking As a Profession, Part 2

Homemaking is a unique profession. If you want the camaraderie of coworkers, you can't just peek over the next cubicle; you have to purposefully seek it out. Confirmation for a job well done doesn't come from next Friday's paycheck but instead comes a couple of decades down the road when you hear the majestic opening notes of "Pomp and Circumstance" or "The Wedding March." Progress in the traditional sense is hard to detect as this morning's clean clothes quickly morph into a heap of dirty laundry, dinner that takes an entire afternoon to make becomes an almost instantaneous jumble of dirty dishes, and shiny floors—for the really advanced—become besmirched just a moment or two after the family walks in the door.

"In the typical Western mode of education," says author Linda Weltner, "tests are taken, grades are given, and the student is finished with the subject. In the workplace, products are manufactured, goals are reached, and if nothing else, money is made."[1] No such measurable luck for homemakers, however, who are rewarded with visible signs of job success about as often as "Who's Who" comes knocking on the door to announce our nomination for

Mother of the Year. (By the way, I believe that washing the red baseball shirt, the white baseball pants, the red socks, and the red and white undershirt some time between Thursday night's and Saturday morning's games without turning everything pink is every bit the "meritorious achievement" deserving of Who's Who recognition; but I digress.)

In truth, the real significant work in a homemaker's day is not the pile of perfectly laundered clothes or a pristine kitchen, but rather a child who got pushed on the swings or who was helped with his algebra homework. Jill Savage, in her book *Professionalizing Motherhood*, says, "We can't buy into the belief that accomplishment is measured by something that stays finished. . . . The profession of motherhood has one primary goal—to see a child grow into a mature, godly, respectful, and loving adult."[2]

Savage urges women to "remember your professional objective: to create a healthy, enjoyable, nurturing environment in which family relationships can thrive. If you become too busy to read your child a book because you must have a perfect house, you've lost your proper focus."[3] While admittedly, creating the perfect house sits on my personal list of temptations somewhere below scarfing down a bowl of Brussels sprouts, Savage's point is well taken: we will grow discouraged in our work as homemakers if we measure success by whether or not the dining room table stays cleared of papers. My dining room table has stayed cleared of papers for a record twenty-seven minutes—and that was one summer when the boys were off at camp.

I need to remember my goal is not to tend a house; my goal is to tend a family. And if that means the washing machine continually swishes, the kitchen counter is littered with snack remnants, and the family room is decorated with tennis shoes, history textbooks, and a forlorn French horn waiting to be practiced—well, so be it. That's what raising a family looks like.

At one point in early motherhood, my goal was simply to keep my boys alive until they reached the age of two. By that time, I figured, their most foolhardy years of investigating electricity outlets and leaping off tall buildings would be over and I could consider my mothering a success.

Eventually the days passed where the job of raising my kids made roping steers look like a staid occupation in comparison. Though my general goal of raising a great family didn't change, the specifics of my job certainly had. It was time to come up with new goals, goals that went beyond mere survival of the species.

It was at that point I read the advice to come up with a family mission statement, cont. ⇒

Quotable

Nobody has so far received a Pulitzer Prize for contriving a poetic boiled custard, in spite of the fact (which I know from experience) that it is a feat less easy to perform than writing a ballade. The Nobel Committee has yet to award any laurels to a woman simply for making her home a place of such peace and delight that her family might rightfully rise up and call her blessed—if such an odd notion ever occurred to them.

to put into writing a specific picture of how we wanted our homes and families to look. While our homes may not live up to the ideal, we might be "hitting the target more often than we're missing it because we're aiming at something," says author Kathy Peel.[4]

Here's the family mission statement I came up with: "I want my home to be a welcoming, comfortable place that reflects Christ and meets people's needs to be loved, nurtured, and listened to."

Welcoming and comfortable—meaning I want to achieve some degree of beauty and order, yet not the spic-and-span cleaning standard I know I could never maintain (if I could even achieve it in the first place). Reflecting Christ—bringing glory to Him in our family's words, actions, and attitudes, so we might "shine like stars in the universe" to a "crooked and depraved generation" (Philippians 2:15 NIV). It's a tall order, I know, and one which I'll shelve by dinnertime if I count on my own abilities. But God can do miracles, and I can trust Him and hope for a miracle beginning in my own sinful, selfish life.

In spite of my and my family's shortcomings, we "press on," in the apostle Paul's words (Philippians 3:12, 14), not giving up as we keep our goal in sight and pray for God's help to get us there.

Why don't you try writing a mission statement for your home? Keep it brief—a sentence or two should do it—and see if it doesn't help you clarify just what your goals are for your home, and for yourself as a homemaker.

As Louisa May Alcott once wrote, "Far away, there in the sunshine are my highest aspirations; I may not reach them, but I can look up and see their beauty, believe in them, and try to follow where they lead."

"The skills of homemaking do not always come naturally in this instant gratification world that we live in. Organization, finances, shopping, cooking, and cleaning . . . are skills that must be learned, which makes them an important part of every mother's career training and development," says Jill Savage in *Professionalizing Motherhood*.[5]

If you never got the chance to learn all the skills you find yourself needing now—how to treat a child with a 102.9-degree fever was surprisingly absent from your business management curriculum—take heart. You can keep improving and getting better at your job. Lots of good books are available to help, on everything from basic health care to cooking to nutrition to communicating with teenagers.

Some of my favorite homemaking authors, I consider personal mentors, on call day or night. Many of them wrote decades ago: Gladys Taber, Phyllis McGinley, Peg Bracken. You can find books by these authors in your local library. You can also start your own personal library by scanning secondhand stores, garage sales, and library sales. Look for books on holiday cookery, cooking on a budget, holiday cooking on a budget, cooking for when you really don't have time to cook, cooking holiday budget meals with no time, no energy, and no working stove; you get the idea. Look for titles on fun activities to do with children, becoming a godly wife, housekeeping, saving money.

Magazines, too, can help you grow in your profession. The suggested menus I find in cooking articles give me ideas for serving my family more balanced meals. (It is rumored that man cannot live on chocolate-chip cheesecake alone, though my son is determined to try.)

Some of my favorite sources of inspiration have been newsletters aimed specifically at homemakers and at-home moms. I look at these as trade journals for my chosen profession. Most fields have professional journals to help employees keep current and get new ideas; we do too. I love articles about other moms at home that let me know I am not some anachronism from another era who does not fit in today's world. I am one of a sisterhood of millions who

Quotable

Nevertheless, ours is a true profession, ancient, honorable, and unique. . . . When some early and talented woman patted her barley cake into a pleasanter shape than her neighbor's, or poured honey on it for a change from drippings, she was advancing her profession and, with it, civilization. When she complained that the floors were cold and persuaded her husband to let her use that extra bearskin for protection against drafts from the doorway, she was progressing another step along the route.[6]

Phyllis McGinley, Pulitzer Prize winner
Sixpence in Her Shoe

have chosen to use our talents and abilities to nurture our families. That's powerful stuff.

According to an article in *Health* magazine, "Any job that involves learning new skills . . . is inherently less stressful than one that's routine and unchallenging."[7] So look at growing in your job as queen as an investment in your health.

Homemaking Magazines and Newsletters

People in other professions may not understand our job, but women who write for homemaking publications do. Since magazines, newsletters, and Web sites change about as fast as a ten-year-old's dinner preferences, you may want to search for the most current resources by signing onto your favorite search engine and typing in a phrase such as "at-home mothering" or "stay-at-home mothers." Here are some publications I have enjoyed:

- ◇ *Hearts at Home* (www.hearts-at-home.org)
- ◇ *P31* (www.gospelcom.net)
- ◇ *Above Rubies* (www.aboverubies.org)
- ◇ *An Encouraging Word* (www.wisgate.com)

"A man has joy in an apt answer, and how delightful is a timely word!" (Proverbs 15:23)

prayer LORD, I DESIRE TO DO A GOOD JOB IN THIS PROFESSION OF HOMEMAKER. THANK YOU FOR PROVIDING TIMELY WORDS OF ENCOURAGEMENT THROUGH THE WRITINGS OF OTHER WOMEN. PLEASE HELP ME AS I SEEK TO IMPROVE MY SKILLS. MAY MY HOME REFLECT YOU.

CHOCOLATE BREAK!

INSTANT CHOCOLATE PUDDING

This dessert, which is as rich as a candy bar, is so simple your kids could make it, providing you supervise the blender part. We loved this pudding so much we went out and bought small covered plastic containers so we could pack it in school lunches.

The recipe comes from Ann Hodgman's excellent and very funny cookbook, *Beat That!*[9] Even if you don't make any of the recipes in the book (which you *should*) it is worth getting simply to read them.

INSTANT CHOCOLATE PUDDING

Place in blender (or food processor):

12 oz. chocolate chips

½ cup sugar

3 eggs

1 T. rum (optional)

1 t. vanilla

Pinch of salt

Pour over all:

1 cup boiling milk (can heat in microwave)

and blend for one minute. Pour into small serving cups and chill for an hour. Serves eight.

week 36

new word

for the week:

Halcyon (hăl′ sē-ən).

Calm and peaceful; tranquil. As in, *"I plan to enjoy these last **halcyon** summer mornings before we have to deal with alarm clocks and homework and making it to the car pool on time."*

alternate

new word:

Importunate

(ĭm-pôr′ chŏŏ nĭt).

Urgent or persistent in requesting, sometimes annoyingly so. As in, *"Once school begins, I will pray **importunately** for my children; I know God doesn't want me to worry but to bring all my concerns to Him."*

The Party's Over: School Days

"Sometimes, when I consider the schools my children enter each fall, I am a bit shaken," admits Dr. Mary Manz Simon, author of *The Year-Round Parent*.[1] Simon mentions that posted at the school's entrance are zero-tolerance drug and alcohol policies, and that hanging above doorways are flags to signify classrooms which during the previous month were "fight-free." It is not a comforting picture.

Though our family's been incredibly blessed in sending our kids to Christian schools and in general I'm confident about their environment, I understand Simon's anxieties. I worry too. Every parent worries.

Will our children have friends to eat lunch with? Will they fit in with their peers? Will they have courage when they need it, be appreciated for the unique individuals they are, be appropriately challenged? Will they succeed socially, athletically, spiritually, academically?

I talked on the phone this week to some friends and was amazed at all the changes this school year brings. Linda's daughter is away at college, getting ready to transfer from one school to another and contemplating marriage(!). Jackie, whose youngest son just entered first grade, begins a new life as she shifts from stay-at-home mom to employed schoolteacher. Kim's number one son is in his last year of high school while number two son attends a new school with a new football team and a new coach.

So many changes.

I think about my own children, beginning a new year at new school buildings with new teachers and new expectations. Uncertainties circle my head like the brim of a hat, making me excited and anxious and sometimes just plain upset. So much is unknown. Last year may not have been perfect, but we're not at all sure we're going to like what's coming. New is hard, especially for those of us whose idea of radical change is to vote out the incumbent every thirty years or so.

I want to be there for my children always, running interference to protect them from bad things the way a good offensive line keeps the guy with the football from getting mauled. But I can't be there always. That's not the way God designed parenthood.

In Philippians 4:6, Paul tells us to "be anxious for nothing." In the Greek language, my pastor tells me, words in a sentence can be placed in whatever order the writer wishes. The most important ideas were saved for two places, the beginning of the sentence and the end. "Nothing," in this verse, is actually the first word. Nothing should we be anxious about, the verse says, because all our concerns we can bring before God.

It's a good reminder this week as my kids embark on yet another school year. I will pray for them and for their teachers and for our friends. I will ask God to fill us with His peace about all this newness. As the halcyon summer days flutter off like butterflies, I will be importunate in my prayers.

Every year after dropping my boys off at school on that first day, I go home and write them a letter. A love letter, I guess you'd call it, where I chronicle my feelings as I watch them head off for new adventures with new stature, new responsibilities, new pants. I confide my hopes and prayers for them for the coming year. And always, it seems, I tell them how very proud I am of the fine young men they're becoming.

Year after year, curled up on my sunny couch writing these letters, I start to cry. Yesterday's superhero lunchbox is gone. Yesterday's boys, shorter than me, trundling off to elementary school, then junior high, then the first day of high school—they're gone. In their place are young men, tall and muscled and shaving. I have only the briefest of moments with them still at home. Time has zoomed by.

It's almost a physical ache, releasing my children into their world that, more and more, does not include me. Writing the letters helps me let go.

I plan to give them the letters at some future date, maybe as they head off to college, or perhaps when they have kindergarteners of their own. (Though my son at twelve asked, "And we would want those, why?") Someday, I hope, they will read the words I've written and know that, no matter how indifferent the rest of society is to their sparkling uniqueness, in their mom's eyes they were treasures of the most special kind.

Don't let the first day of school go by without somehow marking it in highlighter. Even if you're not the type to weep on the couch writing sappy letters, snap your child's picture as he leaves the house. (He can hold up fingers to show what grade he's in.) Plan a special first-day-back dinner or a favorite dessert. Serve sparkling apple juice in goblets. Put the stuffed animals in the window (see week 23) and prop textbooks and footballs in the animals' laps to commemorate the occasion.

Because your child is growing up, and before you know it, you'll have run out of first days to celebrate.

Sniff.

Getting into a routine for the school year is hard, especially if you've had a proper summer with 9 p.m. dinners followed by late-night movies. We are sleepy around here the first week of school, trying to adjust to the early morning reveille. Mornings go better, we discover, when the kids completely pack their backpacks the night before, including lunch money and permission slips.

Also helpful is stocking the kitchen with everyone's favorite breakfast cereals, along with some quick bring-in-the-car breakfast foods (Pop-Tarts™, muffins, bagels) for those mornings we're hopelessly, desperately late.

When the children were younger, we posted a morning checklist, where each person marked the appropriate box as he brushed his teeth, gathered his homework, took his vitamins, and collected his trumpet or sports gear. The chart saved me from being the family nag, and it made the routine more fun as small rewards could be earned for consecutive days of all tasks completed. (Though even with the chart, there were a couple of times we were all the way to school before realizing someone was missing vital clothing items; I think I'll never be totally free of the compulsion to quiz my passengers, "Everybody have two shoes? Two socks?")

In a few weeks we'll be settled into the routine, I'm sure, but for this week we're still getting used to speaking in complete sentences when it's barely light out, and turning lights out at a decent hour at night, even if there are "just two more chapters left!"

A few suggestions to ease the school-year transition:

◇ Some parents take the week or two before school to gradually taper back to an earlier bedtime and to start getting up earlier as well.

◇ Families with younger kids can set out cereal boxes, bowls, and spoons the night before.

◇ Likewise, you can lay out tomorrow's clothing.

◇ Timers in the morning can help keep everyone on track. When the timer goes off, for example, Suzy should be done with breakfast and heading to the bathroom.

◇ If who gets to sit in the front seat of the car is a recurring squabble, try the odd-even trick, where one gets the front seat on odd days, the other on even. If you're driving more than two kids, assign each a day of the week and tape the list to the dashboard to avoid conflicts. You may want to allow the front seat queen or king the privilege of choosing which CD or radio station gets played (or none at all).

In his wonderful book *Raising Musical Kids: Great Ideas to Help Your Child Develop a Love for Music*, Patrick Kavanaugh says, "Studies show that even listening to great music can help children in their studies. A 1993 study at the Center for Neurobiology of Learning and Memory at the University of California, Irvine, showed that students consistently scored higher on tests when Mozart was played in the background. Wolfgang would have loved it!"[2]

This book, by the way, also contains ideas for getting kids to practice their instruments, as well as a terrific appendix listing classical music that appeals to kids.

Lunchbox Ideas

In late elementary school, when my children were at their pickiest and sandwiches I sent to school returned home like undeliverable packages, I came up with a lunchbox strategy that worked brilliantly for several years. I had the boys pack their own school lunches. I provided several options for each category: main dish (including the favorite, peanut butter and crackers), fruit, dessert, and a drink. The boys were to stock their lunches with one item from each category.

The method worked well for several years. Once they reached junior high, however, and the list of what they needed to remember each morning grew longer than their sneakers,

I took pity and started making their lunches again. I figured they'd learned their lesson about griping about my lunches. And what do you know, they had.

Here are some quick lunchbox ideas that might spark up that daily duty:

◇ Cut sandwiches into shapes with cookie cutters to disguise the fact your kids are eating the same sandwich they've eaten the last 364 days of the year.

◇ According to *The Taming of the C.A.N.D.Y. Monster* by Vicki Lansky, "Peanut butter sandwiches freeze well and are easy to make ahead. They are especially easy to make on bread still frozen. . . . Make up the whole loaf (do not slice sandwiches) and return them to the original plastic bag and store in the freezer. Remove as needed—slice—and wrap to go."[3]

◇ A fun lunchbox snack is to peel and core an apple. Mix some peanut butter and raisins and stuff this mixture into the apple's core. Slice the apple in half and poke each half with a Popsicle stick.[4]

◇ Include in your child's lunch the occasional note, riddle, comic strip from the paper, new vocabulary word, encouraging Bible verse, or tiny unexpected candy bar, just to let him know you're thinking of him.

If your kids come home from school "starving," give this recipe a try. It may not be health food, but considering two of the three ingredients are Rice Krispies® and peanut butter, I deem it an acceptable after-school snack. It mixes up quickly, and if there are any left the next day, it would make a fine addition to the lunchboxes. But don't count on it.

SCOTCH TREATS:

In large mixing bowl, pour: **3 cups Rice Krispies®**

In saucepan over low heat, melt:

1 cup butterscotch chips

½ cup peanut butter

Stir constantly. Once mixture is smooth and melted, pour over the cereal. Stir well, then press mixture evenly in buttered nine-by-nine-inch square pan. Chill until firm (one hour, if you can stand it), cut into squares, and serve.

A reminder for moms of college-aged kids: make appointments now for your kids to visit the dentist when they're home at Thanksgiving or Christmastime. Holiday appointments fill up quickly, and the offices may be closed for part of your child's vacation. Also, check into airline reservations now, to give you the most choices and a chance at the lowest fares.

"Be anxious for nothing, but in everything by prayer and supplication with thanksgiving let your requests be made known to God. And the peace of God, which surpasses all comprehension, will guard your hearts and your minds in Christ Jesus." (Philippians 4:6–7)

prayer LORD, THANK YOU FOR THE SUPREME PRIV-ILEGE OF RAISING MY CHILDREN. PROTECT THEM DURING THIS YEAR AND HELP THEM MAKE WISE CHOICES. HELP THEM GROW INTO ADULTS WHO LOVE YOU AND DESIRE TO SERVE YOU ABOVE ALL ELSE.

week 37

new word

for the week:

Chary (châr'ē).

Careful; wary. As in, *"If our family is not chary of overscheduling ourselves this school year, we will hardly recognize each other by the time Christmas comes."*

alternate

new word:

Chivvy (chĭv'ē).

To chase or harass. As in, *"I hope the school boosters won't chivvy me if I turn down the job of PTA treasurer."*

Schedules (or, Which of the 568 Volunteer Opportunities Should I Sign Up For?)

September has always felt more like the beginning of the year than New Year's. The kids go back to school. They have new teachers, new schedules, new carpools, new sports seasons.

And so many choices. It's as though our family were standing in the middle of a field, surrounded by acres of wheat, and we're supposed to choose only those few stalks meant for us. We need God's wisdom in deciding which ones to pick.

Can the kids really handle flag football and still stay on top of their homework? Do they have the time (and motivation) to practice those trumpet lessons we're considering? Are we pursuing an activity for them because everyone we know is signing up, or does the activity really reflect their natural "bent"?

We need to count the cost as a family, too, recognizing that a yes to one activity means a no to other things. Many of the kids' activities include weekend commitments. We need to be aware of exactly what we're signing up for.

I get myself in the most trouble when I forget to pray, when I forget to ask God for His guidance in our schedules. Then I find myself juggling too many after-school sports and wondering whose bright idea it was, anyway, to have the kids pursue organized basketball, wrestling, and baseball, all at the same time.

Oh yeah. Gulp. Mine.

I need wisdom in steering not only my children's activities but my own, as well. There are so many options on what I could do with the hours my children are in school, from church Bible studies to local community college classes to various aerobics offerings. Not to mention the myriad pleas for help from the schools: do I want to aid in the library on Mondays, the office on Wednesdays, the classroom on Fridays?

So many choices, and all good ones.

Some years I have overvolunteered, excited at the opportunities to serve and to try new things. In the end, I learned being room mom/soccer mom/field-trip mom/ Sunday-school mom, all in the same year, made me not super mom but super crabby mom. Hours I should have spent shopping for groceries were given away to other causes. More than once I've found myself filing papers for teachers in my sons' classrooms and wondering why on earth I wasn't home filing my own paper heaps.

An older friend whose children are grown encouraged me recently to put most of my time into being with my children rather than volunteering for various causes. "Because in two years," she said, "you'll have forgotten 98 percent of those people you accomplished things with. But you'll have a relationship with your kids until you're in the grave."

So now I try to be prudent in my volunteering. I volunteer at my children's school for jobs that put me in direct contact with the kids (driving on field trips or helping during classroom parties) and turn down requests to word-process

> ## Quotable
>
> *Vegetables that are planted too close together jam each other so tightly that none develop properly. In order to have full, healthy vegetables, some good plants have got to go to leave room for the others. Some of us have so much jammed together that none of our activities are really producing well. The quality of life improves as the quantity of activities is reduced, if we have overscheduled ourselves.*[1]
>
> **Sandra Felton,**
> *The Messies Manual*

> ## Quotable
>
> *How we spend our days is, of course, how we spend our lives.*[2]
>
> **Annie Dillard,**
> *The Writing Life*

in the office away from the children. I've cut back on church commitments that took me away from my family too many evenings when I should have been home helping the kids study for a science test. I'm trying to be wiser with my time. Because if I'm elected volunteer of the year but neglect to feed my family a decent dinner this fall, I'm spending too much of my energy in the wrong place.

The woman described in Proverbs 31 "looks well to the ways of her household" (v. 27). While she also did many other things, she did not take lightly her responsibilities at home. I, too, want to prize my family, not chasing after the glittering baubles of the world's praise ("Wow, you're such a good organizer—we couldn't have put on the luncheon without you!"), but instead truly valuing the genuine treasure God has given me: my family.

Some advice from Christian speaker and writer Kathi Lipp:

Ask these three questions before agreeing to a commitment:

1. Is this commitment in line with my gifts?
2. Will this help or hurt my family (will my husband or kids be picking up the pieces of the fallout of this decision)?
3. Am I doing this for my own glory, or will it bring glory to God?

I've never forgotten an exercise we did in a college study skills class I took. We were to write down, minute by minute, how we spent our time for an entire week. Not a list of what we were *supposed* to be doing; a list of what we actually *did*.

The results were amazing. I'd had no idea I spent so much time schmoozing with roommates when I was supposed to be studying for my next class. Many snippets of my day I allowed to float out of the room and blow away like dandelion fluff.

I don't mean to hint that anyone's schedule should be

Quotable

The Wise Woman develops the habit of graciously not committing to a responsibility when she is first approached. An example of responding graciously might be to say, "Thank you so much for considering me for this opportunity. I would like to spend time praying about this opportunity, check my calendar, and seek the counsel of my husband. May I respond to your invitation by the end of the week?" Develop the habit of waiting to commit to an obligation until you have allowed yourself to think about it thoroughly.[3]

Pat Ennis and Lisa Tatlock,
Becoming a Woman Who Pleases God

devoid of time for schmoozing. Raising a family and running a home are filled with unplanned moments and opportunities, many that cry out for some good, honest schmoozing. I don't think God would commend us for telling our children, "Not now, dear, Mommy time isn't scheduled until four o'clock."

But I do believe that we can benefit from occasionally tracking our time on paper and seeing exactly where it goes. We can relieve ourselves of the pressure to make beautiful from-scratch dinners when we see that we're not home on weekday afternoons for more than forty minutes at a stretch. Tracking our time can help us gain perspective.

It can also uncover surprises. Incoming phone calls, for example, may take up more time than we'd realized. We may notice repeated shopping trips over the week that indicate we should develop a more-efficient errands route. Recently I counted the hours I spent in the car Monday through Friday and was shocked to see it totaled thirty-one. (We live a long way from our kids' school.)

See if any information emerges from your tracking experiment that can help you use your time in ways that better fit your priorities. If you spot even ten-minute periods that you're held captive on hold on the phone or waiting for a prescription to be filled, you may start to view these as opportunities you've been looking for to read to your child or help him learn his multiplication tables.

Happy tracking. ♥

"So teach us to number our days, that we may present to You a heart of wisdom." (Psalm 90:12)

pra**y**er LORD, PLEASE HELP MY FAMILY AND ME TO MAKE WISE CHOICES IN OUR SCHEDULES FOR THE COMING YEAR. STEER US IN THE UNIQUE DIRECTION YOU WANT US TO GO. SHOW US IF WE'RE TRYING TO DO TOO MUCH. AND HELP ME TO LISTEN.

Quotable

I have changed over the years. I used to think I could do everything, that my babies would be fine squeezed into the rest of my To Do list. Today I know that children must rise to the top of the list, and that list must dwindle considerably. [4]

Iris Krasnow,
Surrendering to Motherhood

Quotable

Jackie Wellwood writes "STAY HOME" two or three times each week on her calendar. "If I am to be a homemaker, then I need to be home. Errands can be run on certain days. On my 'STAY HOME' days, if something comes up I can say no." [5]

Jackie Wellwood,
The Busy Mom's Guide to Simple Living

week 38

Grocery Shopping and Meal Planning

Grocery shopping when my sons were preschoolers was an experience I'd just as soon forget. Not only was there the overturned cart but also the episodes of in-cart hair pulling and scratching, the broken jar of jam (and applesauce, and more jam), and the vomiting in the produce aisle. (I still flinch when I reach that spot.) No wonder the mom you see with little ones in aisle seven looks like she has a migraine. She probably does.

Now that my kids are older, I don't mind shopping for groceries (alone!). But I have discovered some drawbacks to my haphazard shopping methods. I've sometimes gotten in the habit of running by the supermarket almost daily, stopping for items the kids want for school lunch or something quick for dinner. Often I have overbought, and produce such as fruit or lettuce spoils before we have a chance to eat it.

Other times when life is hectic with kids' sports or church activities, I may go a couple of weeks without doing a thorough shopping job. Because there is little at home to eat, we'll swing by a fast-food place far too many evenings. Shopping and meal planning at our house has at times resembled the plaint of Goldilocks: too much or too little, rarely just right.

Recently I've tried a new method, and it's worked smooth as custard. One morning a week, I buy groceries for the entire week. Period. I ask the kids what they'd like for breakfast, lunches, and after-school snacks. Since they know I'm only going once, they also know if they eat all the pretzels by Wednesday they'll have to go without. The rest of the world probably figured this out years ago, but to me it feels like I've discovered a new planet.

Since I've implemented Monday grocery day I've noticed fewer random trips to the store, which saves me time. Also we eat better, and I can better gauge how much to buy. Best of all, when the family starts asking what's for dinner, I don't feel poised for a panic attack. I'm ready.

If you're not already shopping on a set day each week, try it. See if an hour or two of discipline a week doesn't reap a harvest of prandial peace.

When my mom was first married, she belonged to a cookbook-of-the-month club. Being required to buy one book each month, Mom wound up with quite an eclectic collection, among them such titles as *Short Cuts and Left Overs* and *Eating in Bed Cookbook*.

I am the happy recipient of many of these books, their being evicted from Mom's latest kitchen due to lack of space. And I am overjoyed.

My favorite is a volume called *What Cooks in Suburbia*, by Lila Perl ("Presenting more than 225 superlative recipes planned specifically for the basic meal occasions today's busy housewife faces").[2] I love it not so much for the recipes, which are good and simple and don't make my children run screaming from the table, but more for its intended audience. It was boldly and unashamedly written for homemakers, a word scarcely even used in cookbooks today for fear of offending. Hear the lucid and unapologetic dedication: "This book is dedicated to The Modern Suburban Homemaker. She may dwell, of course, in an urban apartment building, a semi-urban garden apartment, or on more spacious acreage of her own in a fashionable exurb. She may pass the major portion of her day in or about her home, or she may spend all or part of it away from home. But if she has a kitchen, a family, and an entourage, large or small, of friends and neighbors, she is—for the purposes of this book—a suburban homemaker."

I also love the idea of cooking from cookbooks that once belonged to women in my family. Along with those from my mom, I've inherited others from my husband's grandma. After years of intending to use them but somehow never managing it, I've finally found a plan that works: on grocery day, I toss a cookbook in the car. Sitting in the store's parking lot, I'll take a few extra minutes to peruse the book and select a couple of likely recipes. There's a special feeling of connectedness with other women in my family as I page through books that once were theirs.

It's fun, too, to call my mom and tell her I've just made Teri's Tuna with Browned Noodles and see if she can guess which of her books it came from.

If you're grocery shopping without kids, make sure on shopping day to bring a cookbook in the car along with your shopping list (and coupons, if you save them). You just may (re)discover a family favorite.

I used to plot out weeknight menus and include all sorts of fancy dishes I'd love to make: boneless chicken breasts stuffed with garlic cream cheese then breaded and served with herbed butter sauce. Sole filets spread with diced shrimp, rolled and fastened with a toothpick, then cooked with a medley of tomatoes, celery, and onion. It all sounded great to me early in the day; I'd buy my ingredients, drop them off at home, then head out for hours and hours of after-school chauffeuring.

For some reason when I slump in the door at 7 p.m., after already putting in a full thirteen-hour day, scads of freeway miles, and forty-five extra minutes in the parking lot waiting for wayward athletes whose practices have run late, my enthusiasm for the complicated dishes has waned. By nightfall, I am predictably at my lowest point of the day, out of gas and facing a tough, steep hill. At that point I am in no shape to put together the fantastic meals I drooled over lo those many hours ago. (As if my family would even like them, anyway; they're basically hamburger and pizza kind of guys.)

I may not be the sharpest crayon in the box, but even I eventually realized I needed to be more realistic in planning meals for the week. It was time to stop setting myself up for failure. Now I actually look at my calendar before I shop and note which nights of the week look most promising in the dinnertime department (and which look least promising). I buy enough food so I'm ready for a few pretty quick meals, but not so much that I wind up with seven dinners we won't even be home to eat. I can buy spaghetti and premade sauce, ingredients for tacos, and whatever I need for Crock-Pot French Dip (see week 39), and be very flexible about which meals I serve when, depending on who's going to be home and who gives me a last-minute call saying don't hold dinner. I can be willing to freeze food if something unexpected comes up. Crazy nights of school open house, debate team practice, and trumpet lessons are no time to worry about gourmet cooking.

A fellow band mom who, like me, spends many nights driving kids to and from evening marching band practice, once explained to me her dinnertime strategy: "At our house," she said, "we have three kinds of food. There's new food, remade food, and Happy Meal Night. This is when I tell my kids, 'You can have anything in the refrigerator that makes you happy.'"

Now there's a strategy that should work.

Tips for grocery shopping and menu planning:

- ◇ If you're very organized, clean out your refrigerator before you shop, freeing up room to store the new food and uncovering expired goodies that should be replaced.
- ◇ Shake bags of flour before purchasing, says one grocery store worker; if flour leaks out, bugs have invaded and left tiny pinprick holes. Pick a different bag.
- ◇ According to the newsletter *An Encouraging Word*, only 31 percent of grocery shoppers arrive with a list, "but it doesn't matter: only a third of your purchases are planned. . . . The vast majority of you who sample a product will then buy it."[4]
- ◇ Also from *An Encouraging Word*, "the choicest elevation on any aisle"—from the store's

point of view—"are between 51 and 53 inches off the floor." So look lower or higher for the bargains.[5]

◇ Shoppers spend an average of thirty-five to forty minutes per visit at the grocery store. For each minute beyond that, shoppers spend two more dollars. "If background music is slowed from a lively allegro of 108 beats per minute to a simple adagio of 60 beats, researchers report, then the speed of the average cart slows, more shots are taken and purchases soar by as much as 38.2 percent."[6]

◇ To save money on grocery shopping, keep a price book, recommends Amy Dacyczyn in *The Tightwad Gazette*.[7] Shopping at a number of stores including grocery stores, warehouse stores, and day-old bread stores, Dacyczyn writes in a small binder the price she pays for different items. Each item has its own page; on it she includes the brand, the store where purchased, the size of the item, the price, and the unit price. When she finds a source that's cheaper than the last, she marks it in her book. Before shopping, she knows which stores offer the best prices on which items.

◇ If making balanced meals is not your strength, look for menus in cookbooks or magazines for inspiration. Even if you don't make the exact recipes, their menus can give you ideas for how to better round out a meal.

◇ Use lots of colorful foods for a balanced menu. A plate with a yellow fruit or vegetable, something red, something green, will tend to provide a good variety of nutrients.

FUN FACT

Studies show that families will eat the same ten main dish foods eighty percent of the time.[8]

Governmental dietary guidelines for Americans are pretty straightforward, according to *Cooking Light* magazine: eat lots of grains, fruits, and vegetables; go easy on fat, sugar, sodium, and alcohol; and keep weight under control. But in other countries? Here are excerpts from some of their guidelines.

GERMANY: Eat not too much and not too little.

JAPAN: Sit down and eat together and talk.

THAILAND: A happy family is one that eats together, enjoys treasured family tastes and good
home cooking.
UNITED KINGDOM: Enjoy your food.[9]

"But they who seek the Lord shall not be in want of any good thing." (Psalm 34:10)

---

prayer LORD, YOU ARE MY GOD AND I KNOW I CAN
ASK YOU FOR ANYTHING. I TRULY DESIRE TO BE A GOOD HOMEMAKER
AND A GOOD STEWARD OF ALL THAT YOU GIVE ME. PLEASE GIVE ME WIS-
DOM AND ENERGY AS I ATTEMPT TO FEED MY FAMILY GOOD FOOD.

week 39

How Can I Make Dinner When I'm Always in the Car? Dinnertime Solutions

In the early years of her marriage, author P. B. Wilson didn't ordinarily bother making dinner. When considering the hours it took to cook and clean up, as well as the wealth of available premade entrees and fast food, she saw cooking as a poor use of her time.

Wilson came to realize as the years passed, however, that by not valuing cooking she was depriving both herself and her family of rich experiences. As she says in her book *God Is in the Kitchen Too*, amid her busy schedule "the conversations, laughter and fellowship were snuffed out."[1] While acknowledging that making meals requires effort that must be subtracted from other activities, Wilson says, "This investment pays very high dividends. Watching the positive, ongoing development of your family unit is priceless. Your family will grow to cherish the times around the dinner table and develop an inner stability they would not have without it."[2]

I, too, am a recent convert to holding family mealtimes in high regard, having thought for years that my children's year-round involvement in band and sports activities made a postpractice stop for McFood virtually inevitable.

Gathering for a family dinner—together, all at the same time, at a table not in the van—seemed like a lot of effort. And frankly, I wasn't sure it was worth it.

I'm not sure when my ideas began to change; maybe it was as the children approached adolescence and it seemed more important than ever to wrest what family time we could from life's increasingly frenetic demands. In any case, somewhere along the line I grew to appreciate the unique camaraderie our family experiences around evening meals.

Research bears out the benefits. According to studies, adolescents who eat dinner frequently with their families are less likely to use illegal drugs, be depressed, or get in trouble with the law. They are also more likely to get good grades. "Surprisingly," notes *Dr. James Dobson's Focus on the Family Bulletin*, "the benefit was seen even in families that didn't eat together at home. Those who met at fast-food restaurants had the same result."[3]

If I'm not making the effort to provide a family dinner-time whenever possible—even if it's frozen pizza and bag salad—my family misses out on that connection of sharing the day's ups and downs. We miss out on the habit (not to mention good manners) of learning to eat what's in front of us, rather than thinking life always includes menu options. We miss out on the benefits of working together to clean up after a meal. Mealtime is family time, plain and simple, and it's something I've realized I'm willing to be inconvenienced for.

My friend Susie, mother of three, told me how she managed to make a special dinner of Chinese duck the other night. "While Emily was at piano lessons and Michael was at high school swim practice, I ran home and cleaned the duck. I picked up Emily and got Allison from her swim club, then got home, boiled the marinade, and started soaking the duck." Her recipe called for scallions, which

Susie didn't have, but after bringing Emily to play rehearsal and picking up Michael from the high school—by this time, it was 6:45 p.m.—she decided to do without. The recipe also called for a marinate/refrigerate/marinate/refrigerate process that would have taken three days, "but I decided marinating for thirty minutes would have to be enough." The duck, as it turns out, was delicious; "The only thing is, by the time Emily got home from play practice at 9:30, there was none left! And she was the one who wanted the duck in the first place!"

The moral of this story is not that one average-sized duck feeds four people not five; it's that cooking in ten-minute snatches is the only way most of us can expect to get any kind of dinner on the table. With children involved in afternoon and evening activities and the constant interruptions to get Cinderella to the ball, producing a midweek dinner is an accomplishment at least as impressive as building those ancient Egyptian pyramids everyone's always gushing over. (Did the Egyptians have to break every half hour to deliver their little mummies to practice? I think not.)

One woman who understands dinnertime difficulties is Rhonda Barfield, a homemaker, mother of four, homeschooler, and author. In her book *15-Minute Cooking*, Barfield says her cooking methods developed out of "pure, desperate necessity."[6] Without a large chunk of time for meal preparation, Barfield figured the best way for her to get a complete meal on the table—including main dish, side dish, quick bread, and homemade dessert—was to work fast and break her preparation into two fifteen-minute bursts. Often, Barfield starts cooking the night before for the next day's dinner. Using these techniques, Barfield's family has been encouraged "to sit down together at relatively calm evening meals because we all have something to really look forward to: good food and fellowship."[7]

Maybe we can't whip up a home-cooked meal every night, but if, like Barfield and my friend Susie, we're willing to work in small snatches; if we're willing to forego the perfectionist mentality, forget the occasional missing ingredient, and forswear those steps we don't have time for, we can feed our families good, solid meals more often.

At least, assuming they're not off at play practice.

Finding a cookbook specific to the time-crunched life can feel like finding a friend who's a good listener. Finally, someone who understands!

Keep your eyes open for titles such as *The Four Ingredient Cookbook, Make-Ahead Cooking,* and *Fast Meals.* Check out books and magazines you own, ask friends, scan the library's selection. Use time waiting for kids in the car to browse recipe possibilities. Note which dishes you can prepare early in the day and reheat later; look for recipes with quick-cooking fish fillets, chicken that's already boned, vegetables that are precut. Accept that you may have to put aside the Julia Child for now and go for *101 Ways to Make Magic with Cream of Chicken Soup.*

When considering recipes, don't forget about the absent cook's best friend, the Crock-Pot. Is there anything more welcoming than returning home from a harried evening to the aroma of dinner that's already cooking? An added bonus is that timing isn't critical; most recipes give you a range of cooking times (four to six hours, for example), so if Coach keeps the kids a few minutes overtime, it's not a big deal.

Some people make extra food on weekends and freeze it for the week ahead, or even the month. (See *Once-a-Month Cooking* by Mimi Wilson and Mary Beth Lagerborg.) My friend Kris, a teacher, tried this the month before school started one year and found the method worked great—"except I accidentally put the chopped onions for all the recipes into the first recipe."

Others double or triple favorite recipes when they make them. "Having a freezer filled with premade dinners," says

---

Ruth Marcus in a *Washington Post* article, ". . . gives me a sense of inner calm, something like survivalists must feel when they have the cabin stocked with enough Spam to survive nuclear winter."[9]

A friend who's a busy homeschooling mom of six likes to fill her freezer with what she calls "Whack-a-Meal." "You brown a whole bunch of hamburger meat at once, put it in Ziploc® bags and smush it down so it's thin, then freeze; when you're ready to use it you just whack it on the counter and heat it up."

My all-time favorite make-ahead-and-freeze dish is Quiche Lorraine. I never make fewer than four at a time (motto: fry bacon once). They make great meals for new moms, can be served any time of the day, and, since each requires only four slices of bacon and plain milk instead of cream, are not expensive. Ask the guy at the meat counter for bacon ends rather than full strips and they're even cheaper.

QUICHE LORRAINE

I buy premade frozen piecrusts. For a complete meal, add a bag of salad, a can of pears or peaches, and a package of rolls.

Thaw **1 deep-dish frozen piecrust** for ten minutes. Poke with fork all over, then bake at 450 degrees for five minutes. Remove from oven and set aside. Reduce oven heat to 350 degrees.

Cook **4 slices bacon** until crisp. Drain; crumble. Reserve 1 T. bacon; sprinkle remaining in piecrust.

Top with **1 cup shredded Swiss cheese** (4 ounces).

In separate bowl, mix:

> **2 t. flour**
> **¼ t. salt**

Stir in: **1 cup milk**

> **2 beaten eggs**

Carefully pour over cheese in piecrust. Bake at 350 degrees for thirty minutes. Sprinkle with reserved bacon. Bake till knife inserted off-center comes out clean, fifteen to twenty minutes more. Serves four.[11]

FRENCH DIP IN THE CROCK-POT

This is flavorful and easy.

Around noon, put in the Crock-Pot:

3 lb. chuck roast, trimmed of any fat

Add: **2 cups water**

½ cup soy sauce

seasonings (1 t. dried rosemary, 1 t. dried thyme, 1 t. garlic powder, 1 bay leaf, and 3 whole peppercorns)

Cook on high for five to six hours. When the meat is tender, take it from the broth and shred with two forks. Serve on hamburger buns or split French rolls, with a cup of "jus" (juice) on the side. Add a salad and sliced fruit to finish the meal.[12] ♥

"There is nothing better for a man than to eat and drink and tell himself that his labor is good. This also I have seen that it is from the hand of God. For who can eat and who can have enjoyment without Him?" (Ecclesiastes 2:24–25)

pra🙷er LORD, THANK YOU FOR GIVING ME A FAMILY TO TAKE CARE OF. HELP ME TO MAKE WISE CHOICES AT THE GROCERY STORE AND TO PUT FORTH MY BEST EFFORTS TO GIVE MY FAMILY GOOD, SOLID NUTRITION SO THEY'LL HAVE THE ENERGY THEY NEED TO GET THROUGH THEIR DAY.

CHOCOLATE BREAK!
CHOCOLATE CHIP CHEESECAKE

As my son said at age eleven, "Anything without chocolate isn't worth eating." I have to agree. This cheesecake is crammed with mini chocolate chips, making it eminently worth eating.

CHOCOLATE CHIP CHEESECAKE

In small bowl, combine:

1 cup graham cracker crumbs

3 T. sugar

3 T. butter, melted

Press onto the bottom of a nine-inch springform pan.

Using electric mixer, beat:

3 8-oz. packages cream cheese, softened

¾ cup sugar

until well blended. One at a time, add:

3 eggs

mixing well after each. Stir in:

1 cup small chocolate chips

1 t. vanilla

Pour mixture over crust. Bake at 450 degrees for ten minutes, then lower heat to 250 degrees and continue baking for 35–45 more minutes. Loosen cheesecake from sides of pan; cool before removing rim. Chill.

week 40

The Joys of Leftovers

"May I take your order, sir?"

My husband reached for the menu I offered, wide-eyed at my appearance in a chef's hat with notepad in hand. The children sat at the dinner table and giggled at my crummy French accent. It was leftovers night, and instead of reciting my usual tired litany of offerings, I decided to write up menus and have some fun. "Le Menu" included several choices of main dish, choices of side dishes, and an optional dessert; taped to the bottom were riddles I'd found in old kids' magazines.

The element of surprise made for a fun evening. We all enjoyed the silliness, even the chef. "What kind of fruit?" asked one son about the dessert. "Zee same kind as lassst night, sir," I answered, dignified for a moment until we all burst out laughing.

Come up with your own "le menu" some evening, based on treasures you find in your refrigerator. And don't forget to practice zat French accent. Bon appétit.

new word

for the week:

Lachrymose

(lăk′ rə-mōs′).

Weeping or inclined to weep; causing tears. As in, *"Children, please don't be lachrymose just because we're having leftovers tonight."*

alternate

new word:

Detritus (dĭ-trī′ təs)

Any disintegrated matter; debris. As in, *"Could you kids please help clear away the postprandial detritus?"*

Sample Le Menu

Main dish (choose one)

❏ Cheese burrito
❏ Cheese and beef burrito
❏ Cheese quesadilla
❏ Cheese & beef quesadilla
❏ French dip

Side dishes (choose one or more)

❏ lettuce (salad)
❏ carrot sticks
❏ sliced peaches
❏ sliced fruit—berries, pears, apples, bananas (circle choices)

❏ Yes ❏ No   I would like a meringue "cookie" filled with fruit and topped with vanilla/raspberry swirl frozen yogurt.

It's been a pleasure being your server. Have a nice day!

Riddle: Q. What is Jack Frost's favorite thing about school?
A. Snow and tell.

FUN FACT

↰

September 28 is National Good Neighbor Day. So if you're home today and have time, stop by a neighbor's with a plateful of cookies. Or maybe just a friendly hello.

One of my most treasured cookbooks, I picked up years ago at that bastion of fine literature, the supermarket. Snagged from a large bin at the front of the store and costing only a few dollars, *Leftovers* by Coralie Castle is probably the most useful in my collection.[1] What I love about it is its practicality. How often have you served a great meal, roast beef or roasted chicken, say, only to be faced with a huge plate of leftovers staring back at you afterward for days? Families can be picky about eating the same food they ate last night, and sometimes it seems easier just to throw something new in the oven and relegate last night's detritus to the dog.

If you find a cookbook where the author's given some thought to the possibility of food that didn't disappear at first sitting, however, you may be in for a pleasant surprise. In *Leftovers*, for example, Castle provides all kinds of unexpected ways to use already-cooked food, from turkey pie with stuffing crust (see week 48) to shepherd's pie (meat in individual serving dishes, covered with mashed potatoes blended with an egg and a few tablespoons of Parmesan cheese and baked). The way she sees it, leftovers, prepared with "imagination and a willingness to engage in a little risk taking with combinations and seasonings," can wind up tasting better than the original meal:

> Those Mexican-restaurant leftovers of half an enchilada, some beans, rice and shredded lettuce, and a couple of tortillas can all be broken up into a rich stock and served as a delicious soup, garnished with freshly shredded cheese and chopped coriander. The leftovers from a dinner at a prime-rib or steak house can just as easily be transformed: cut the meat into strips and marinate for a salad, and brown the skin from the baked potato in butter to eat with fried eggs for the next morning's breakfast. . . .
>
> There are even "planned" leftovers, when one deliberately cooks a larger portion than is needed for a single meal. The "extra" measure then becomes the basis for a dinner on another evening. Planned leftovers save cooking fuel, conserve the time and energy of the cook (who much prefers washing one rice pot to washing two), and makes dinner a more relaxed affair. Before the meal, there's time to play a set of tennis, spend time with the children, sit down to talk with family or guests, or simply relax after a long workday. Develop a planned-leftovers schedule that works for you and you won't feel so "tied" to the kitchen.[2]

Castle goes on to say that the innovative leftovers cook can avoid throwing out food. "My one failure on this front," she says, "is the dressed tossed salad, which is one leftover without a future. That long-held belief that you can whirl it in the blender for a delicious gazpacho will never be proven by me."

Before my family balks at another night of leftover roast for dinner, I'll head for my *Leftovers* book. Maybe we'll have marinated beef salad, or twice-baked potatoes topped with diced beef. With Castle as my guide, I'm betting no one will even realize they've seen this meat before.

Often, perfectly good food is left to die on my refrigerator shelves, because in my rush to get someone to sports practice or to the office supply store for poster board for tomorrow's English project, I haven't taken a minute to peruse the refrigerator

TWICE-BAKED POTATOES

Cut in half lengthwise **4 large freshly baked potatoes**. Scoop out pulp, leaving a 3/8-inch thick shell. Mash pulp while hot.

Stir in **2/3 cup low-fat cottage cheese, sour cream, plain yogurt, or half-and-half**. Add about 1 cup of the following filling suggestions.

Season with **salt and pepper**.

Mound into reserved shells and place on baking sheet. Sprinkle with **grated cheese** and **paprika**, bake at 350 degrees for fifteen minutes. Serves four as a main dish.

Potato Filling Suggestions

◇ shredded **cooked chicken or turkey** and sautéed minced **green onions**

◇ flaked **cooked firm white fish** and sautéed diced **bell peppers and onions**

◇ mashed **ripe avocado**, fresh **lemon juice**, and minced **fresh chives**

◇ sautéed minced **celery** and grated **Gruyère cheese**

◇ **hard-cooked egg yolks** mashed with **anchovy paste or anchovy filets**, added to minced **hard-cooked egg whites**

◇ flaked **crab meat**, grated **onion**, and grated **cheddar cheese**

◇ minced **onions** sautéed in **butter**, grated **Monterey Jack cheese**, minced fresh **parsley** and **chives**, and chopped **walnuts**

◇ crumbled **blue cheese**, minced **chives**, and mashed **garlic**

◇ minced **lamb roast**, chopped ripe **tomatoes**, and diced **bell peppers and onions and garlic** sauteed in **olive oil**

◇ diced **cream cheese or crumbled feta cheese**, fresh **lemon juice**, and **minced chives** [3]

to see what's in there. If I took a morning peek in the fridge and considered the contents not as problematic blobs of decaying food but as a precooked start to tonight's dinner—be it casserole, salad, omelet, quiche, pasta dish, sandwich, or soup—I'll bet I could relieve some dinnertime stress.

"The term 'leftovers' is freighted with negative connotations," says Jay Jacobs in his book *Cooking for All It's Worth: Making the Most of Every Morsel of Food You Buy*, " . . . nightmarish visions of sandwiches, salads and hashes begat generation upon generation by the Thanksgiving turkey, Easter ham or Sunday roast; offerings that grow progressively more monotonous and less palatable with each succeeding day until, finally fed up with this dreary parade of anticlimaxes, we escape to a fine restaurant, there to dine elegantly on *bisque d'homard, émincés de boeuf bordelaise* . . .—in plain English, recycled leftovers."

Jacobs points out that the American cook buys food with only one meal in mind. "Whatever is not finished off on the occasion either is trashed or disdainfully suffered, like a guest who has overstayed his welcome."[4]

He urges us to think differently. A single ham, for example, could yield enough leftover meat to make eggs Benedict for breakfast, ham and winter melon soup, a ham mousse, soufflé, or the beginnings of a chef's salad. "All those ragged little scraps will go into future gumbos and jambalayas, quiches and omelets, stuffed artichokes and—blended with bits of chicken salvaged from the stockpot—*tortellini* filling. . . . The bone—precious bone!—will add resonance and character to my black bean or split-pea soup. I and mine will sup superbly off and on for months on this ham, conferring virtual immortality on the pig whence it came, and never know gastronomic ennui."[5]

Granted, this fine cooking takes time, time that we may not have at this point in our lives. But Jacobs's point is well taken: leftovers are a happy thing, the beginning of the next meal, and by no means destined to reappear time and time again in exactly the same form. If nothing else, we can chop up what our family doesn't eat, measure it in quantities of one cup, and freeze in plastic containers until we figure out what to make with it. (Don't forget to label and date.)

Let's heed the words of *The Joy of Cooking* author Irma S. Rombauer, from the book's 1946 edition: "Some of the most tempting . . . dishes are made from icebox scraps. Do not disdain them."[6]

JAPANESE SAUCE FOR COLD NOODLE SALAD

This recipe comes from my mom, and it's really, really good.

When you've got **leftover cooked pasta** or **cooked meat** or **seafood**, mix up a quick batch of this sauce. Add it to pasta and meat, throw in some **diced green onion** and **diced cucumber** if you have them, then enjoy this meal that'll be better than the one you ate the first time.

Combine: **1/3 cup rice vinegar**

   3 T. Memmi (Noodle soup base, made by Kikkoman and found in the supermarket)

   1 T. sugar

   1 T. sesame seeds, toasted under the broiler until brown (watch closely; takes less than a minute)

   1 T. oil

   ½ t. sesame oil

Stir until sugar dissolves.

Pour over cooked pasta, diced cooked meat, chopped green onions, and diced, peeled cucumber. Refrigerate.

"And do not be conformed to this world, but be transformed by the renewing of your mind, so that you may prove what the will of God is, that which is good and acceptable and perfect." (Romans 12:2)

Quotable

In her book, 1,001 Bright Ideas to Stretch Your Dollars, author Cynthia Yates suggests living off what you have in your refrigerator, freezer, and cupboard for a time without buying anything new unless absolutely necessary. "Try it. Start with a week, then longer. Using things up gets to be a habit, as does creativity."[7]

prayer

LORD, THANK YOU THAT YOU ARE CONSTANTLY TRANSFORMING ME, WITH "IMAGINATION AND A WILLINGNESS TO ENGAGE IN A LITTLE RISK TAKING," TILL I END UP BETTER THAN I WAS IN MY ORIGINAL FORM. THANK YOU FOR NOT DISCARDING ME. YOU ARE THE BEST!

week 41

The Seasons Are Changing: Homemaking in the Fall

In her book *A Family Raised on Rainbows*, Beverly Nye says, "I love the fall season. . . . It's a change of pace. After the care-free outdoor days of summer, I start feeling like the squirrels. Time to get my nest ready for winter and the holidays ahead. . . . I love to smell the bonfires, the crispy apples in the orchards, and as funny as it may seem, the dried cornstalks in the fields. Somehow it gives me the feeling that everything and everybody have done their duty, and all is right with the world."[1]

I love the fall too. It's the time of year I feel especially domestic, as though there's nothing I should be doing that's more important than simmering a stew or baking a pie. Something about the crisp air, which seems to have cooled overnight; the fallen leaves, which scuttle end over end down our long country driveway; the sound of chain-saws echoing through our mountain community as people stock their woodpiles for the winter ahead. Everything about the season makes me want to nest, to make my home cozy, to withdraw from the approaching cold and settle in for winter.

It's a great time to pull out a jigsaw puzzle—preferably,

new word

for the week:

Sough (sŭf).

A soft murmuring sound, as of the wind or gentle surf. As in, *"The sough of wind rustling through the October leaves is such a peaceful sound."*

alternate

new word:

Rhizome (rī′ zōm).

A thickened stem growing under or along the ground and sending out roots from its lower surface and leaves or shoots from its upper surface; bearded iris, for example. As in, *"This fall I'm going to plant some flowering bulbs, even if I don't know a rhizome from a rhinestone."*

one with a fall scene—to stop at a local pumpkin patch and buy some mini pumpkins and gourds for the table, to wear yellow, orange, or red. It's a great time to try a new cookie recipe, to dig out the heavy comforters, to bake bread. It's a great time to clear off the dining room table and give it a gleaming rub of lemon oil.

Fall is a great time to make mulled apple cider, to listen to Vivaldi's "The Four Seasons," to picnic by the fire or to go watch a high school football game. It's a great time to gather an impromptu bouquet from interesting leaves or blooms found in the yard.

It's a great time to call the chimney sweep.

If you're dying to nest but find your primary perch is not home but the driver's seat of your car, don't despair; do what one woman did: before leaving home she kneaded bread dough then brought it with her in the car, to rise and punch down as she was out and about. The car is "usually nice and warm—a good place for bread to rise," says author Rosalind Creasy in *Cooking from the Garden*.[2] Assuming, that is, you can protect your dough from any wriggling passengers and their muddy cleats.

Fall ideas:

◊ Gather seeds from the spent flowers in your garden; bag up and label, to plant in the spring.

◊ Pull out candles to dine by.

◊ Serve an all-orange dinner, with the kids devising the menu. Possibilities include orange juice, carrot sticks, grilled cheese, orange-colored pasta with Parmesan cheese, orange Jell-O®, orange sherbet.

◊ Hike with your family on a woodsy trail. Look for big leaves to grace your table.

◊ If you've carved a pumpkin, sprinkle cinnamon (or nutmeg) on the inside of the lid. When you light the candle, it'll smell like pumpkin pie.[3]

◊ If your freezer resembles the black hole, start clearing it now in preparation for make-ahead Thanksgiving dishes you plan to make.

◊ Bury your hands in the dog's thickening fur.

◊ Make up the beds with flannel sheets so everyone's nice and comfy.

◊ Buy small, round loaves of bread, one for each family member, and hollow out leaving a thick crust; fill with chili or stew and serve to applause.

◊ Buy a jug of fresh apple cider from the market.

◊ Pull out your slippers and curl up on the couch with a blanket, a good book, and a cozy fire.

❖ Celebrate Get Organized Week (founded by the National Association of Professional Organizers). Each day this week, set aside fifteen minutes to sort through your piles of mail.

When planting flowering bulbs, many gardeners recommend tossing them onto the ground and planting them wherever they land. I tried that one October, planting fifty irises that, from the picture on the package, looked irresistible. Apparently they *were* irresistible as the gophers ate them whole before I could see whether random garden design actually works.

Gophers notwithstanding, bulbs seem relatively foolproof, growing without persnickety water or soil requirements. In fact, when my husband laid down a new gravel driveway one year in a slightly wider configuration than our old one, some diehard daffodils poked up the next spring amid the gravel. You've got to love tenacity like that.

I think of bulbs as a fall investment that will reap rewards in the spring. But as I saw recently from one Web site (www.whiteflowerfarm.com), some bulbs can be planted in fall and they'll bloom that same fall! I whipped out my credit card and ordered some colchicum lilac wonders, colchicum the giants, and Sternbergia luteas.

Daffodils, narcissus, and colchicums are supposed to be repellent to deer and rodents; critters apparently do like tulips and crocuses, so be aware as you make your bulb purchases. My mom foils the critters by planting her tulips in large pots that she keeps out of reach on her deck. An added advantage is she can roll the pots out of sight once the tulips are spent.

Don't forget: plant bulbs pointy side up! If it's not obvious which end is which, plant on their side, and count on the shoots being able to figure it out. A general rule is to plant the bulbs three times as deep as the bulb is tall. And wait to plant until the weather's turned cool.

Quotable

The earlier you make your bulb selections, the better. . . . With bulbs, first pick is important, even if it's too early to plant. . . . Make sure they are nice and plump, and not mushy. Check for mildew, insects, or other signs of disease. Smell them. Apply the same standards that you would to an onion that you might buy at the market. . . . Once home, store your bulbs . . . in a cool dry place until you are ready to plant (don't let them freeze, of course).[4]

Christine Allison,
365 Days of Gardening

In climates with mild winters, tulips, crocuses, and hyacinths should be refrigerated for six or more weeks before planting, to trick them into thinking they've experienced a cold winter underground and now it's time to get growing. But according to Bulb.com, you should remove fruit, especially apples, from the fridge during that time as the fruit emits a gas that will kill off the flowers inside bulbs.

Author Christine Allison, in her book *365 Days of Gardening*, advises you to plant bulbs in groups. "One tulip here or there looks foolish," she admonishes. Plant odd numbers together, it being "much more natural to see 5 or 7 or 9 bulbs planted together than the same bulbs in even sets."[5]

So let's get out there and dig. Gophers, be warned. We are serious here.

A few years back as I sat at my kitchen table munching leftover pizza for lunch, I looked up at the window and stopped midbite; a dark, odd-looking cloud floated up the hill. *That's an odd-looking cloud!* I thought, and went outside to investigate.

Sure enough it was an odd-looking "cloud," mainly because it wasn't a cloud at all but a pile of smoke coming from the house down the hill.

Smoke isn't uncommon where we live. Many in our neighborhood use their fireplaces for heat, and on county-declared "burn days," attended piles of burning leaves can be spotted around the neighborhood. But this time something was different. The air smelled of cinders; the heat, the floating black ash, the popping sounds followed by the sound of my neighbor's frantic yelling, all confirmed that something was very wrong.

I called 9-1-1; I tried to contact a nearby neighbor, who wasn't home; I called my husband at work; then I gathered the dog and leash and drove away.

Our road was closed and more than ten fire trucks arrived on the scene, so we didn't know for hours if we'd return to find our home as we'd left it, belongings intact, or if we'd come back to ashes. It was a good time to pray.

In the middle of it all, I realized that everything of value to me was already safe. My kids were off at school. My husband had come from work to meet me. Our dog was in the car. And my eternal future was safe, sealed in heaven with Christ (I Peter 1:3–4).

Later, a friend who volunteers with the Red Cross was aghast. "You just drove away?" she asked. Next time, she exhorted, "make sure to bring your important papers!" An emergency preparedness class teaches you to collect those papers in one place (wills, insurance policies, passports, bank account numbers, credit card information, social security cards, birth and marriage certificates) so they're ready *before* a disaster. Then, if a quick evacuation ever becomes necessary, you can just grab the container and go.

Fire Safety Tips

Fall is a good time to think about fire safety. My neighbor's fire started when she cleaned her fireplace and put still-warm ashes into a plastic bucket. The bucket caught fire, which caught her garage on fire, which caught her house on fire. (She was unharmed, but her house was destroyed; the popping noises I'd heard were her windows breaking from the heat.) The lesson, of course, is to dispose of hot ashes safely. (The U.S. Fire Administration recommends soaking hot ashes in water and disposing in a metal container outside your home.)

Other important fire safety tips:

◇ If you use your fireplace regularly, call a chimney sweep each fall to have it cleaned. Creosote, a by-product of wood-burning fires, can build up in chimneys and stovepipes and start a fire.

- Your home should contain at least one easily accessible all-purpose fire extinguisher. I've used ours only once, when sesame seeds I was broiling burst into flames and threatened to ignite the wood cabinets around the oven. But I've always been grateful I had it.

- Make sure smoke detectors are installed in your home, at least one on every floor and preferably one by each bedroom. They should be placed on the ceiling or high on a wall, six to twelve inches from the ceiling. If they're battery operated (some are not; they are electrically wired into the house), check regularly to make sure they work. Replace the batteries each year; make a note on your calendar so you won't forget. (Warning: the alarm is [obviously] excruciatingly loud, so don't be so overwhelmed by the din when testing that you accidentally tear it out of the wall. Ahem.)

- Discuss fire safety basics with your family: If you suspect a fire, feel the door. If it's hot, don't open it but escape through an alternate route. If it's necessary to travel through smoke to get out, crawl on all fours as the air will be clearer by the floor.

- Have your children practice opening their bedroom windows and demonstrating how to remove screens in case evacuation through the window becomes necessary.

- Plan an outside spot where your family will meet in case of emergency evacuation—maybe the driveway. Practice a fire drill when no one's expecting it.

"By wisdom a house is built, and through understanding it is established; through knowledge its rooms are filled with rare and beautiful treasures." (Proverbs 24:3–4 NIV)

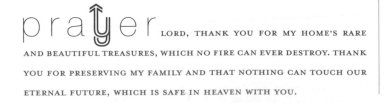

prayer LORD, THANK YOU FOR MY HOME'S RARE AND BEAUTIFUL TREASURES, WHICH NO FIRE CAN EVER DESTROY. THANK YOU FOR PRESERVING MY FAMILY AND THAT NOTHING CAN TOUCH OUR ETERNAL FUTURE, WHICH IS SAFE IN HEAVEN WITH YOU.

week 42

Friendship

When one of my dearest friends recently had surgery, I was frustrated that I didn't have time to bring over a homemade meal. We had been pregnant together and had watched our children learn to swim, memorize Sunday-school verses, and play hundreds of innings of Little League baseball together. And I couldn't bring over a meal?!

Sad but true. Between carpooling kids to and from baseball / football / wrestling / band practice, not to mention youth group, doctors' appointments, and the ever-important, unremitting school, it sometimes feels like my fanny is permanently attached to the front seat of the van. Throw in those extras like out-of-town visitors, a family member's birthday, or the kitchen being re-sheetrocked, and it's apparent that sometimes it's all we can manage just to send a card.

I am not always the friend I want to be. I frequently can't return phone calls for several days because I'm not home, or I am but I need to catch up on laundry, supervise homework, grab a quick shower, etc. I am often disappointed with myself; I am not always the friend I want to be.

But I've decided that sometimes I need to be willing to settle. To be satisfied with the small gesture if it's the best I can do. A friend who's been sick for the last five years says, "It amazes me how much power there is in a phone call, a

new word

for the week:

Amity (ăm′ ə-tē).
Peaceful relations, as between nations; friendship. As in, *"Without the **amity** of women in my life, I'd surely be in the corner of a room somewhere, babbling incoherently."*

alternate

new word:

Recondite (rĕk′ ən-dīt′).
Not easily understood by the average person. As in, *"Just how we're supposed to find time for friendships is a **recondite** mystery, but it's one worth pondering."*

card, or someone praying with me on the phone. It's not always the big things that make the difference." Her words reassure me that God can use my humble offerings, like He did the two small coins offered by the widow, which were all she had to give (see Mark 12:41–44).

Ideas for five-minute friendship:

- ◇ Order a pizza and have it delivered to a friend's house.
- ◇ Buy her a gift certificate at the local coffee place or ice cream shop and pop it in the mail.
- ◇ Pray for her via e-mail or by leaving a prayer on her answering machine.
- ◇ Leave a "have a good day" sticky note on her door or her car if you're close by.
- ◇ Send stickers in the mail to cheer her on.

When time for friends is extremely limited, follow Cynthia Heald's advice: Meet some classic Christian authors through your reading. You'll never be without a wise friend, day or night.[1]

Since the job of homemaker comes with no built-in co-workers or lunch breaks, we have to be as deliberate about meeting our social needs as we are about keeping enough chocolate ice cream in the house. But how, with intense family responsibilities, can we find time to meet our very real needs for connection with people who don't have to be reminded to use their inside voices or flush? It's a challenge that sometimes seems insurmountable.

James 1:5 advises us that "if any of you lacks wisdom, let him ask of God, who gives to all generously."

Who, God? Who should I seek to be friends with? Is there someone You want to bring into my life that I need to be open to?

And how, Lord? How can I find time for friendships when it's all I can do to keep up with the laundry?

When my children were preschoolers, most of my friends were women I knew from weekly Bible study. Most of us were young moms awash with similar struggles. It was an invaluable gift not to have to explain why you were twenty minutes late, your hair was unkempt, your T-shirt was appliquéd with baby spit-up, and your lesson was done only to question two. Everyone was in the same boat; we were all just trying to stay afloat.

As that first summer drew near, we realized if we didn't keep meeting through the break we'd spend the next few months prolonging conversations with the grocery bag boy or wrong numbers simply because they were the only grown-up voices we were likely to hear all day. For sanity's sake, we couldn't afford to quit gathering. So we drew up a list of the best parks in the county (ones with bathrooms and lots of play equipment) and continued to get together, exploring a different park each week. We brought with us bag lunches, kids of all ages, and questions about potty training, sibling rivalry, and PMS.

In the ensuing years, I've found other ways to connect with friends: craft nights at one another's homes, aerobics class, photo crops, occasional lunches out, season tickets for Sunday matinees to our local regional theater.

Coming up with friendship solutions that work for you may take some time, some thought, and some experimentation. But persevere. Don't give up. Friendships are important. They help us get through life's stages, the good and the rocky. They are worth pursuing, in spite of the obstacles.

"Try it!" urged my thirteen-year-old as we stood in line at the big warehouse store. "Try it on the checkout guy!"

We had been listening to a book on tape that gave instruction in making friendly conversation with just about anyone. I'd checked it out from the library because I've

Quotable

Paul exhorts us to "carry each other's burdens" (Galations 6:2 [NIV]). The word he uses for burdens refers to the temporary "overburden" that a sister may be carrying, as distinct from the "everyday load" he refers to in Galatians 6:5. When we are temporarily overburdened due to the stress of death, divorce, illness, and so on, we definitely need the supportive help of our sisters. We need someone to come alongside and help shoulder the overburden.

The best way to do that is by empathizing, weeping with those who weep. Your quiet and listening presence will help absorb some of the pain and relieve some of the burden. If we attempt to deny the burden by pointing out blessings, we add to the pain. . . . Too much cheerfulness or the offering of solutions intensifies grief.[2]

Dee Brestin,
The Friendships of Women

Quotable

I have rarely met a person or been in a situation where there was not something valuable worth learning. . . . I like to ask men and women about their jobs, where they met their spouses, what they have been reading about, what they consider their greatest present challenges, and where they find God most alive in their lives.[3]

Gordon MacDonald,
Ordering Your Private World

always felt inadequate at making small talk; I never know how to talk to new acquaintances, short of playing newspaper reporter (my job in a former life) and bombarding them with questions.

"I don't know . . ." I was whining now. As one who freezes when strangers strike up a conversation with me—how do you answer a lady who pulls you aside in the produce aisle and confides she's trying to lose weight but her family won't cooperate?—I had a hard time envisioning anyone being overjoyed at personal comments from a stranger. But my son's encouragement—or maybe it was goading—was working. Maybe it's not too late to change, I thought. After all, I had been the one who'd checked out the tape from the library; why had I done that if I wasn't at least willing to try?

As we approached the checkout guy, my heart beating louder than normal, I opened my mouth to speak: "Pretty busy today, huh?" I said. Argh. Not exactly the brilliant repartee I had hoped for.

"Yeah," he answered, then added a few comments of his own. When our transaction was complete, I glanced at his nametag and said a quick "Thank you, Joe," which may seem like no big deal but is as out of character for me as if I'd stripped naked and sung an aria right there on the warehouse floor. I'd called him Joe! I didn't even know him and I'd called him Joe!

I was amazed at how richly I'd been rewarded for my unspectacular attempt. My new best friend Joe and I had actually had a conversation. My son, who happens to be immensely at ease talking in front of absolutely anyone, eyed me with a smile. I learned something that day about starting a friendship. You just start.

I am fairly certain I'm in no imminent danger of becoming a daytime talk show host or a slick salesman who can convince you that a timeshare in Tuscaloosa is just the thing for your retirement years. But I'd like to think that I can become a little less fearful in unfamiliar social settings. After all, isn't the definition of a stranger just a friend you haven't met yet? I'll get back to you on that, right after I discuss it with my thirteen-year-old and our new best friend Joe. ●

"A friend loves at all times." (Proverbs 17:17)

prayer LORD, PLEASE "FORTIFY MY SPIRIT SO THAT I MAY MEET LIFE HOPEFULLY AND BE ABLE TO ENDURE EVERYTHING WHICH THOU MAYEST BE PLEASED TO SEND ME."[4] HELP ME TO BE A GOOD FRIEND, AND TO BE ALERT TO POTENTIAL FRIENDS YOU SEND MY WAY. HELP ME TO CARE MORE ABOUT THE PERSON I'M TALKING WITH AND NOT SO MUCH ABOUT MYSELF.

week 43

Insuperable

(ĭn-sōō′ pər-ə-bəl).

Incapable of being overcome; insurmountable. As in, *"My lack of training for this job of homemaker is not insuperable; I am continuing to learn more every day."*

alternate

new word:

Sedulous (sĕj′ ōō-ləs).

Diligent; industrious; the sense of earnest, persistent labor. As in, *"If I continue to be sedulous in my homemaking efforts, I am bound to become competent at my work."*

Old-Fashioned Homemaking

Before I got married, my list of hoped-for wedding gifts included a popcorn popper and small glass dishes for serving shrimp cocktails. On my entire bridal registry list, there was not a single request for pot or pan.

My older and wiser female relatives found much merriment in my omission, joking, "What will you eat when you get tired of popcorn and shrimp cocktails?" Though I already possessed a certain deftness with banana bread, somewhere around the last bridal shower it began to dawn on me that the learning curve for my new role might be a bit steeper than I'd imagined.

Needless to say, my shift from young woman to wife was more like a stumble than a glide. I had studied and prepared for a career in the working world. But I was completely unequipped for this vast job of taking care of a home and family. (*Vast*: very great in extent or scope; immense; enormous; boundless.)

I suspect most of us are in the same boat when we first get married—and often for long afterward, unless we make real efforts to improve our homemaking skills. Just how exactly are we supposed to know the difference between a chuck roast and a rump roast, a chef's knife and a paring knife, a meat thermometer and a candy thermometer? How are we to know how much meat to expect each person at the dinner table to eat? And how, exactly, are we to come up with a balanced menu and then perform the magical feat of getting everything prepared and hot and ready to eat at precisely the same moment?

Getting food on the table involves many, many steps, from grocery shopping to following a recipe to setting the table. There's a lot to know. Just when, exactly, were we supposed to have absorbed all these lessons? Somewhere between calculus and Canadian history exams?

I recently enjoyed reading a book that helped me see that mine is not the first generation to be daunted by the demands of domesticity. The book tells not only the history of *The Joy of Cooking* cookbook and its authors but also the culinary climate of the times in which it was originally written—1931.

I'd always assumed that previous generations of American women had been well schooled in the domestic arts. So it was fascinating to learn that this simply wasn't so. According to *Stand Facing the Stove: The Story of the Women Who Gave America the Joy of Cooking (The Lives of Irma S. Rombauer and Marion Rombauer Becker)* by Anne Mendelson, many middle-class American women in the 1800s and early 1900s had domestic help.[1] While the mistress of the house might oversee the cooking and occasionally pitch in for big meals, in general she knew very little about day-to-day meal preparation.

As the culture and economy changed (the Depression of 1929 and the 1930s was a factor) and these women no longer employed hired help, they realized they were sorely lacking in kitchen skills. They hadn't grown up watching and learning how to cook from female relatives; they were faced with having to do a job for which they were ill prepared.

Enter *The Joy of Cooking*—a book written by a woman who, up until her fifties, had had little interest in cooking. Irma S. Rombauer, a new widow, needed to find a way to make a living, and she decided that writing a cookbook would be it. An amateur writing to other amateurs—and imbuing the subject of cooking with an air of excitement and adventure, to boot—Irma Rombauer was to find in *The Joy of Cooking* both a means of support and a consuming interest for the rest of her life.

Somehow, knowing that the author of one of the most exhaustive cookbooks ever written didn't know much about cooking until she was in her fifties makes me feel better. Given enough time and desire, even those of us whose cooking repertoire includes little more than cookies will eventually be able to turn out a decent meal. Our families will survive as we painfully figure out what we are doing, one dinner at a time. (Assuming, of course, that they can last for a while on popcorn and shrimp cocktail.)

Home, after all, wasn't built in a day.

As I walked through the kitchen one recent evening, I was dismayed to see the table I'd cleared less than an hour before was now littered with cups and paper plates—leftovers from the every-man-for-himself pizza we'd had for dinner. Why didn't anyone ever clean up after himself? What was so tough about throwing away a paper plate and sponging off the table, anyway? I grumbled as I cleaned up the latest in the never-ending series of messes.

Kitchen duty done, I sat down with *Pioneer Women* by Joanna L. Stratton.[2] I read of the women who hauled their family's cooking and drinking water from springs that were up to a mile away. I read of women who had to make meals for their families almost entirely from foods they could produce themselves (think cornbread, corn grits, corn mush, corn pudding). I read of women whose laundry chores began with making soap (technically, it began with collecting the right wood to make the fires to produce the right ashes from which to make the soap).[3]

Homemaking has always involved hard work. And in previous generations, it was very, very hard work. According to *Perfection Salad: Women and Cooking at the Turn of the Century* by Laura Shapiro, women in the eighteenth century were responsible for producing "nearly everything their families consumed. . . . The wife, with her daughters and the other women of the house, took charge of spinning, weaving and sewing, making the family's clothing, linens, and quilts. She gardened and perhaps did some back-yard butchering, made soap and candles, preserved the fruits and vegetables, salted and pickled the meat, churned butter, and baked enormous quantities of bread, pie, and cake."[5]

In the next century, life for the homemaker didn't get any easier. "During much of the nineteenth century,"

FUN FACT

In the 1860s, the European immigrants who pioneered the American West "experienced culture shock when they discovered how they would need to bake bread. Scandinavians, Germans, and Czechs were used to an abundance of wood to fire stone or brick-lined ovens. Not only did they have to learn the peculiarities of the more elaborate cook stove, they also had to learn to cook with corncobs or dried manure as fuel."[4]

writes Maxine L. Margolis in *Mothers and Such*, "washing clothes involved chopping wood to heat the water that was drawn by hand. . . . Laundry day was so named because doing the family wash did take an entire day."[6]

Before cooking in days of old, "Someone must pluck, cleanly disembowel, and behead poultry; scale and gut fish; rinse or scrub vegetables (which commonly arrive with the dirt of the garden and perhaps a few snails still clinging to them); . . . boil the hard loaf sugar to clarify it of scummy impurities and often insects; . . . shell every nut."[7]

I thought again of my grumbling at having to clean up after a dinner I hadn't made or even bought (my husband had picked up the pizza on his way home from work). My entire contribution had been clearing off the table and, later, clearing it again. I felt more than a little sheepish.

I'm glad on hectic days I can buy premade food. Sometimes I need perspective on how good I have it, living in the time and place that I do. We have our own unique pressures today, to be sure—like carpooling from sunup to sundown (and later)—but they're not the backbreaking seven days a week of hard labor faced by homemakers of the past.

As the pillow on my bed says, I am the "Princess of Quite A Lot." I need to remember that.

In the mountain community where we live, the power generally goes out a few times a year, sometimes for a couple of days at a time.

It's kind of fun on these sporadic occasions to live without electricity for a while. No TV or computer means my husband and my sons and I leave our separate stations and seek one another's company, all in the same room at the same time (oh my!). We might play a board game or read books by flickering flashlight. The kids do algebra by candlelight, gathered around the kitchen table with a motley assortment of half-burned turkey candles from last Thanksgiving and stubs of almost-finished votives clustered on aluminum foil for added brightness. No heat means we head for the wood-burning stove in the living room, where we sit close for warmth, mesmerized by the flames.

I wouldn't want to live without my conveniences for long, but I've got to admit, the temporary break from automation always comes as a welcome lull. I'm unable to run the washing machine, dishwasher, or vacuum; the evening immediately becomes simpler and quieter, as our options diminish and darkness becomes the impetus to actually climb into bed.

"We are told that 'There is no great loss without some small gain,'" says Laura Ingalls Wilder in the book *Little House in the Ozarks: The Rediscovered Writings*. "Even so, I think that there is no great gain without a little loss. We do not carry water from the spring anymore, which is a very great gain, but it was sometimes pleasant to loiter by the way and that we miss a little."[8]

Maybe I shouldn't wait for a serendipitous power outage to bring my family a quiet island of peace. Maybe I should just gather up the candles and firewood some evening and pull the plug myself. We can enjoy an old-time weenie roast in the fireplace and listen to the peaceful quiet of a house that's gone to bed and is urging its human inhabitants to follow suit. ♛

"Every good thing given and every perfect gift is from above, coming down from the Father of lights, with whom there is no variation or shifting shadow." (James 1:17)

Quotable

How few cooks, unassisted, are competent to the simple process of broiling a beef-steak or mutton-chop! [9]

Catharine E. Beecher and Harriet Beecher Stowe,
American Woman's Home

prayer

LORD GOD, I AM SO THANKFUL FOR ALL THE MANY GIFTS YOU HAVE BESTOWED UPON ME AND MY FAMILY. YOU HAVE PROVIDED FOR OUR EVERY NEED. THANK YOU THAT ALL THAT WE HAVE THAT'S GOOD COMES FROM YOU.

week 44

Planning Ahead for a More-Relaxed Christmas

Right around December 15 the first year I was married, I was horrified to realize I was the one in charge of "making Christmas happen"—a Christmas, incidentally, that now included brothers- and sisters-in-law, nieces and nephews, aunts-, uncles-, mothers-, fathers-, grandmothers-, and grandfathers-in-law. I was completely overwhelmed.

My husband, however, had discovered to his happy surprise that his Christmas responsibilities had all but disappeared.

He was not so happily surprised, though, when December 24 rolled around and he saw me still lurching for boxes and mailing tape, making hopeless last-ditch runs to the post office to mail packages that wouldn't arrive till after the New Year. Things were not going well.

This being my first year in charge, and with two fairly large families between us, I'd had no idea the enormous amount of planning that goes into choosing presents for scores of people, wrapping them, and getting them to their scattered destinations on time. On top of that, my groom and I had naively decided to make most of our gifts. What were we thinking?!

Since then, things have changed. As our families have grown, we have simplified, now drawing names for gift

new word

for the week:

Tchotchke (chäch′ kə).
An inexpensive souvenir or trinket. As in, *"Let me know, kids, if you see any **tchotchkes** in this catalog you think your teachers might like for Christmas."*

alternate

new word:

Gewgaw (gyo͞o′ gô).
Something gaudy and useless; a decorative bauble. As in, *"But let's try and make it something useful, not just some **gewgaw."***

exchanges with brothers and sisters, nieces and nephews. We still like to make gifts at Christmastime, but we now aim for a more reasonable number and set our sights on simpler projects.

I start thinking about gift shopping early now too—maybe compulsively early—and aim to end early. I know I cannot wait until December. The overseas gifts alone need to be bought, wrapped, packed, and mailed by mid-November just to make sure they arrive by Christmas. And knowing we'll see some families at Thanksgiving whom we may not see at Christmas prompts me to get those presents ready early to save post-office trauma later.

So while it may seem strange to start focusing on Christmas when it's only October, I've learned by experience it is not, by a long shot, too early for me. As the Chinese proverb says, "Prepare your silken coat before it rains, and don't wait until you are thirsty to dig a well."[1]

And don't wait until December to start your Christmas shopping either.

Q u o t a b l e

The Christmas spirit seems far away when we are caught in a last-minute rush, with its traffic jams and aching feet and that awful moment when we discover, late at night, that we still have six presents to wrap and no more Scotch tape anywhere in the house.

A few well-organized people avoid all this by planning ahead, but most of us are caught, year after year. But then as we tie a red bow around the jar of spicy cranberry relish that was simmered in our own kitchen last fall, we suddenly imagine the smile that will light the face of the receiver . . . and somehow, we begin to feel in a Christmas mood after all. And when we open the

cont. ⇨

My organized friend Cat swears she needs to complete her Christmas shopping by the end of October if she's to have any hope of focusing on the holiday's real meaning come December.

I've never been able to duplicate her impressive feat (though there was that one August when I sat on a grassy hill selecting Christmas gifts from catalogs while my children splashed happily through the local water slides). Most years, come December I'm still shopping for at least a few gifts. But in the same spirit as my friend, I do try to finish most of my Christmas shopping as early as I can, knowing it will ease the December craziness and give me that much more time later to focus on cheery details like snuggling on the couch reading Christmas picture books.

When those first catalogs bursting with personalized ornaments start crowding my mailbox, I begin to fold back pages and make notes on who I think would like what. I make a long list of people I'd like to give presents to, trying to remember teachers and friends I often forget to thank the rest of the year. I star the names of overseas family members, knowing gifts for them must be sent earliest (by November 11, according to the post office, for packages to reach my sister's family in Norway by ship in time for Christmas). I mark the names of other gift recipients across the country, as well as those I'll be able to deliver to in person at Thanksgiving. These are my top priority.

Just where the gifts are going is important, a fact I didn't fully appreciate until the year I bought ceramic coffee mugs to send to relatives across the country. Upon realizing I had neither the proper packaging nor the confidence I could do the job without turning the mugs into raw material for mosaics, I turned to a storefront shop that packages and mails for you. In a flash of brilliance, I didn't think to ask the price. I've never made that wallet-shocking mistake again. Now as I shop for far-off relatives, I think lightweight: tapes, CDs, books, and calendars, which can ship in padded envelopes rather than boxes scrounged from shopping-mall dumpsters. I also give extra consideration to mail-order companies that can ship directly to the recipient.

I know that no matter how prepared I try to be, life in a few weeks will still be hectic. I will still lunge for last-minute purchases in the checkout lanes, fearing that my homemade felt ornament isn't gift enough and must be supplemented with the nifty rolling-ball massager. But by finishing as much of my shopping ahead as I can, I'm guaranteed at least a little more time in December for banging out off-key Christmas carols on the piano, making hokey clay ornaments at the kitchen table, and partaking of special Christmas programs at church where little cherubs in lamb costumes nudge the furry ears out of their eyes and I wistfully remember those not-so-long-ago Christmases when the little lamb onstage was mine.

Gift-giving tips:

◇ Some of the most memorable gifts are homemade. Start now if there are hats to crochet, candles to mold, Christmas pillowcases to stitch.

◇ Don't forget about food gifts as possibilities (try chocolate butter, CHOCOLATE BREAK after week 30). Experiment soon; if a recipe flops, you'll have time for plan B.

◇ Make a gift budget along with your list of recipients. Can you get by with perhaps ten dollars per gift? Run the plan by your husband so you'll be in agreement before you shop.

◇ Photos of friends or family make great presents. Take pictures now, get them reprinted or enlarged, and start looking for frames.

◇ Buy a few generic gifts to have on hand (a coffee mug, scented candle, box of chocolates). Later, when you realize you've overlooked your son's soccer coach, you'll be ready.

◇ For next year: Pam Young and Peggy Jones, authors of *The Sidetracked Sisters' Happiness File*, among other books, recommend buying two gifts when you shop for birthdays during the year. Save one for Christmas and you've got a head start.

With all the upcoming Christmas plays, parties, and programs, a family could easily find itself committed to attending holiday hoo-hahs every single night in December. But whose idea of a great Christmas is that? Saying yes to every invitation, filling every square on the calendar, is a sure road to siphoning off the joy and peace of the Christmas season.

The only way I've found to avoid the December frenzy is to give the schedule some deliberate thought now. By having a plan ahead of time, when the invitations come later it's easier to decide which to accept and which to decline.

If we're hoping for a calmer, more peace-filled Christmas, the first thing to ask is what we want this year's holiday to look like. Here are some questions to start with, from *Great Christmas Ideas: Hundreds of Ways to Bring Christ Back into Christmas and Discover New Joy in the Holidays*, by Alice Chapin:

◇ Do I want to spend lots of time at home in family fun activities?

◇ Do I want to be creative in making and giving gifts that cost less or nothing at all?

◇ Do I want to slow down and avoid December pressure by doing other activities ahead? Which ones?

◇ Do I want to entertain in my home?

◇ Do I want to experience the peace of Christmas? How?

◇ Do I want to do more for others, to give more of my time and talent?

◇ Do I want to send Christmas cards?

◇ Do I want to do a great job of decorating my house?

◇ Do I want to get through December without gaining weight?[3]

Our ideal holiday should include activities we really want to do, not just those we've always done. If you don't look forward to attending the annual company Christmas party or making a fancy Christmas dinner, who says you have to?

List whatever activities sound like they'd bring you joy, even if you're not sure you'll have time for them: driving around the neighborhood to see Christmas lights, bringing homemade cookies to friends, attending a local church's Nativity production, seeing the *Nutcracker* ballet. Ask each family member to do the same. What would they love to do this Christmas? What means Christmas to them? Their answers may surprise you.

My husband's list was incredibly short (making gifts in the garage with the kids, getting a tree, and sending Christmas cards); one of my sons listed ice-skating (something we rarely do) and receiving lemon drops in his Christmas stocking (something I didn't realize we did—my mom must sneak them in). By checking your family's lists, you may find yourself free of certain activities you'd thought were "musts." That heirloom plum pudding you make every year may be cherished by absolutely nobody. Including you.

"X" off calendar squares for those activities that survived the pruning—an afternoon for Christmas baking, for example, or the Saturday when you'll choose your tree. And leave lots of blank squares. You can even write, "Stay Home" to keep you from overscheduling.

Christmas card strategies:

◇ If you're sending Christmas cards, buy them early so you can start addressing. Don't let the quest for the perfect card keep you from buying any.

- ❖ Order Christmas return-address labels if you need them.
- ❖ Pick a day in October or November and write on your calendar, "Start addressing Christmas cards." (I shoot for the World Series in October.) Bring cards and addresses in the car and work as you wait for kids to be done with music or sports practice. Kathy Troccoli's CD *A Sentimental Christmas* (Reunion Records) is good company.
- ❖ If you're addressed by Thanksgiving, reward yourself with a scented candle or some holiday stickers.
- ❖ Buy Christmas stamps, available mid- to late October.
- ❖ Assign your husband the cards for people he has the biggest connection to. My husband may simply sign "The Walkers" rather than give a play-by-play of the year, but he gets more cards finished in ten minutes than I do in three evenings. So hand a few over to the big guy and watch him fly.
- ❖ Don't make yourself crazy with perfectionism. Your yearly effort may lack the charm of the homemade cards of your dreams, but that's OK. You can opt to print mailing labels on your computer; you can photocopy a newsletter or a family pictures page, eliminating time-consuming personal notes. Do what you can at this stage in your life; relax; your best is good enough.
- ❖ If you're having a tough year, put the cards away and try again next year. Cross that puppy off your list.

Check your closet for any holiday party clothes you may need. Far better to shop for black heels now than to panic the afternoon of the big company shindig. ♛

"And the Word became flesh, and dwelt among us, and we saw His glory, glory as of the only begotten from the Father, full of grace and truth." (John 1:14)

prayer FATHER, THANK YOU THAT YOU CARE SO DEEPLY FOR EACH OF US THAT YOU SENT YOUR SON, JESUS CHRIST, TO DIE TO PAY FOR OUR SINS. HELP ME TO COMMUNICATE YOUR LOVE THROUGH THE CHRISTMAS CARDS I SEND. HELP THOSE I LOVE TO ACCEPT THE INCREDIBLE GIFT YOU'VE GIVEN US IN CHRIST.

CHOCOLATE BREAK!

PECAN FUDGE PIE

This is a wonderful recipe from my aunt Li (pronounced "lie"). Li has been known at holidays to swear that she would eat highly salted, sodium-packed Virginia ham "if it kills me," so you know that when it comes to food, she is serious.

This fudgy pie is simple to make. It's a great addition to a Thanksgiving dessert table, but it'd be a shame to serve it only once a year.

PECAN FUDGE PIE

Remove from freezer:

1 unbaked pie shell

Set aside. Melt:

2 squares unsweetened chocolate

1 stick butter

1 ¼ cups sugar

on medium-low heat, stirring constantly. Still stirring, add:

2 eggs

¼ cup milk

1 t. vanilla

½ t. instant coffee granules

½ cup chopped pecans (optional, if your cherubs hate nuts)

Cook only until ingredients are well blended. Remove from heat. Prick pie crust all over with fork. Pour chocolate mixture into crust. Place:

8 whole pecans on top in center, fanning out like a star. Bake at 350 degrees for 35 minutes. Serves eight.

week 45

Keeping Christ in Christmas

"How do you celebrate Christmas?" asks James Montgomery Boice in *The Christ of Christmas*. "If we are honest, we must admit that many persons, even Christians, celebrate it most by watching football games on television, decorating their houses, visiting relatives and friends, or buying presents."[1]

Decorating and presents are certainly part of my celebration, but I don't want them to take over, squeezing Christ right out of Christmas. I will have enough time to meditate on Jesus and His coming if I begin early, before the season creeps up on me like a stealthy teenager ready to pounce from a darkened laundry room with a heart-stopping "BOO!" These weeks really are a time of preparing our hearts, getting them soft and ready, like soaking raisins before throwing them into muffin batter.

The year my women's Bible study group studied the book of Luke led up to one of my most meaningful Christmases ever. We'd spent the fall months immersed in Jesus' life. We had experienced our Savior's birth and were making the inevitable march with Him toward crucifixion. By the time December came, we were somewhere around chapter 10; and while we knew the end of the story, our months of study had made us entranced by the Man whose story it was.

I've often thought a fine Advent tradition would be to read a chapter of Luke each day of December, ending with the last chapter, chapter 24, on Christmas Eve. The whole family could gather around the Christmas tree, maybe right before bed, and hear more about our wonderful Savior. "For the Mighty One has done great things for me; and holy is His name" (Luke 1:49).

Alice Chapin, in her wonderful book, *Great Christmas Ideas: Hundreds of Ways to Bring Christ Back into Christmas and Discover New Joy in the Holidays,* has this to say:

> Christmas ought to be very, very merry. But when we celebrate lightly, without reflecting much of the deeper meaning of the season, we are cheating both ourselves and others. Each Yule season brings new opportunities for spiritual renewal and for passing on precious parts of our faith to new generations. For their sakes, and for Jesus' sake, we dare not allow Christmas to become distorted until it is little more than a time of empty festivities. . . . We must not confuse celebration with entertainment. We must learn creative ways to tell often the Good News about God in our midst during the Yule season. Then Christmas will take on new meaning and bring personal fulfillment for everyone involved.[3]

The weeks leading up to Christmas can be a special time of drawing close to God. Here are a few suggestions:

◇ Purchase an Advent calendar, with a little flap to open each day of December until Christmas Day. Look for a calendar that depicts the Nativity scene with Scripture readings behind each window.

◇ Read about Mary and Martha (Luke 10:38–42), a perfect

story for this time of year when our preoccupation with to-do lists can crowd out time with God. In the story, Jesus reprimands Martha for being "distracted with all her preparations." Martha's sister, Mary, meanwhile, is commended for choosing "the good part," which was listening at His feet. (For more on Mary and Martha, see week 7.) Like Mary, I want to choose the good part this Christmas, even if it means some cards I'd like to send will have to wait.

◇ Consider how your Christmas tree decorations can point to Christ. In *Celebrating the Christian Year*, Martha Zimmerman suggests that the first ornament you place on the tree be an apple, to remind you of Adam and Eve's sin, which made it necessary for Jesus to come in the first place. Lights on the tree signify Christ, the Light who comes into a dark world. "Select symbols that tell the Christmas story and are reminders of Christ's life," says Zimmerman, "such as angels, bells, candy canes, lambs, hearts, doves, and candles. Top off the tree with a star. Read Matthew 2:2, 'Where is the baby born to be the king of the Jews? We saw his star when it came up in the east, and we have come to worship him' (TEV)."[5]

◇ Play Christmas carols that tell the story of Christ, paying special attention to the words.

Another great way to prepare for Christmas is to purchase an Advent wreath, a tabletop wreath with four candle holders spaced around it and room for a fifth candle to be placed in the center. (The word *advent*, by the way, comes from Latin words meaning "to come.") Starting on the fourth Sunday before Christmas, which falls somewhere around November 30, light one of the candles (purple, to signify royalty) and hold a short family worship service with Scripture reading, singing, and praying.

"Before lighting the first Advent candle, turn out all the lights in the house and see how dark it really is!" suggests Martha Zimmerman in her book *Celebrating the Christian Year*.

"This experience of physical darkness reminds us of that time before Christ, when humanity was sitting 'in darkness and the shadow of death . . .' (Luke 1:79, NASB)."[6]

The following Sunday, light the first and second candles. Again, use purple to represent royalty and, again, read Scripture, sing, and pray as a family. Keep going for four Sundays; the fifth and final candle, the center one, is lit along with the others on Christmas Eve or Christmas Day. White to symbolize purity, this last candle represents the coming of Jesus, the Light of the world.

A number of books give detailed guidance on Advent ceremonies, complete with suggestions for scriptures and songs. But there's no reason your family can't devise your own ceremony, using songs and scriptures about Christ that are most meaningful to you. (For starters, see Isaiah 7:10–14; 9:6; 11:1–2; 40:9–11; Micah 5:2–5; Malachi 3:1; Matthew 1:18–25; Luke 1:26–35; 2:1–20; John 1:14; and Philippians 2:5–11.)

Don't stress over the need to "do Advent" perfectly. One of Satan's favorite tricks is to whisper, "You blew it! You failed! You might as well give up!" Even if you skip a Sunday or two because life got hectic or you just forgot, start wherever you are. Less-than-perfect efforts still bring us closer to God.

> ## Quotable
>
> *No longer need we pray, Come. He has come. He is here.*[7]
>
> **Walter Wangerin Jr.,**
> *Preparing for Jesus*

This time of year brings so many opportunities to serve with so many different organizations that many Decembers I'm caught off guard with requests from all directions. Truth be told, I get a little resentful that so many people with good intentions wait until mid-December to announce their projects, many with deadlines like "*no later than Friday morning!*"

"Why did you wait until now?" my inner Scrooge complains. "Where were you back when squeezing an extra shopping trip into my schedule wouldn't have hurt like a pinched shoe?" My response is ungracious and miserly, I know. (What would Jesus do? Probably not grumble and complain.) But it's how I feel.

As I have recognized my tendency toward late-hour holiday resentment, I've tried to remember to pray occasionally during autumn about how our family can participate in the coming gift drives and service opportunities. I've been astounded at God's graciousness in answering my meager prayers.

When I precede the Christmas season by asking God where and how our family should serve, my attitude is transformed. No longer the stressed-out Scrooge, one recent mid-December I responded with true excitement to the lady soliciting gifts for Angel Tree's Prison Ministry. "This is an answer to prayer!" She looked at me, clearly puzzled as I tried to explain that I'd been asking God to steer our family to just the right opportunity.

I know I am selfish with my time, especially when I'm already feeling overcommitted. But when I've prayed ahead of time just a few simple prayers for guidance, God graciously gives me a new heart, one that is willing to serve in a way that, believe me, does not come from me. As author Walter Wangerin Jr. so eloquently put it in his book *Preparing for Jesus: Meditations on the Coming of Christ, Advent, Christmas, and the Kingdom*:

> So when peace comes into me, though I had been desperately restless and afraid; and when I, who am weak, act with surprising strength; and when faith arises in my hopeless soul; and when I, whose heart was filled with hatreds, suddenly find forgiveness there; . . . and when what I am is what I ought to be—when*ever* the impossible gift arrives for me, it is God. . . . It is his mercy so great, that those around me (my neighbors and relatives) are astonished to find me in such a blessed condition after all. [8]

If you commonly find yourself with the mid-December grumbles, start praying now for "your" family—the needy one He's going to show you. You might even want to buy and wrap gifts before you've learned of specific needs, asking God to direct you in your purchases. When your opportunity arises, you'll know it. You'll be able to say with confidence, "This is an answer to prayer!"

If you've never asked God into your life, to forgive you of your sins and make you His child, you can do it right now. It doesn't take special, fancy words. All it takes is a humble heart that's willing to admit that you miss the mark, that you are not perfect, that you are a sinner. You recognize that He is holy, that you cannot live up to His standard of holiness, and that you need Him. You recognize that He sent His Son, Jesus Christ, to take the punishment that should have been yours, for your sin. And you want His forgiveness. You want Him to be in charge of your life from now on. You accept the gift of eternal life He offers you through Jesus Christ. That's it. It's as simple as that.

"But seek first His kingdom and His righteousness, and all these things will be added to you." (Matthew 6:33)

prayer LORD, THANK YOU FOR COMING. THANK YOU FOR YOUR INDESCRIBABLE LOVE, WHICH, AS A SINNER, I SO CLEARLY DO NOT DESERVE, BUT WHICH YOU HAVE LAVISHLY BESTOWED ON ME ANYWAY. HELP ME TO TAKE THE TIME THIS CHRISTMAS TO SIT AT YOUR FEET, IN WONDER AND WORSHIP.

week 46

Company's Coming! Hospitality

"I appreciate this group so much and look forward to it all week," says one fellow who's been coming to our house for several years for a weekly men's Bible study.

A mixture of feelings comes over me when I hear this. I'm often overwhelmed on school-day afternoons with picking up kids, getting them snacks, bringing them to sports practice, rushing home to feed them, helping them with homework, then realizing the house is a mess and the men are coming in five minutes. There are many times, to be honest, I wish they weren't coming. I am embarrassed, often, that my house isn't vacuumed or even picked up. Laundry and paper piles abound.

Although I recognize my home is as neat as I can make it, given my family's current stage and kid-oriented priorities, it is still uncomfortable to welcome people when the house isn't party ready. It's uncomfortable letting them walk by homework projects that have taken over entire rooms, unfolded clothes, dinnertime chaos. Opening my home when it doesn't look so hot is hard—like appearing in public in a bathing suit, flaws exposed.

I've been surprised over the years by visitors' reactions when they're brought in amid the chaos. They've run the gamut, from "Boy, your house is messy!" (from a five-year-old who was deeply troubled by dog hair on the carpet and the piles of clean, folded clothes stacked by my son's bedroom door), to "Wow, I don't know how you keep your house looking so nice" (from a dad with five children under the age of ten and a homeschooling wife). One man with grown kids makes a beeline for my sons every time he visits, no matter what room they're in or what messes they're amid; no doubt the hum of activity brings back happy memories of his own family in younger years.

Though I dread any critical comments, spoken or only imagined, I believe most people really are fine with walking into a home that's obviously lived in. Good, they think (or at least I think they think), we're not the only ones with clutter.

As Doris W. Greig points out in her book *We Didn't Know They Were Angels: Discovering the Gift of Christian Hospitality,* "We are called to be hospitable in Christ's strength, by His power and not by our own. As we give ourselves to God, we discover that He gives back to us a wonderful present of . . . the ability to demonstrate Christ's love to those He sends our way."[1]

If we let Him, God can change our imperfect attitudes and use our imperfect homes to bring a blessing to others. Somehow, I think that's more important than whether the carpet is free of dog hair.

At least I hope so.

I remember well the company dinners I used to attempt when I was first married. From the stuffed acorn squash to the homemade Cracker Jacks®, my strenuous efforts included complicated recipe after complicated recipe. I didn't have time to sit and chat with my guests; I was too busy fretting at the oven over the fresh peach cobbler that refused to puff (I had no idea you couldn't substitute regular flour for

Quotable

Well, now. I probably shouldn't have curdling milk in the fridge if I'm inviting someone over for tea, and it might be nice if I emptied the kitchen trash can and didn't leave dirty clothes all over the bathroom floor. But to be a hostess, I'm going to have to surrender my notions of Good Housekeeping *domestic perfection. I will have to set down my pride and invite people over even if I have not dusted. This is tough: My mother set a high standard. Her house is always immaculate, most especially if she's expecting company. But if I wait for immaculate, I will never have a guest.*[2]

Lauren F. Winner,
Mudhouse Sabbath

"self-rising"). Though on that particular occasion dessert was salvaged by rechristening it "Peach Goo" and serving it over ice cream, I'm certain those early attempts at hospitality would have been more rewarding, for me and my guests, had I scaled down my culinary efforts.

According to Karen Mains, author of *Open Heart, Open Home*, when we're stressed at inviting others to our home, pride may be at the root. "A good barometer to measure whether pride is rising in me is to ask two questions: Am I nervous? Am I fussing? . . . Am I afraid the new recipe will flop or that someone might wander into an unclean room and people will think less of me? . . . If I find myself fussing too much about spots on glasses, getting upset because I have to clean the bathroom sink *again*, going wild because someone has walked on the freshly vacuumed carpet—what does it mean? Who is coming that I am trying to impress with all these efforts?"[3]

Mains says that as she's matured, she's learned a lot about letting go—"letting go of props that bolster one's ego, letting go of ploys and gambits that vault us in the eyes of other people, letting go of many of the material means that become so important in our eyes. How lovely to be able finally to laugh at our disasters!"[4]

I like to reflect on her conclusions, especially when I'm expecting company for Thanksgiving or Christmas. Hospitality is not about trying to impress or competing to see who's the best housekeeper or the best cook. It's simply about opening the home God has given us, grand or humble, and welcoming others in.

As Thanksgiving approaches and I begin to drool over recipes for vegetable-herb purees and homemade cranberry cheesecakes, I need to remember that I can make these some other time. For now, I am better off spending my energy praying that I would have a good attitude and a calm spirit that focuses not on myself but on my guests.

One of the best examples of hospitality I've ever heard was of an elderly lady who opened her home to a couple of teenage girls traveling on a high school choir trip. Miriam Huffman Rockness, one of those girls, recalls the story in *Home, God's Design: Celebrating a Sense of Place:*

> Carefully instructed by our leaders that "service" did not end with the concert but extended into the homes that hosted us, my roommate and I were nonetheless taken aback by the shabby and crowded dwelling to which we were assigned one night. Even the warmth of the hot chocolate served by our elderly hostess could not remove the chill of the Canadian evening from this unheated apartment. . . .
>
> With relief we sank at last into the double bed that filled the tiny room separated from the kitchen by only a curtain. I lay in bed listening to our hostess wash the cups and saucers, straighten the chairs around the table. Finally the lights were switched off. The only sound was the ticking of a clock. Slipping out of bed to visit the bathroom, I groped my way into the kitchen and stumbled into a large object. I adjusted my focus to the moonlit room. Sound asleep in a straight chair was our hostess, a blanket wrapped around her street clothes! Totally absorbed in the discomfort of our "unlucky draw," it hadn't occurred to me to wonder where *she* was sleeping. "Jean," I whispered, returning to our room, "we have *her* room. She's sitting up all night!"
>
> Early the next morning we woke to the wonderful aromas of sizzling bacon and English muffins toasting on an oven rack. Two humbled girls sat at the kitchen table trying now to give of our-

selves in some small way to one who had given us her rare gift—all that she had.[7]

It's easy for me to find excuses not to be hospitable. Hospitality costs me something. It takes effort, sometimes more energy than I feel I have to give. But God will bless those efforts when I'm obedient.

I love the story in 1 Kings 17, where a widow in the midst of a drought, down to her last bit of oil and flour, reluctantly opens her home to a hungry houseguest. "I can't feed you," she tells Elijah at first. "In fact, my son and I are about to eat the last of our own food, and then we're ready to die."

"Don't be afraid," Elijah answers. "God says your bowl of flour and jar of oil won't ever be empty until we have rain again."

The widow did as Elijah directed, making him a bread cake and then making one for herself and her son. And "the bowl of flour was not exhausted nor did the jar of oil become empty, according to the word of the LORD which He spoke through Elijah" (1 Kings 17:16).

How often have I missed out on blessings God had planned for me when I refused to open my home or my life to others? Even a tentative yes, God blesses. ♛

Quotable

Remember hospitality comes in many forms.

Sometimes hospitality means weeping with a friend or a neighbor, or staying up extra late just to listen to the story of the pain in someone's life. It may be watching the neighbor's children when their mother is ill, or taking food to the home of a new neighbor. . . . We need to pray, "God, please make me willing to see, and then grasp, the opportunities you send my way."[8]

Doris W. Greig,
We Didn't Know They Were Angels

Some verses on hospitality:
◊ Romans 12:10–13
◊ Matthew 25:35–40
◊ 1 Peter 4:9–10

"Do not forget to entertain strangers, for by so doing some people have entertained angels without knowing it." (Hebrews 13:2 NIV)

prayer THANK YOU, LORD, FOR THE OPPORTUNI-
TIES YOU GIVE ME TO LOVE AND SERVE OTHERS. HELP ME TO BE WILLING
TO ANSWER "YES!" WHEN YOU ASK ME TO SHOW HOSPITALITY, AND RE-
PLACE MY GRUMBLING ATTITUDE WITH A CHEERFUL HEART. STRENGTH-
EN ME TO DO WHAT YOU ASK.

Quotable

*Host– and hostessing, as
we know, is often a heroic
endeavor, requiring daring,
ingenuity, a desire to take
chances and a concern for
others. These traits are
also called for in saints and
Nobel Prize winners.*[9]

Laurie Colwin,
Home Cooking

Quotable

*To invite people into our
homes is to respond with
gratitude to the God who
made a home for us.*[10]

Lauren F. Winner,
Mudhouse Sabbath

week 47

Cozen (kŭz′ən).

To deceive, by means of a petty trick or fraud. As in, *"I am tempted to cozen my guests into believing I made homemade gravy when I actually just opened a can."*

alternate

new word

Sapor (sā′ pər).

A quality perceptible to the sense of taste; flavor. As in, *"Don't you just love the sapor of homemade gravy?"*

Thanksgiving, Part 1

Well-known chef Julia Child and coauthors Louisette Bertholle and Simone Beck, in their book *Mastering the Art of French Cooking, Volume One*, have this to say: "If you are not an old campaigner, do not plan more than one long or complicated recipe for a meal or you will wear yourself out and derive no pleasure from your efforts."[1]

They were talking about cooking in general, but their words seem especially appropriate this time of year, when we may anticipate hosting a big holiday meal such as Thanksgiving dinner.

This year as I begin thinking about the Thanksgiving meal I will orchestrate in just another week, I am grateful for rolls that can be store bought and for stuffing mixes. I am grateful for my friend Pam's make-ahead mashed potato and gravy recipes. I am grateful for a cousin who is bringing yams and for a mother-in-law who cheerfully pitches in wherever needed. I am grateful for frozen vegetables.

I probably won't be winning any best of show in the assorted pies Thanksgiving competition, but that's just the point. Thanksgiving isn't a competition. It's a time to gather with family we love and give thanks to our Father, who is the giver of all good gifts. A Father who loves me no matter what—even if I use store-bought piecrust.

To me, the most nerve-wracking part of cooking Thanksgiving dinner—aside from the whole vacuuming thing—is preparing those last-minute dishes. Now, thanks to my friend Pam, who gave me these potato and gravy recipes, I no longer have any last-minute dishes.

This can be made a week ahead and frozen, then later thawed and baked; or, make one or two days ahead and refrigerate until time to bake.

MAKE-AHEAD MASHED POTATOES

Peel and cut into chunks:

5 pounds potatoes

Place in large pot, cover with water, and boil, until easily pierced with fork (about thirty minutes). Drain, then mash potatoes in the hot pan, together with:

1 stick butter

8 oz. cream cheese

1 cup milk

½ t. salt

Place mixture in casserole dish. Cover with plastic wrap and refrigerate overnight (or freeze, if desired). Bake at 350 degrees for thirty minutes. Before serving, sprinkle with **½ t. fresh, chopped chives**, if desired. Serves eight to ten.

If the pressure to produce greaseless, lumpless gravy with eighteen pairs of eyes watching brings back that same panic you felt when first testing for your driver's license, try this recipe, which you can make and freeze up to three months ahead. You'll never have to face gravy stress syndrome again.

This takes several hours to cook, then more time to refrigerate (to allow fat to congeal), so a Friday evening, Saturday morning cooking timetable works well. On Thanksgiving morning, remove from freezer and refrigerate; when close to dinnertime, heat in large pan. At that point, you can add turkey drippings if you want (or not).

DELICIOUS MAKE-AHEAD GRAVY

Preheat oven to 400 degrees. Get a large roasting pan ready.

Arrange **4 turkey wings** (about 3 pounds) in single layer in pan.

Scatter **2 medium onions,** peeled and quartered over the top.

Roast for 1¼ hours, until wings are brown. Remove wings and onions to a six-quart pot.

Add **1 cup water** to roasting pan and stir to loosen any browned-on bits. Add to pot.

Next, add:

> **6 cups chicken broth** (of 8 cups total; refrigerate the remaining 2 cups)
>
> **¾ cup chopped carrot**
>
> **½ t. dried thyme**

Bring to a boil, then reduce heat and simmer 1 ½ hours, uncovered. Remove wings; you can pick off meat and save for another use, if desired.

Strain the broth into a saucepan, pressing on the vegetables to get as much liquid as possible. Discard the vegetables. Refrigerate broth (overnight is good) so you can skim off the fat more easily. (The fat will congeal to a thin layer on top when chilled; just pitch it in the garbage as it will clog your drain if you put it down the sink.)

Whisk **¾ cup flour** into remaining **2 cups chicken broth**.

Stir until smooth. Bring the broth in the pan to a gentle boil, then stir in flour-broth mixture. Boil five to eight minutes, stirring, to thicken.

Stir in:

> **2 T. butter**
>
> **½ t. pepper**

Refrigerate up to a week, or freeze up to three months. Makes eight cups.

On Thanksgiving Day, once the turkey's cooked, remove turkey from roasting pan, then skim the fat off the pan juices and add juices to the heated gravy, if desired.

(Note: If cooking makes you cry, please, just buy instant mashed potatoes and canned gravy, or order a complete takeout meal from a restaurant or grocery store, as one friend does, then bring it home and serve.)

My friend Karen, whose home is always beautiful, told me by phone how her Thanksgiving plans were progressing.

"I bought a cute cornucopia for the centerpiece. And I have two new sets of pretty dishes I'm going to alternate.

Oh, and I'm painting the downstairs! The walls are taupe, with the trim done in white. It really sets off the woodwork."

"It sounds beautiful," I replied, suddenly realizing that though Thanksgiving was less than a week away, I hadn't thought about a centerpiece and wasn't even sure I owned enough dinner plates. We would be hosting thirteen, and since many of our recent holiday dinners had taken place in my in-laws' or parents' homes, I was out of practice. And also, as I realized later, out of drinking glasses.

After I hung up the phone, I was glad I'd talked with my organized friend who has such a flair for making things beautiful. This year for me there would be no ninth-hour scrounging in the yard for leaves to plop on the table and declare a centerpiece. I spent the morning arranging tables, pulling out tablecloths to see what I had and what needed to be washed and ironed, and playing with arrangements of mini pumpkins and Indian corn I'd bought earlier. I tried some fancy napkin folds I'd be too busy to mess with later in the week. And I made a mental note: shop for cornucopia.

If you're hosting Thanksgiving dinner, take an hour or two today to pull out what you have and do a quick run-through. If you need to borrow chairs or silverware, make the calls now. Polish any silver you'll be using, iron your tablecloths, do what you can ahead of time. You'll be that much more relaxed and ready to focus on your guests when Thanksgiving Day arrives.

Three quick ideas to fancy up your table:

◇ Look for chocolate turkey lollipops that stores such as See's sell this time of year, to place next to each person's silverware.

◇ Hand your kids a packet of photograph "doubles," have them cut out the heads of guests who are coming for Thanksgiving dinner, then glue the heads onto cardboard to make holiday place cards. If they're feeling especially silly (and if family members are silly enough to appreciate it), have them attach the heads to bodies of people and animals cut from old magazines—the wilder, the better.[3]

◇ Try the "water lily" napkin fold, with a gold or silver chocolate candy kiss placed in the center of each person's napkin. (Choose whichever color kiss goes best with your china.)

Take a large, square cloth napkin. Fold each corner into the center so all four corners meet at one point. (You should have a square.) Fold all four corners again to meet in the middle. (You have a smaller square.) Turn napkin over. Fold all four corners to meet in the middle one last time. (You may want to put something in the center to "weight" it for a minute.) Holding the center, pull out each corner from underneath, to make four "petals." From underneath once more, pull four remaining "petals" out and to the front. (These will form smaller petals, in between the larger ones.) Remove whatever you used to weight the napkin, and place candy kiss in center.

Traditional Thanksgiving dinner, in my mind, includes turkey with stuffing, mashed potatoes and gravy, a green vegetable, cranberries, rolls, and pie. But how many of these dishes were really part of the first Thanksgiving?

It's hard to know. According to the historical living history museum Plimoth Plantation, Inc. in Plymouth, Massachusetts, "There is no exact record of the bill of fare of the famous first harvest festival of 1621, often referred to as the 'First Thanksgiving.'" From the two written records that exist of the event (one from William Bradford's book, *Of Plimoth Plantation*, the other from a 1621 letter by Edward Winslow), we do know that deer, cod, sea bass, and wildfowl such as ducks, geese, turkeys, and swans were included in that historic meal. Also included was cornmeal.

If vegetables were included, they would not have been called vegetables, but instead roots, pot herbs, or "sallet herbs." "The herbs were either boiled along with the meats as 'sauce' or used in 'sallets,'" according to Plimoth Plantation's Carolyn Freeman Travers. "A sallet was a vegetable dish either cooked or raw, and either 'simple' or 'compound' (that is, made from one ingredient or several). The popularity of sallet or vegetable dishes was not great at this time. Therefore, they are not always mentioned, although they were served fairly frequently."[4]

Not included at that first harvest would have been apples, pears, and other fruits not native to New England;

sweet corn on the cob (the corn the English colonists and local Native Americans grew was a "flint" variety, good for making cornmeal but not for eating on the cob); potatoes and sweet potatoes, which were not available in early New England; flour-thickened sauces or gravies (in 1621, they used bread crumbs or egg yolks as thickeners); and cranberry jelly or preserves (sugar was too scarce, though the colonists may have used cranberries in stuffings, which were called "puddings in the belly").

Not to be difficult, but I believe I'll leave the deer and the swans for another time. I'm kind of partial to the turkey tradition myself, along with good old unauthentic, flour-thickened gravy. Made ahead, of course.

One more great Thanksgiving recipe. I know, I know, the pilgrims probably didn't have Jell-O® either.

MOM'S SPARKLING JELL-O SALAD

In large bowl, stir together:

2 3-oz. packages sparkling white grape gelatin

1 ½ cups boiling water

Stir until dissolved. Refrigerate fifteen minutes. Gently stir in:

2 cups cold club soda or seltzer water

Refrigerate for thirty minutes, or until slightly thickened. Open and drain:

1 20-oz. can pineapple chunks

Reserve 1 cup pineapple for garnish. Gently stir rest of pineapple into gelatin, along with:

1 11-oz. can Mandarin oranges, drained

½ cup dried cranberries

Spoon into oiled six-cup mold. Cover and refrigerate four or more hours. Unmold and garnish with reserved pineapple. Serves twelve.

A few more Thanksgiving thoughts:

◇ Robb Forman Dew, author of *A Southern Thanksgiving: Recipes and Musings for a Manageable Feast*, suggests serving Thanksgiving dinner at 4 p.m. or later, to give you plenty of time in the morning to get the turkey in the oven. "If you have to get up at the crack of dawn in order to have the meal ready at midday, you'll feel disgruntled and grudging the next day. But if the meal is to be ready between three and four, the turkey doesn't have to go in the oven until eleven, or not until noon if you plan to serve dinner between five and six."[5]

◇ As for cranberry sauce. The kind you buy in a can, whether jellied or whole, is delicious. If you want to make your own, it is super quick and easy; you basically boil, stir, and re-frigerate. Pick up a bag or two in the produce section and follow the cranberry sauce recipe on the package.

◇ If you have holiday cookie cutters (stars, turkeys, etc.), use them to cut fancy shapes from jellied cranberry sauce (the kind that comes in a can) that you've sliced to ¼-inch thickness. Place shapes on turkey platter for an easy, festive garnish. ♥

"Whatever you do in word or deed, do all in the name of the Lord Jesus, giving thanks through Him to God the Father." (Colossians 3:17)

prayer DEAR LORD, HELP ME TO STAY CALM THIS THANKSGIVING, TO NOT TRY TO IMPRESS ANYONE WITH MY WONDERFUL MEAL, BUT TO FOCUS INSTEAD ON THE MANY WAYS YOU HAVE BLESSED US. THANK YOU FOR MY FAMILY. THANK YOU FOR YOUR PROVISIONS. THANK YOU FOR YOUR MERCY AND COMPASSION, WHICH ARE NEVER ENDING. THANK YOU MOST OF ALL FOR JESUS.

week 48

Thanksgiving, Part 2

new word
for the week:

new word
for the week:

Fadge (făj).

To fit, to suit. As in, *"It simply will not fadge for me to get all worked up over producing the perfect gourmet Thanksgiving dinner."*

alternate
new word:

Borborygmus

(bôr′ bə-rĭg′ məs)

Intestinal rumbling caused by moving gas. As in, *"Goodness! Excuse my stomach's borborygmus!"*

One year in an attempt to make Thanksgiving more meaningful, we asked dinner guests to write on a piece of paper what they were most thankful for. Later, sitting around the table, we read the slips aloud. "One more year," read the shaky script of my husband's elderly grandmother.

I've never forgotten that simple praise for the gift of life that, most of the time, I take for granted. It reminds me of the Old Testament character Job, who realized when all his worldly goods were taken away and his ten sons and daughters were tragically killed, "Naked I came from my mother's womb, and naked I shall return there. The Lord gave and the Lord has taken away. Blessed be the name of the Lord" (Job 1:21).

Job had a deep understanding, in a way I do not, that life on earth is fleeting and every day is a gift. Rather than complain about his loss, which was huger than I can imagine, he was simply thankful for the past blessings he had enjoyed and acknowledged God's right to give and to take away. All he could do, says author Ray C. Stedman, "is say 'Thank you' for having had [the gifts] as long as [he] did."[1]

This Thanksgiving, I want to hold Job's humble spirit of thankfulness; to take it out and dwell on it, turn it around, looking intently, examining. God has given us so many blessings. All that we have is from Him.

One more year. Blessed be the name of the Lord.

"For every cup and plateful, God make us truly grateful."[2]

A few ideas to promote thankfulness:

. . . .

◇ Find Bible verses that focus on praise and promises from Jesus. Write the verses on small slips of paper, roll them into tiny scrolls, and insert them into homemade rolls before baking. At Thanksgiving dinner, have each person break into the roll and read his "thankfulness fortune" out loud before the blessing.[3]

◇ Listen to a praise tape or CD at breakfast. *A Classic Thanksgiving: Songs of Praise* is a peaceful, uplifting CD that includes some wonderful hymns and classical pieces.[4]

◇ Take Thanksgiving guests one at a time into another room, ask them what they're thankful for, and tape-record their responses. Play back the tape for everyone between dinner and dessert.[5]

◇ Read aloud a favorite psalm before dinner.

The First Thanksgiving

Though exact numbers vary depending on your source, the "housewives" who cooked for that first three-day Thanksgiving celebration in 1621, feeding at least 140 guests (ninety or so native Wampanoag men and fifty-two English colonists), were probably only four (the rest of the colonists' wives had died), with perhaps some children and others aiding in the food preparation. The women used no cookbooks. Forks were not used for eating, only knives and a few spoons. Hands were used to both serve and to eat; the diners may have sopped themselves dry with huge, three-foot-square napkins.

A lot has changed since that celebration. (It only *feels* like you're feeding 140 people for three days.) But one thing remains the same—the spirit of thankfulness that comes from recognizing the tremendous gifts we've been given by our heavenly Father.

According to Plimoth Plantation, Inc.'s Carolyn Freeman Travers, the English colonists' faith "permeated their daily lives. Undoubtedly, some sort of grace or prayer would have preceded their feasting. A typical 'Thanksgiving before meate' incorporated these themes:

> O Lord our God and heavenly Father, which of Thy unspeakable mercy towards us, hast provided meate and drinke for the nourishment of our weake bodies. Grant us peace to use them reverently, as from Thy hands, with thankful hearts: let Thy blessing rest upon these Thy good creatures, to our comfort and sustentation: and grant we humbly beseech Thee, good Lord, that as we doe hunger and thirst for this food of our bodies, so our soules may earnestly long after the food of eternal life, through Jesus Christ, our Lord and Saviour, Amen."[6]

One year when my husband and I were in charge of the church youth group, we supervised the teenagers as they helped conduct the Thanksgiving week church service, complete with one brave fellow who dressed up like a turkey in front of the congregation and clucked. (It's hard to forget those yellow tights.) The kids called on people to volunteer things they were thankful for, using the letters T-H-A-N-K-S-G-I-V-I-N-G. ("Who can think of something they're thankful for that begins with the letter T?") It was a fun opportunity to take time out for thankfulness amid the feeding frenzy.

It was thankfulness that Abraham Lincoln had in mind when he wrote his Thanksgiving Proclamation in 1863, which said, in part, "The year that is drawing towards its close, has been filled with the blessings of fruitful fields and healthful skies. To these bounties, which are so constantly enjoyed that we are prone to forget the source from which they come, others have been added, which are of so extraordinary a nature, that they cannot fail to penetrate and soften even the heart which is habitually insensible to the ever watchful providence of Almighty God."

Lincoln wrote this in the middle of the Civil War years; his beloved son Willie had died in 1862, just one year before. This great president truly understood suffering. Yet he also understood the need to be humble before God and give thanks for His many blessings. "I do therefore invite my fellow citizens in every part of the United States, and also those who are at sea and those who are sojourning in foreign lands, to set apart and observe the last Thursday of November next, as a day of Thanksgiving and Praise to our beneficent Father who dwelleth in the Heavens."

From then on, the event became an annual celebration for the entire nation.

I am thankful we've elected presidents throughout our history who not only believed in God but honored Him with their words and their lives. I am also thankful for this holiday, which gives us a chance to reconnect with family near and far. As my friend Pam says, "For parents of college kids, it's a really special holiday because it's usually their first time home." So I guess you could say that what I'm thankful for that begins with the letter T is . . . Thanksgiving.

On Being Thankful

I LOVE THE MESS TO CLEAN AFTER A PARTY BECAUSE IT MEANS I HAVE BEEN SURROUNDED BY FRIENDS.

I LOVE THE TAXES I PAY BECAUSE IT MEANS THAT I'M EMPLOYED.

I LOVE THE CLOTHES THAT FIT A LITTLE TOO SNUG BECAUSE IT MEANS I HAVE ENOUGH TO EAT.

I LOVE A LAWN THAT NEEDS MOWING, WINDOWS THAT NEED CLEANING AND GUTTERS THAT NEED FIXING BECAUSE IT MEANS I HAVE A HOME.

I LOVE ALL THE COM-PLAINING I HEAR ABOUT OUR GOVERNMENT BE-CAUSE IT MEANS WE HAVE FREEDOM OF SPEECH.

I LOVE THE SPOT I FIND AT THE FAR END OF THE PARKING LOT BECAUSE IT MEANS I AM CAPABLE OF WALKING.

cont. ➡

The dinner guests may be gone, but that doesn't mean the leftovers are—unless, of course, you've thought ahead and done what author Robb Forman Dew does: dispensed with the overabundance by stocking up on disposable aluminum cake pans and sending your guests home with mini-meals they can enjoy the next day, keeping just enough food for "one lazy day of snacking on leftovers" for whoever's at your house."[7]

Some years our day-after meals have been turkey soup and turkey sandwiches. Other years, it's turkey sloppy joes and turkey burritos. One nifty creation is **turkey pie**, with a crust of leftover stuffing smushed into a greased pie pan and baked at 350 degrees for fifteen minutes, and for the filling, ½ cup grated cheese, 2 eggs, and 1 cup milk (or ½ cup milk, ½ cup gravy) poured over 1 cup shredded turkey and baked at 350 degrees for thirty-five minutes or till knife inserted in the middle comes out clean.

Turkey curry is another hit. Served over a bed of rice with tasty garnishes of slivered almonds, flaked coconut, golden raisins, and leftover cranberries, "You don't even know you're eating turkey!" says one (relieved) houseguest.

QUICK TURKEY CURRY

(It goes without saying that you can omit the onions if eaters at your house will complain.)

In medium saucepan over medium heat, sauté:

¼ cup chopped onion

in: **1/2 T. butter** until soft.

Add: **1 10 ½-oz. can condensed cream of chicken soup**

¼ cup milk

Stir well, heating through. Stir in:

1 cup light sour cream or plain yogurt

½ t. (or more) curry powder, to taste.

(If too thick, add more milk.)

Add: **1 cup shredded turkey**.

Heat. Serve over:

Cooked rice

Serve with condiments: **raisins, slivered almonds, flaked coconut, leftover cranberries**.

Serves four.[8]

Two quick turkey sandwich ideas:

◆ Spread cream cheese on bread; top with layer of cranberries and layer of turkey. Top with second piece of cream-cheesed bread.[9]

◆ Place sliced turkey on lightly toasted bread. Top with thinly sliced cheddar cheese and broil until melted. Add thin slices of Granny Smith apples and top with another piece of toasted bread.

I LOVE MY HUGE HEATING BILL BECAUSE IT MEANS I AM WARM.

I LOVE THE LADY BEHIND ME IN CHURCH WHO SINGS OFF KEY BECAUSE IT MEANS THAT I CAN HEAR.

I LOVE THE PILES OF LAUNDRY AND IRONING BECAUSE IT MEANS MY LOVED ONES ARE NEARBY.

I LOVE WEARINESS AND ACHING MUSCLES AT THE END OF THE DAY BECAUSE IT MEANS I HAVE BEEN PRODUCTIVE.

I LOVE THE ALARM THAT GOES OFF IN THE EARLY MORNING HOURS BECAUSE IT MEANS THAT I'M ALIVE.

—AUTHOR UNKNOWN

"Make a joyful shout to the LORD, all you lands! Serve the LORD with gladness; come before His presence with singing. Know that the LORD, He is God; it is He who has made us, and not we ourselves; we are His people and the sheep of His pasture.

Enter into His gates with thanksgiving, and into His courts with praise. Be thankful to Him, and bless His name. For the LORD is good; His mercy is everlasting, and His truth endures to all generations." (Psalm 100:1–5 NKJV)

prayer THANK YOU, LORD, FOR YOUR ABUNDANT LOVE, YOUR TENDERNESS AND COMPASSION FOR YOUR CHILDREN. THANK YOU THAT NOTHING—NEITHER DEATH, NOR LIFE, NOR THINGS PRESENT, NOR THINGS TO COME—CAN SEPARATE US FROM YOUR LOVE.

FUN FACT

According to *Thanksgiving 101* by Rick Rodgers, "about 675 million pounds of turkey are served each Thanksgiving."[10]

Quotable

In a letter to his daughter, Benjamin Franklin complained about the eagle's being selected as our national symbol. "I wish the bald eagle had not been chosen as the representative of our country; he is a bird of bad moral character. . . . In truth, the turkey is in comparison a much more respectable bird, and withal a true original native of America." [11]

CHOCOLATE BREAK! stop!

CROOKIES

A wonderful Christmas candy that makes a great gift, these take only about ten minutes to make, then another thirty minutes to chill. Break them into pieces then package in holiday tins or gift bags. If you store your chocolate chips in the freezer, take them out as soon as you know you're going to make this so they'll melt better.

CROOKIES

On baking sheet, spread out:

1 "sleeve" of Saltine crackers

In small saucepan over medium-low heat, melt:

1 stick butter

1 cup brown sugar

Once the mixture is gooey, pour evenly over crackers. Bake at 350 degrees for five minutes, until bubbly. Remove from oven, and sprinkle on top:

2 cups chocolate chips

As the chocolate melts, spread it with the back of a spoon. Pop into the refrigerator until set, then cut apart the candy and put into gift containers.[12]

week 49

for the week:

Discommode

(dĭs′ kə-mōd′).

To inconvenience; disturb. As in, *"I trust you won't be too **discommoded**, kids, to put your dirty socks in the laundry room before Grandma gets here."*

alternate

new word:

Bonhomous (bŏn′ə-məs).

Possessing frank and simple good-heartedness. As in, *"Thanks, kids, for being so **bonhomous** and pretending to eat Great Aunt Agnes's Crock-Pot Scalloped Pineapples."*

Christmas Is Here! Last-Minute Ideas

Most of my family's attempts at homemade gingerbread houses have not remotely resembled the candy-covered masterpieces you see on magazine covers. The absolute worst was one year when the kids and I followed an article's cheerful instructions to use a shoebox as the base rather than gingerbread, since the whole creation would be covered with frosting anyway and no one would ever know. No one would have, either, except for the sad fact that within hours the boxes collapsed and the heat in the house made the frosting and candies melt down the sides of our wonders like the face paint of a clown who had cried too many tears. In the end our creations looked exactly like what they were—a trio of sagging orange shoeboxes adorned with pathetic globs of dripping frosting.

Determined to orchestrate fun family time with my children if it killed me, I never gave up on the gingerbread house fantasy. After years of modified yet still-disastrous attempts, I finally came across the gingerbread secret I'd been waiting for. You can make cute little houses ornate as any magazine editor's, with lemon drops and M&Ms®, and cereal-thatched roofs, without devoting two days of your life to making and chilling dough, enlarging patterns, measuring walls and roofs, baking, mixing frosting with powdered sugar flying, and swatting at the hands of little ones who want to help in this thirty-seven-hour project, not including decorating. I am about to divulge the secret that will wipe away your gingerbread traumas forever.

Ready? Here it is.

Shh. Quiet on the set.

(Whisper.) Graham crackers.

That's it. And store-bought frosting. There. Done. You can now make twinkling "gingerbread houses"—a whole village if you want!—and virtually skip all the tedious, not-fun parts. With graham crackers as the base, even the littlest kids can fashion a simple structure. If ceilings collapse during construction, just grab some more graham crackers and start over. For a couple of dollars spent in the cracker aisle, you can outwit your overworked, overwrought inner mother who's grimly determined to do all the traditions "right." (Maybe that's just me.) You'll end up with a calmer, gentler yuletide you, and candy-covered results that look surprisingly magazine cover-ish, considering how little effort the whole thing actually took.

Gingerbread fun. Let the games begin.

Gingerbread House Specifics

Of my many attempts to entice my sons to bond with me over craft projects, gingerbread houses is one of the few areas where I've succeeded. "Didja buy the gingerbread stuff yet, Mom?" they ask, confirming that just a bit of candy goes a long way toward convincing the two young men who tower over me to join in for an hour of kitchen-table bonding.

Start with a large piece of cardboard (the 8 ½" x 11" back of a pad of paper works fine) and cover it with foil, one for each person who's making a house. (Alternatively, grab a plate you won't be needing and cover it with foil.) This is your base.

For each house, you'll need four full-sized graham crackers (two for walls, two for roof) and two graham crackers you cut with a serrated knife. (Place the full-sized graham cracker in front of you with the short side toward you; cut off the top right and top left corners of the graham cracker, to resemble a pitched roof. You should have a square on the bottom and a triangle on top, connected to it, to make the slanted sides on which the roof will sit.) Use light pressure and a sawing motion to minimize breakage. If a cracker breaks, simply grab another one.

With a can of store-bought white frosting, "glue" the cottage pieces together along the edges. Start with one wall and one side. Glob it together with plenty of white frosting (also known as "snow"). Then do the other wall and side. Now glob those two sections together to form a rectangle—the four walls of your "house." Last, stick the roof pieces on top.

All this will probably take about ten minutes. Now you get to decorate! Working one section at a time, use your tub of white frosting to stick small candies all over your house: chocolate chips, jelly beans, M&Ms®, white and green Tic Tacs®, mini marshmallows, red cinnamon candies, lemon drops. Line the house seams with candies, decorate the roof, create doors, windows, flower boxes, wreaths. Add a Tootsie Roll® chimney, gumdrop bushes, Life Saver® wreaths, toothpick crosses. Chocolate nonpareils make great rooftop décor or walkways. Drip frosting off your cottage for "icicles." Around your cottage, build pretzel fences and marshmallow snowmen. Decorate inverted ice cream cones for trees. Sprinkle glittery colored sugar with abandon.

Stock up on extra graham crackers and frosting in preparation for visits from nieces or nephews, a grandma, a pal from the basketball team. Prepare for a bonhomous evening, complete with nibbling.

To those conscientious waist watchers who protest the idea of a cookie swap, I say, "You've got to be kidding! It's Christmas!" How can a home have too many cookies? And who says you have to eat them all?! Feed them to your family, give away small bagsful to neighbors, bring some to the kids practicing for the church Christmas pageant. A once-a-year cookie orgy will not kill you. (At least I'm fairly certain.)

Christmas cookie swaps are not only fun but, at their most basic, they're a cinch to organize. Simply invite as many friends as you want, asking each guest to bring six dozen cookies, all of one type, whatever type she chooses. (Guests can also bring copies of their recipes, if they wish.) Ask each person to also bring an empty cookie tin, which she'll fill with everyone else's offerings. As hostess, make sure to provide festive heavy-duty paper plates or large reclosable plastic bags for guests who forget to bring containers.

Once everyone has arrived, lay out all the cookies on the table. You will be surprised: some people will have made fewer than six dozen, some will have made more, some will have run out of time to make any but still wanted to come, and some will have misunderstood the instructions and brought several different varieties. The beauty of this get-together is: it doesn't matter! Simply count the number of cookies of each type, divide it by your number of guests, and write on a small piece of paper by the plate how many each person can take. (So thirty-six chocolate crinkle cookies, say, divided by ten guests means everyone gets to take home three chocolate crinkle cookies. If the plate next to it holds eighty Russian tea cakes, each of your ten guests can add eight Russian tea cakes to her stash.) When everyone has circled the table, filling their buckets with the allowable number of treats, there will be the odd cookies left—those six extra chocolate crinkles, for example. At this point, you can eat whatever's left, or let everyone sneak a few more of her favorites into her container.

This is a great evening get-together, after guests have already eaten dinner. In way of refreshments, simply provide drinks, and maybe a bowl of grapes or a plateful of orange slices. Play festive Christmas background music and you've got a fun, lively party where everyone goes home feeling like they've won the door prize.

And those family members at home, who are eagerly waiting for the cookie lady's return? They'll think they've won the door prize too.

Five or ten dollars might not seem like much to spend on a gift, but when you start multiplying it by all the friends, neighbors, and teachers you'd like to lavish, the total dollar figure can bring on a surge of panic.

Amy Dacyczyn, author of *The Tightwad Gazette* books, addresses frugal gift giving. "If you buy yourself expensive goods from Bloomingdale's, people will justifiably feel that it's inconsistent for you to buy them bargains from the dollar store. In contrast, if you always seek out bargains for yourself, others will be far more likely to accept them as presents from you."[2]

Dacyczyn's ideas for inexpensive gift giving include giving "services" such as babysitting; buying secondhand items at yard sales; drawing names to limit the number of presents you give; and making gifts.

This last idea is my favorite tightwad strategy, since making presents is not only budget friendly but also supremely satisfying. Though I don't have time to make all the gifts I'd like, I do have time to make some. If I find an idea that's quick and inexpensive, I make several. I've bought inexpensive glass balls from the craft store and decorated them with glittery Christmas paints and gold-ribbon bows; I've filled jars with powdered "milk bath" ingredients; I've given homemade jams and cappuccino mix; I've painted soaps (you simply scrape off the brand name, use acrylic craft paint to make a design of hearts, stars, or Christmas trees, then cover the paint with a layer of melted wax).

One great gift, especially when kids are young and produce mountains of masterpieces daily, is to print up pads of paper, personalized with their very own artwork. Simply have the child draw a picture in pencil, then go over it in black ink. Bring the drawing to your local copy shop, which can shrink or enlarge it to size, and have the shop print it up on pads. These make terrific presents for proud grandparents, teachers, or even the kids' friends. Be sure to save one for yourself.

It's time to:

◇ Mail those Christmas packages.

◇ Put card writing into high gear.

◇ Wrap gifts as you purchase them—at least some—so you won't be faced later with an overwhelming jumble of bags. Save your receipts, all in one place.

◇ Make wrapping paper. Cut open brown paper bags, bring out the puff paints, cut up old Christmas cards, and glue away. When the kids were small, I bought a roll of white paper and dipped their little hands and feet in red and green paint, which made splendid wrap. Another year we used cookie cutters as stencils and colored with colored pencils and markers.

◇ Wrap gifts with oversized artwork your kids may have made at school. One year we added gold ribbons with gift tags stating, "Artwork provided by Ben and Jake." After Christmas, my mother-in-law told us she'd ironed the pictures and displayed them on her wall. You can't buy fans like that.

◇ Start those Advent wreaths and calendars.

◇ Buy extra nylons if you're attending any dress-up holiday events.

◇ Make sure the kids have appropriate clothes (that fit!) for the school musical or excursion to *The Nutcracker*.

◇ Plan Christmas menus (see week 51 for holiday food ideas).

◇ Get kids to help decorate. One year my boys adorned the large houseplant in our living room with felt poinsettia napkin rings and my Christmas earrings; they put the Nativity scene on a holly-rimmed serving platter that I usually reserve for food, and stuck Christmas cookie tins on living room tables rather than in the kitchen where I'd have stashed them. Fresh eyes make imaginative decorators. ♥

"So Jesus said to the twelve, 'You do not want to go away also, do you?' Simon Peter answered Him, 'Lord, to whom shall we go? You have words of eternal life. We have believed and have come to know that You are the Holy One of God.'" (John 6:67–69)

prayer LORD JESUS, THANK YOU SO MUCH FOR COMING TO EARTH, LIVING HERE AS A MAN, AND GOING TO THE CROSS TO PAY FOR MY SINS SO I CAN HAVE A RIGHT RELATIONSHIP WITH GOD. LORD, TO WHOM SHALL WE GO? YOU AND ONLY YOU HAVE THE WORDS OF ETERNAL LIFE.

week 50

Slow Down

for the week:

Festoon (fĕs-tōōn′).

To decorate with a garland of leaves or flowers or the like, suspended in a loop between two points. As in, *"A living room festooned with evergreen boughs across doorways and windows would be lovely."*

alternate

new word:

Surfeit (sûr′ fĭt).

An excessive amount; overabundance. As in, *"If I go overboard, will someone help me tone down my surfeit of holiday ambition?"*

As I watched my son and his teammates play their first basketball game of the season, I heard the coach urge from the sidelines, "Slow it down!" He wanted the ball handler, my son, to take his time getting from one end of the court to the other, spending a few extra seconds appraising the situation before plunging in with a course of action.

That's what I want to do this Christmas. Slow it down. Slow it down by praying over which Christmas activities I should participate in before jumping in and committing myself. Slow down the panic that sets in when I'm at the store filling my basket with extra gifts that I'm not sure I even need because I haven't taken the time at home to see what gifts I already have. Slow it down by reading scripture about the Messiah as I watch our Advent candle burn, stopping what I'm doing for a few minutes of quiet attention on things that really matter.

Much as I try every year to refine my Christmas expectations, to plan ahead and organize and pare down my lists, I still have a tendency to overdo. For some reason, Christmas brings out the overachiever in me. I agree with Dean and Grace Merrill, who say in their book, *Together at Home*, "Why is it we all seem to have sixty days' worth of Christmas tradition and activity to fit into the thirty days between Thanksgiving and Christmas? We know such a packing job is impossible, but every year we keep trying anyway."[1]

Thankfully, along with the wrinkles comes a little wisdom. I'm beginning to see that the "perfect Christmas" may not exist outside of my imagination. I will probably never have time to see *The Nutcracker*, the living Nativity scene, and the city's Christmas lights display all in the same year. I will probably never have an opportunity to bake fancy holiday goodies with my children the week before Christmas. I will probably never have energy to festoon my mantel with swags of fresh greenery.

I'm lucky to remember to water the tree.

I try to remind myself that the December 25 deadline for love and togetherness and goodwill toward men is not a deadline at all. There is no time limit on doing good deeds, on giving people notes or tokens of appreciation, on making an out-of-the-ordinary meal and taking time to enjoy it with my family.

As the coach's words echo in my head, I breathe an amen of agreement. Slow it down. I don't need to run wildly downcourt with a long, unfocused list of must-dos. Only by slowing down and looking at where I want to end up—sitting at the feet of my heavenly Father, appreciating the magnitude of the gift He's given me in Jesus Christ—will I have a truly successful season.

Much like the basketball team, I'd say.

> ### Quotable
>
> *It seems strange that the Lord should tell people confronted with earthquakes and floods and assorted disasters to do exactly the opposite of what their instincts tell them to do. "Run," says instinct. "Be still," says the Lord.* [2]
>
> **Stuart Briscoe,**
> *What Works When Life Doesn't*

BE STILL, AND KNOW THAT I AM GOD.—PSALM 46:10 NIV

Slow it down!

- ◇ Spend a few minutes outside, bundled up against the cold.
- ◇ Make Christmas music as a family. If anyone plays an instrument (even badly), bring it out. Sing some carols.
- ◇ Work on a holiday jigsaw puzzle.

◇ Pull out holiday videos or photos from years past and reminisce.

◇ If you happen to be awake between 1 and 3 a.m. on December 13–15, check out the meteors in the night sky. Look south to see the Geminid shower of fifty to eighty meteors per hour.[3]

◇ Stare into the fire and spend some silent, thankful moments thinking about all God has done for you.

As I woke up this morning with a sore throat, I realized that some version of this scenario plays out nearly every year. Somehow, between the late nights watching the children's Christmas programs and the way-more-to-do-than-actual-time-to-do-it list, I wind up staying up too late too many nights in a row. My body reacts predictably, with a sore throat or the sniffles or some other sign it's being overworked.

When my husband, in a genuine attempt to help, suggests the two of us stay up late to get some gift-wrapping done, I snap at him. Very quickly our home's atmosphere changes from one of excited Christmas activity to one of tension and fatigue.

Though the scenario is getting to be as familiar as a well-worn pair of flannel pajamas, each December I'm still surprised by the month's tidal wave of activity and my resulting case of the drags. My annual sore throat tells me I'm trying to do too much, and I'm not taking care of myself.

It also reminds me that, much as my lists and organizational attempts delude me into thinking I am steering the boat, I'm not really the master of my own ship after all. Life is full of unexpected squalls, which seem less an adventure in December than in the other eleven months. It may be a child with a poorly timed case of the chicken pox, which means we can't get out to do the shopping we'd planned. It may be an emergency visit to the music store to get the trumpeter's valve unstuck in time for the big concert. It may be a simple sore throat. Whatever it is, I'm beginning to wonder if it isn't God's way of reminding me once again that my life is not my own, that my days are His, and that He's the one in charge, not me.

If dinnertime at your house is more dashing than dining, it may be time to check the family calendar for an upcoming Friday or Saturday night when the whole family will be home. Mark the date with "family dinner," then unearth your dusty fondue set and prepare for a nice, slow meal that's perfect for families who need to reconnect.

All you need for **meat fondue** is small cut-up cubes of **steak meat (about ¼ to 1/3 pound per person), olive oil** for boiling the meat, and any **vegetables** that sound like good accompaniments (**mushrooms, green peppers** cut in squares, **zucchini** sliced ¼ inch thick). Optional additions to the oil are a spoonful of **minced garlic** and a can or two of **anchovies**, oil and all.

You simply bring the olive oil to a boil in a saucepan on the stove, add your garlic and anchovies (no need to dice; the boiling oil disintegrates the fish, lending a tasty, unidentifiable flavor), and slowly cook until the seasonings are infused into the oil. Then transfer the oil to a fondue pot in the middle of the table, pass around the raw meat and vegetables, skewer the food with long fondue forks, and cook.

I've used a can of Sterno® underneath the fondue pot as a heat source, but some experts recommend denatured alcohol, found in hardware stores, as a better, hotter fuel for cooking meat. One note of caution: make sure your fondue pot is metal, not ceramic, for meat fondue, as the heated oil can crack ceramic.

As an accompaniment to the meat and vegetables, serve **fresh crusty sourdough bread** and cheeses such as **Gorgonzola** (blue) and **fontina**, which are passed around and sliced at the table.

This meal was one Italian family's traditional Christmas Eve dinner for four generations, and it's easy to see why. A fondue dinner forces you to slow down. Each piece of meat takes a couple of minutes to cook. Two minutes is enough time to ferret out quite a few details about your child's English project or the coach's latest motivational speech. With the lights turned low, the world slows down and the dinner table becomes an exotic restaurant you're reluctant to leave. The added novelty of each person cooking for himself, plus the mystery of whether or not your food will still be on the fork when you lift it from the pot, make for a magical evening. (If your fork comes up empty, by the way, you owe the person on your left a kiss.)

If your family enjoys this fondue evening, find a book of fondue recipes at the library or bookstore and experiment. Rick Rodgers's *Fondue: Great Food to Dip, Dunk, Savor, and Swirl* is full of good information.[6] Who knows, you might decide to make dunking and swirling a new annual tradition.

Not to be confused with dunking and dribbling, of course, which is what the basketball team will be doing. ♛

"Do not fear, for I am with you; do not anxiously look about you, for I am your God. I will strengthen you, surely I will help you, surely I will uphold you with My righteous right hand." (Isaiah 41:10)

pra**y**er LORD, HELP ME TO BE CALM IN THESE DECEMBER DAYS, RECOGNIZING THAT THERE IS ENOUGH TIME TO DO ALL YOU WANT ME TO DO. HELP ME TO FOCUS MY THOUGHTS ON YOU.

week 51

Eating Our Way Through the Holiday: Christmas Foods

I can't think of a soul who at this time of year has extra hours for concocting ultra fancy holiday desserts. Yet one of my favorite Christmas pastimes is to drool over holiday cookbooks, and most years I can find time to try at least one or two festive new recipes, especially if they're not too fussy and contain chocolate.

A charming Christmas Eve custom in Provence, France, is to serve thirteen Christmas desserts at once, representing Christ and His twelve disciples. Why has this lovely custom not caught on? We could start with a store-bought bûche de Nöel, the traditional French log-shaped cake, then continue right through to selected Christmas cookies and fudge, maybe throw in an orange or two, some mixed nuts, then conclude with a scrumptious Hot Fudge Upside Down Cake.

Hot Fudge Upside Down Cake does meet the criteria of "special yet not fussy" and contains a good amount of chocolate. I first tasted it at my sister's house when her kids were small. To deter them, she called it "nut cake," at which point they, like proper children everywhere, immediately fled to the next room. Meanwhile, she and I hid in the kitchen and scarfed it down before you could say glutton. (Don't tell me you've never done this.)

Calling it "nut cake" worked for a while, but her kids are bright and eventually the jig was up. Now we have to share the cake (though I suppose we could pretend it dropped on the floor, but that would be lying).

This is cakelike and gooey at the same time, just like a hot fudge cake should be. The nuts, by the way, are optional. But you don't have to tell anyone that.

HOT FUDGE UPSIDE DOWN CAKE

About 1 ½ hours before serving, preheat oven to 350 degrees. In large bowl, measure:

¾ cup flour

⅔ cup sugar

½ t. salt

½ cup milk

¼ cup butter, softened

1 square unsweetened chocolate, melted

1 ½ t. baking powder

1 t. vanilla

Mix with mixer at low speed. Once ingredients are mixed, increase speed to medium and mix for four minutes. Pour into an eight-by-eight-inch baking dish.

Into medium bowl, measure:

½ cup sugar

¼ t. salt

½ cup packed brown sugar

3 T. cocoa

½ cup walnuts, coarsely chopped (optional)

and mix. Sprinkle over chocolate mixture. Do **not** stir. Pour over all:

1 ½ cups boiling water

Again, do **not** stir. Bake sixty minutes. Cool slightly and serve warm with ice cream and spoons.

An annual Christmas tradition at our house is to set out an easy brunch that family members can enjoy all morning long—when they first get up, while presents are being opened, and after the gift giving is completed.

The night before, I cut up small wedges of cantaloupe and wrap them in slices of prosciutto. Some years we serve coffee cake, if a spare mom or grandma happens to be around and wants to make one. Sometimes we serve a hot main dish, such as an egg and cheese casserole. We always offer bagels, cream cheese, and lox, as well as juice and coffee.

And always, always, always we have orange rolls.

These are so simple to make because they start with canned refrigerated biscuits. And they're so yummy it's hard to believe how easy they are. Basically you take refrigerated biscuits, dip each one in a melted butter/sugar/orange rind mixture, and bake. For simplicity's sake, grate the orange peel the night before and refrigerate; first thing in the morning, put the recipe together and pop it in the oven. (If the timer goes off mid-present opening, halt the proceedings for a second to take out the rolls.) The recipe is from Beverly K. Nye's book, *A Family Raised on Rainbows,* where it's called Sherry Jones's Orange Bubble Loaf.[2] Thank you, Sherry, wherever you are, for a wonderful Christmas morning tradition.

> ## Quotable
>
> *I'm always asked what the dominating factor in American cuisine is, and my reply is that it's the many ethnic groups, each of which brought its own ideas of food to this country.*[1]
>
> **James Beard,**
> *The Armchair James Beard*

ORANGE ROLLS

Pull out a Bundt pan (or pie pan). Combine:

1 stick butter, melted

1 cup sugar

1 orange rind, grated

Open: **3 cans refrigerator biscuits**

Dip biscuits one by one into the orange butter mixture. Stand each one on end in the pan. Bake at 350 degrees for thirty to forty minutes. Turn out on platter and serve hot.

Note: If you're serving only a couple of people, you can divide the recipe and use only one or two cans of biscuits. Cut down on the baking time, though; the fewer the rolls, the faster it cooks.

MAKE-AHEAD EGG AND SAUSAGE CASSEROLE

My mom makes a great night-before egg and sausage casserole that we sometimes have on Christmas morning. You can cook the sausage ahead of time and assemble the casserole partway the night before, then add the milk and eggs and bake on Christmas morning. Even if you generally avoid spicy food, don't be scared off by the hot sausage; the flavor is just right, even for kids.

In large skillet, cook thoroughly:

2 lb. sausage (1 regular, 1 hot)

until no pink is left. Drain and crumble. Grease nine-by-thirteen-inch baking dish. Place in dish:

About **6 slices of bread,** crusts removed and each slice cut in half.

Alternate over bread:

cheddar cheese, sliced

swiss cheese, sliced

Spread sausage over cheese. (Can make recipe the night before up until here. Refrigerate overnight.)

The next morning, beat:

6 eggs

2 cups milk

and pour over all. Bake at 325 degrees for one hour. Let cool, then cut into squares to serve.

Note: You can substitute any grated cheese you have on hand for the cheddar and swiss.

Unlike Thanksgiving, where almost every American eats the identical meal of turkey, mashed potatoes, and cranberry sauce, Christmas dinner can be all over the map. Ask a hundred people what they're eating and you'll probably get a hundred different answers. From sheep parts (Norwegian) to braised carp (Austrian), it seems every heritage has its own Christmas traditions.[3]

A dish that keeps cropping up in holiday magazines is Christmas goose. Never having eaten goose myself, I started asking around. What, exactly, do people think of

Christmas goose? And how do they cook it? What do they serve with it?

Funny thing is, no one seemed to know. I couldn't find anyone who'd ever made a Christmas goose or even eaten one. The closest I came was my friend Pam, who had seen a gourmet cooking show once that featured a dish called turducken: a boned turkey stuffed with a boned duck stuffed with a boned chicken—and each with its own stuffing. But I digress.

This goose dinner, the supposed "quintessential American Christmas meal," is apparently beloved only by food editors. Not to be diverted in my quest for the perfect holiday dinner, however, I decided to give goose a try. (A new bumper sticker possibility: "Give goose a chance.")

I selected a recipe from one of my fancier cookbooks ("Roast Goose with Sausage/Pistachio/Kumquat Stuffing"). Figuring only a lunatic would attempt a complicated new menu on Christmas Day, I planned my feast for the weekend before Christmas. I ordered an eleven-pound goose from the local fancy grocery store (nine to eleven pounds is optimal, apparently, for the goose to be big enough to feed us yet not so big that it would be tough). The bird would arrive frozen, and I could pick it up the day before my dinner to ensure plenty of time for defrosting.

After much anticipatory buzz, the day finally arrived for me to meet my goose. I headed to the grocery, where the white-aproned butcher, consulting his clipboard, declared I must have already picked up my goose as my name was crossed off his list. After assuring him that I had not yet procured my poultry—and spending more minutes than was good for my blood pressure debating just how such a misunderstanding could have occurred—the butcher finally, reluctantly handed me my goose. I scurried for the checkout line posthaste.

The next twenty-four hours were a bit of a blur as I spent most of it chopping and stirring and trying to find my gold-rimmed plates. But the upshot of the goose experiment is (1) an eleven-pound goose barely feeds eight (with no leftovers); (2) roast goose even with a fancy stuffing is nothing special; and (3) turkey is a much better buy (my businessman husband kept muttering under his breath "price performance").

So if you've never cooked a goose, or even eaten one, don't worry; you haven't made an egregious error of omission. If you took a vote around my house, we'd tell you goose is vastly overrated and you're better off buying a Christmas turkey.

Or better yet, see if any friends are cooking prime rib for dinner and are willing to invite a few extra stomachs. ♛

FUN FACT

"*Christopsomo*, the Christmas bread of Greece, is flavored with chopped orange peel and the dough is rolled in sesame seeds before being formed into the shape of a cross and sprinkled with chopped almonds."[4] Christopso-mo, by the way, means "Christ bread."

At the elaborate Polish Christmas Eve dinner called Wigilia, "it is customary to have an even number of dishes and an odd number of guests, allowing one extra place for the Holy Spirit." [5]

"Eels are almost compulsory Christmas eating in parts of France and Italy." [6]

"In the same region there were some shepherds staying out in the fields and keeping watch over their flock by night. And an angel of the Lord suddenly stood before them, and the glory of the Lord shone around them; and they were terribly frightened. But the angel said to them, 'Do not be afraid; for behold, I bring you good news of a great joy which will be for all the people; for today in the city of David there has been born for you a Savior, who is Christ the Lord.'" (Luke 2:8–11)

prayer LORD, HELP ME NOT TO GET SO CAUGHT UP IN MY CHRISTMAS PREPARATIONS THAT I FORGET WHAT THIS HOLIDAY REALLY COMMEMORATES. THANK YOU SO MUCH FOR BEING WILLING TO COME TO EARTH AS A BABY TO SUFFER AND DIE FOR MY SINS. THANK YOU FOR SACRIFICING YOUR LIFE SO THAT I MIGHT HAVE LIFE, TOGETHER WITH YOU IN HEAVEN FOREVER.

week 52

Bringing in the New Year

When I was a child, I loved to set up a small tabletop Christmas tree in my bedroom each year, its twinkling lights and ornaments adding a festive air to my already-cluttered room.

Unfortunately, true to my sidetracked nature, I often left this holiday cheer to twinkle away until well after May Day. It was quite a shock to me one of my first Christmases as a married woman when my husband suggested, rather forcefully I thought, that January 1 was a prime day for taking down Christmas decorations. But they'd only been up a few weeks! It couldn't possibly be time to end the festivities!

In recent years, I've come to appreciate the wisdom of my husband's ways. Now when January 1 creeps up on us, I am a bit relieved, truth be told, to reclaim my tabletops and shelves, putting away the Christmas tchotchkes and replacing them with photos or books or, better yet, nothing at all. It feels good to clear out the old in readiness for the new. Isn't that what the New Year is all about?

This last week of the year is a great time to clear out excess in other areas, as well, such as all that stuff clogging the cupboards. As you put away Christmas gifts, remem-

new word
for the week:

Habiliments
(hə-bĭl'ə-mənts).
Dress or garb associated with an occasion. As in, *"Good, I guess it doesn't matter that I don't have any New Year's habiliments since we're not doing anything for New Year's, anyway."*

alternate
new word:

Coruscate (kôr'əs-kāt').
To give forth flashes of light; to sparkle, glitter. As in, *"If I did own any coruscating sweaters, this would be the perfect time of year to wear them."*

ber the old adage of one item in, one item out. As you put a new sweater away, throw out an old one you no longer wear. New soup bowls for Christmas? Ditch the long-retired lunchboxes or the egg poacher that's covered with fifteen years' worth of dust. Cart some of your overflow to charity, where it can be useful to someone else. (And if you hustle and get it done by December 31, you can write it off on this year's taxes too.)

Take advantage of the post-Christmas calm and go through your file cabinets, too, purging papers you no longer need. (One organizational expert claims you should do this every year!) Recently when I looked through a file of craft ideas I'd started saving back when I was still worrying about biology exams (my own, not my kids'), I was surprised at how many projects I just plain didn't want to do any more. Styles change, hobbies change, tastes change. I am no longer interested in making huge fabric bows to adorn my already-overburdened Christmas tree. I am no longer interested in waltzing through the mall wearing a handmade belt made from old orange peels.

When I toss out the old, I make room for the new. I make room for the hobbies and tastes that reflect who I am now, not who I was when disco was king.

So have the family gather round, mix up some hot chocolate, and put on a zippy CD. Then get to work, taking down decorations and sorting through drawers. Ho, ho, ho, and a happy new year.

About those Christmas thank-you notes: don't procrastinate too long or the job will grow till it's big as a boulder. Just write a couple a day until you're done. You can write notes on the Christmas cards you didn't get around to sending; that way you're not stuck with storing cards for next year that you'll never be able to find anyway.

Younger kids might find the thank-you job easier if you type up a basic form letter on the computer, leaving blanks for them to fill in for the name of the recipient, the present that's being acknowledged, and room for a couple of personal sentences.

I THANK MY GOD IN ALL MY REMEMBRANCE OF YOU, ALWAYS OFFERING PRAYER WITH JOY IN MY EVERY PRAYER FOR YOU ALL. —PHILIPPIANS 1:3–4

If you can't bear to throw out all the Christmas cards you received, save a few favorites to use as bookmarks during the year. Every time you see your aunt Rachael's handwriting, it'll remind you to pray for her and maybe drop her a quick card in the mail.

Most of our friends are pretty low-key when it comes to celebrating the New Year. A bottle of sparkling cider, the unusually wild prospect of keeping eyelids propped open till midnight—that's about all the excitement we can handle.

But a couple of years ago, a friend issued a New Year's invitation that called to me like a lilting flute melody. "We're not doing anything for New Year's," Kris began, "and wondered if you guys might want to come over and do nothing with us." Can an invitation get any better than that? There wasn't even time to stress over not owning a glittery black top hat.

That year several families, including kids, showed up at Kris's house with food to munch and board games to play. As *Private Benjamin* and other movies played in the background, it seemed no time at all before battles of Mancala and Chinese checkers were interrupted by the announcement that it was time to pull out the confetti-filled plastic poppers. We gathered on the back deck, snapped pictures, and yelled, "Ten, nine, eight . . ." in unison as we toasted in the New Year.

Different families celebrate the holiday differently, of course, depending on the ages of their children, their tolerance for late hours, and where they fall on the introvert/extrovert scale. When children are little and making them stay up hours past their bedtime seems like the worst idea you can imagine, it's fun to pretend you're in a different time zone and count down as though it were midnight. It may be only 9 p.m. in California, for example, but it's midnight in New York.

It's also fun to spend time just talking through the last year's happenings—trips taken, children's accomplishments, new job or volunteer opportunities. And also to dream about the future.

To help celebrate the New Year in Greece, a special cake called vasilopita is baked, which contains a hidden coin that's said to bring good luck to its finder.

Eating something sweet is said by the Greeks to bring a sweet New Year. Twelve grapes popped into one's mouth as the clock strikes midnight (one grape per strike) is said to bring twelve months of good luck.[1]

My ninety-six-year-old grandma tells me that where she lives in Florida, "Hog jowl and black-eyed peas are the New Year's favorite." I'm not sure I'd recognize a hog jowl if it jumped up and bit me. But I could definitely go for a New Year's

Blessing Cake, where each family member lights a small candle and places it on the cake as he describes something he's thankful for from the last year.

At our church near New Year's, we sometimes sing the Lord's Prayer to the tune of "Auld Lang Syne." (Try it; it's amazing how the words and tune fit.) Which sounds like the perfect ending to a perfectly splendid New Year's celebration, even if you weren't able to stay awake until midnight in your coruscating habiliments.

When my son was in fourth grade, his class spent time each week drilling new vocabulary words.

"Can anyone use the word priority in a sentence?" his teacher asked.

My son's hand shot up. "I am my mom's priority."

His teacher was so taken aback by his confident assertion she didn't know how to respond. She stammered out a few syllables, then quickly moved on to the next word.

When my son reported the incident to me later that afternoon, I felt like he had handed me a bouquet of roses. We had been talking about that very thing earlier in the week—how I didn't want the kids to ever feel as though they were getting in the way of my work. They were my work, I told them. Whatever else I did had to fit around my priorities of taking care of them and my husband.

The lesson had stuck. My son's confidence that he is indeed my priority was one of those wonderful, yes-they're-really-listening moments—like the first time they flush without prompting. Some of what I'm trying to impart to my children is, astonishingly, getting through.

We've heard it a million times and are sometimes tempted to use the stray sock lying on the floor of the car to gag the next person who brings it up. But there's no escaping the fact that our children do grow up. Though a rainy Candyland day with a preschooler may feel like it lasts fourteen years, before we know it those days are over. The kids are in school. They have their own friends. They play on sports teams with their own practice schedules. They engage in their own phone conversations, they want their own lunch money, and rumor has it, someday (soon!) they'll have their own driver's licenses.

Ready or not, in the blink of an eye, someday comes.

Don't face it with regrets. Make your children a priority. Make loving your husband a priority. Don't let the opportunity slip away to show love to those God has given you, making a home that's filled with love and laughter and warm memories. You will never regret your efforts.

Because we homemakers have a vital job. We are wise women, committed to building our homes (Proverbs 14:1). We are Queens of the Castle. ♥

"An excellent wife, who can find? For her worth is far above jewels. The heart of her husband trusts in her, and he will have no lack of gain. . . . She looks well to the ways of her household, and does not eat the bread of idleness. Her children rise up and bless her; her husband also, and he praises her, saying: 'Many daughters have done nobly, but you excel them all.' Charm is deceitful and beauty is vain, but a woman who fears the Lord, she shall be praised." (Proverbs 31:10–11, 27–30)

prayer DEAR FATHER, THANK YOU SO MUCH FOR GUIDING ME IN THIS JOB OF WIFE AND MOM AND HOMEMAKER. THANK YOU FOR YOUR TENDER SHEPHERDING, WHICH GIVES ME A PERFECT EXAMPLE OF HOW I AM TO TEND THOSE IN MY CARE. THANK YOU FOR THE INCREDIBLE OPPORTUNITIES YOU GIVE ME IN MY HOME FOR DOING GOOD. AS I TAKE CARE OF MY HOME AND FAMILY, HELP ME TO REFLECT YOUR GOODNESS, KINDNESS, AND LOVE.

CHOCOLATE BREAK!

MISSISSIPPI MUD CAKE

This cake is rich and yummy, and I hope you love it as much as I do. It comes from Mable Hoffman's book *Chocolate Cookery*, and if you haven't already overstuffed yourself on holiday goodies this would be a fine way to do so. If you have, then wait a week or two and try the cake anyway. You'll be glad you did.

MISSISSIPPI MUD CAKE

Grease and flour a thirteen-by-nine-inch baking pan. Preheat oven to 350 degrees. In large mixing bowl, beat until thick:

4 eggs

Slowly add: **2 cups sugar** and stir well. In a separate bowl, combine:

1 cup butter, melted

1 ½ cups flour

⅓ cup unsweetened cocoa powder

1 t. vanilla

1 cup flaked coconut

½ cup chopped pecans

Add to egg/sugar mixture. Stir well. Pour into prepared pan. Bake thirty minutes. Remove from oven and immediately spread gently over top:

1 (7-oz.) jar marshmallow crème

Prepare frosting.

Frosting: In medium bowl, beat together:

½ cup butter, melted

1/3 cup unsweetened cocoa powder

1 t. vanilla

6 T. milk

1 (1-lb.) box powdered sugar (4 cups)

Spread frosting over warm marshmallow crème, swirling as you go so it looks marbled. If desired, sprinkle on top:

1 cup chopped nuts (optional)[3]

notes

Week 1 (*January*)—**Who, Me? A Homemaker?!**

1. Printed by Proverbs 31 Ministries, (704) 849-2270.
2. Mary LaGrand Bouma, *The Creative Homemaker* (Minneapolis: Dimension Books, 1973), 169.
3. Cheryl Mendelson, *Home Comforts* (New York: Scribner, 1999), 10–11.
4. Linda Weltner, *No Place Like Home: Rooms and Reflections from One Family's Life* (New York: Arbor House, 1988), xii–xiii.

Week 2 (*January*)—**Giving Homemaking Our Best**

1. Pam Young and Peggy Jones, "Sidetracked Sisters," audiotape from March 1998.
2. Catharine E. Beecher and Harriet Beecher Stowe, *American Woman's Home* (Hartford, CT: Harriet Beecher Stowe Center, 1869; rep. 1998), 220–21.
3. Dr. Mary Ann Froehlich, *What's a Smart Woman Like You Doing in a Place Like This? Homemaking on Purpose* (Brentwood, TN: Wolgemuth & Hyatt, 1989), 35–36.
4. Laura Ingalls Wilder, *Little House In the Ozarks: The Rediscovered Writings*, ed. Stephen W. Hines (Nashville: Thomas Nelson, 1991), 64. Originally written in 1916.

Week 3 (*January*)—**Achoo! I Feel Fine: Fostering Our Health**

1. National Osteoporosis Foundation, www.nof.org.
2. Deborah Shaw Lewis, with Gregg Lewis, *Motherhood Stress* (Grand Rapids: Zondervan, 1989), 150.
3. National Institutes of Health Osteoporosis and Related Bone Diseases National Resource Center, www.osteo.org.
4. Stefi Weisburg, "Sleep Starved"; statistic quoted from University of Pennsylvania biological psychologist David Dinges, PhD.
5. Stefi Weisburg, "Sleep Starved," *Redbook*, September 1992; statistic quoted from Thomas Roth, PhD, director of the Sleep Disorders Center at Henry Ford Hospital in Detroit.
6. Cal Fussman, "And I in My Cap," *Esquire*, April 1998.
7. Ruth Bell Graham and Gigi Graham Tchividjian, *Mothers Together* (Grand Rapids: Baker, 1998), 108.

Week 4 (*January*)—**Delighting in the King: Building Healthy Spiritual Habits**

1. Ray C. Stedman, *Secrets of the Spirit* (Waco, TX: Word, 1977), 63–64.
2. Joanna Weaver, *Having a Mary Heart in a Martha World* (Colorado Springs: Waterbrook, 2000), 102.
3. Daily Walk devotional materials are available at http://home.navigators.org/us/devotion, or write The Navigators, P.O. Box 6000, Colorado Springs, CO, 80934, (719) 594-2371.
4. Tjitske Lemstra and Baukje Doornenbal, *Homemaking* (Colorado Springs: NavPress, 1997).

5. Dru Scott Decker, *Finding More Time in Your Life: With Wisdom from the Bible and Tools That Fit Your Personality* (Eugene, OR: Harvest House, 2001), 105.
6. Debra Waterhouse, *Why Women Need Chocolate: How to Get the Body You Want by Eating the Foods You Crave* (New York: Hyperion, 1996).
7. *Cooking Light*, October 1999, 146.
8. Sharon Tyler Herbst, *The Food Lover's Guide to Chocolate and Vanilla* (New York: Morrow, 1996.

Week 5 (*January/February*)—**Celebrating Creativity in Small Snatches**

1. Susan Branch, *Girlfriends Forever* (Boston: Little, Brown, 2000), 55.
2. Valerie Schultz, "Reckless Abandon," published in *Welcome Home*, "Dr. Laura Perspective" as "Giving It Your All: Mothering Is a Woman's Most Creative Act," May 1999. Sent via personal e-mail to author.
3. Anne Morrow Lindbergh, *Gift from the Sea* (New York: Pantheon, 1955; rep. 1975), 47.
4. Claudia Arp, *Beating the Winter Blues: The Complete Survival Handbook for Moms* (Nashville: Thomas Nelson, 1991).
5. Beverly Nye, *Everyone's a Homemaker* (New York: Bantam, 1982), 160.
6. *Prevention*, May 2000.

Week 6 (*February*)—**Valentine's Day**

1. Bruce Larson, *My Creator, My Friend* (Waco, TX: Word, 1986), 130.
2. Amy Dacyczyn, *The Tightwad Gazette III: Promoting Thrift As a Viable Alternative Lifestyle* (New York: Villard, 1996), 95.
3. Helen Handley, ed., *The Lover's Quotation Book* (New York: Pushcart Press, 1986).
4. *Sunset* magazine, February 1979. Used by permission.
5. Gladys Taber, *Stillmeadow Sampler* (Philadelphia: J. B. Lippincott, 1966), 2004.
6. W. H. Lewis, ed., *Letters of C. S. Lewis* (New York: Harcourt Brace Jovanovich, 1966).

Week 7 (*February*)—**It's OK to Say No: Managing Our Time As Homemakers**

1. Ruth Bell Graham, *Legacy of a Pack Rat* (Nashville: Oliver-Nelson, 1989).
2. Carl Sandburg, as quoted on www.quotationspage.com.
3. Gordon MacDonald, *Ordering Your Private World* (Nashville: Thomas Nelson, 2003), 78.
4. Anne Ortlund, *Disciplines of the Beautiful Woman* (Waco, TX: Word, 1977), 51.

5. Dorothy Lehmkuhl and Dolores Cotter Lamping, *Organizing for the Creative Person* (New York: Crown, 1993), 45.

6. Charles E. Hummel, *Tyranny of the Urgent!* (Downers Grove, IL: InterVarsity, 1994), 25–26.

Week 8 (*February*)—Pray First, Act Later

1. Evelyn Christenson with Viola Blake, *What Happens When Women Pray* (Wheaton, IL: Victor, 1975), 93.

2. Ray C. Stedman, *Jesus Teaches on Prayer* (Waco, TX: Word, 1975), 41.

3. Brother Lawrence, *The Practice of the Presence of God*, excerpted in *The Treasury of Christian Spiritual Classics* (Nashville: Thomas Nelson, 1994), 578.

4. John Rutter, "Gloria," Hyperion Records Ltd., London, www.hyperion-records.co.uk.

5. Evelyn Christenson with Viola Blake, *What Happens When Women Pray*, 26.

6. Gladys Hunt, *Honey for a Woman's Heart* (Grand Rapids: Zondervan, 2002), 159.

Week 9 (*February/March*)—When There's No Way Around the Busyness

1. Pat King, *How to Have All the Time You Need Every Day* (Wheaton, IL: Tyndale, 1982), 23.

2. Barbara Curtis, *Lord, Please Meet Me in the Laundry Room: Heavenly Help for Earthly Moms* (Kansas City: Beacon Hill Press, 2004), 61.

3. Joanna Weaver, *Having a Mary Heart in a Martha World* (Colorado Springs: Waterbrook, 2000), 58.

Week 10 (*March*)—Taking a Sabbath

1. Trent C. Butler, ed., *Holman Bible Dictionary* (Nashville: Holman Bible Publishers, 1991), s.v. "Sabbath."

2. Lauren F. Winner, "In Today's Culture, What Does It Mean to Keep the Sabbath Holy?" *Today's Christian Woman*, Jan./Feb. 2004.

3. Kim Thomas, *Even God Rested: Why It's Okay for Women to Slow Down* (Eugene, Oregon: Harvest House Publishers, 2003), 94.

4. Gordon MacDonald, *Ordering Your Private World* (Nashville: Thomas Nelson, 2003), 174.

5. Max Lucado, *Traveling Light for Mothers* (Nashville: W Publishing Group, 2002), 61.

6. Debbie Barr, *A Season at Home* (Grand Rapids: Zondervan, 1993), 168–69.

Week 11 (*March*)—Celebrating St. Patrick's Day and Purim

1. Dorothy Rhodes Freeman, *St. Patrick's Day* (Springfield, NJ: Enslow, 1992), 37.

2. These Irish blessings come from: *Irish Proverbs*, illustrated by Karen Bailey; Mary Murray Delaney, *Of Irish Ways*, 333; Jason S. Roberts, ed., *Irish Blessings, Toasts and Traditions* (New York: Barnes & Noble, 1993), 112; Liam Mac Con Iomaire, *Ireland of the Proverb* (Grand Rapids: Masters Press, 1988).

3. Mary Murray Delaney, *Of Irish Ways* (New York: Kilkenny, 1985), 336.

4. James O'Connel, *Classic Irish Proverbs* (San Francisco: Chronicle, 1997).

5. Mary Murray Delaney, *Of Irish Ways*, 334.

6. Edna Barth, *Shamrocks, Harps, and Shillelaghs* (New York: Clarion, 1977), 30.

7. Ibid., 33.

8. Donna Rathmell German, *The Bread Machine Cookbook* (San Leandro, CA: Bristol Publishing, 1991), 117.

Week 12 (*March*)—In Search of the Peaceful Home

1. Walter Wangerin Jr., *As for Me and My House* (Nashville: Thomas Nelson, 1987), 170.

2. Trent C. Butler, ed., *Holman Bible Dictionary* (Nashville: Holman Bible Publishers, 1991), s.v. "peace."

3. Terry Willits, *Creating a SenseSational Home* (Grand Rapids: Zondervan, 1996), 15–16.

4. Claire Cloninger, *When God Shines Through: Seeing God's Patterns in the Broken Pieces of Our Lives* (Dallas: Word, 1988).

5. Catharine E. Beecher and Harriet Beecher Stowe, *American Woman's Home* (Hartford, CT: Harriet Beecher Stowe Center, 1869; rep. 1998), 212.

6. Gladys Taber, *Stillmeadow Sampler* (Philadelphia: J. B. Lippincott, 1959), 34.

Week 13 (*March*)—Easter, Part 1

1. Linda Ebert, original source unknown.

2. Becky Stevens Cordello, *Celebrations* (New York: Butterick, 1977), 50.

3. Beverly K. Nye, *A Family Raised on Rainbows* (New York: Bantam, 1981), 122.

4. Julee Rosso and Sheila Lukins, with Sarah Leah Chase, *The Silver Palate Good Times Cookbook* (New York: Workman, 1984), 54–55.

5. Statistic quoted in *Parade*, 23 October 2005.

6. Susan Branch, *Girlfriends Forever* (Boston: Little, Brown, 2000).

Week 14 (*April*)—Easter, Part 2

1. George Frideric Handel, *La Resurrezione*, trans. 1988 by Anthony Hicks and Avril Bardoni; published by Erato-Disques S.A. 1991, 81.

2. Patrick Kavanaugh, *The Music of Angels: A Listener's Guide to Sacred Music from Chant to Christian Rock* (Chicago: Loyola Press, 1999).

3. Walter Wangerin Jr., *Peter's First Easter*, illustrated by Timothy Ladwig (Grand Rapids: Zonderkidz, 2000).

4. Becky Stevens Cordello, *Celebrations* (New York: Butterick, 1977), 51.

5. Jane Breskin Zalben, *To Every Season: A Family Holiday Cookbook* (New York: Simon & Schuster, 1999).

6. Ibid.

Week 15 (*April*)—Adventures in Gardening

1. Edith Schaeffer, *The Hidden Art of Homemaking* (Wheaton, IL: Tyndale, 1971), 85–86.

2. Celestine Sibley, *Small Blessings* (Garden City, NY: Doubleday, 1977), 144.

3. Rosalind Creasy, *Cooking from the Garden* (San Francisco: Sierra Club, 1988).

4. Ibid., 5.

5. *Reader's Digest Atlas of the Bible* (Pleasantville, NY: The Reader's Digest Association, 1981), 22.

6. Thalassa Cruso, *To Everything There Is a Season* (New York: Knopf, 1974), 46–47.

7. Martha Stewart, *Martha Stewart's Gardening: Month by Month* (New York: Clarkson Potter, 1991).

8. Ibid., 84.

9. Allen Lacy, ed., *The American Gardener: A Sampler* (New York: Farrar, Straus, Giroux, 1988).

Week 16 *(April)*—**The Simple Secret to Omitting Stress from Your Life**

1. Deborah Shaw Lewis, with Gregg Lewis, *Motherhood Stress* (Grand Rapids: Zondervan, 1989).

2. Ruth Bell Graham and Gigi Graham Tchividjian, *Mothers Together* (Grand Rapids: Baker, 1998), 62.

3. Deborah Shaw Lewis, with Gregg Lewis, *Motherhood Stress*, 89.

Week 17 *(April)*—**So You're a Sidetracked Home Executive™?**

1. Dorothy Lehmkuhl and Dolores Cotter Lamping, *Organizing for the Creative Person* (New York: Crown, 1993), 209–10.

2. For more information, check out www.messies.com, or write *Messies Anonymous*, 5025 S.W. 114th Ave., Miami, Florida, 33165.

3. Pam Young and Peggy Jones, *Sidetracked Home Executives* (New York: Warner, 1977).

4. Sandra Felton, *The Messies Manual* (Grand Rapids: Revell, 1984), 72.

5. Marla Cilley, *Sink Reflections* (New York: Bantam, 2002).

6. Pam McClellan, *Don't Be a Slave to Housework* (Cincinnati, OH: Betterway, 1995), 69.

Week 18 *(May)*—**Housework, Done Correctly, Can Kill You**

1. John E. Frook, "How to Clean Your House from Top to Bottom in Two Hours," *Family Circle*, 5 April 1988, 20–24

2. Cindy Tolliver, *At-Home Motherhood: Making It Work for You* (San Jose, CA: Resource Publications, 1994), 81.

3. Kathy Peel, *The Family Manager* (Dallas, TX: Word, 1996), 304.

4. Sandra Felton, *The Messies Manual* (Grand Rapids: Revell, 1984), 57.

5. Stephanie Culp, *How to Conquer Clutter* (Cincinnati, OH: Writer's Digest Books, 1989), 33.

6. Kathryn Donovan Wiegand, *Finding God at Harvard*, ed. Kelly Monroe, (Grand Rapids: Zondervan, 1996), 147.

7. Benjamin Franklin, *The Autobiography of Benjamin Franklin* (New York: P. F. Collier & Son Corporation, New York, 1787; rep. 1937, 1963), 85.

8. Sue Bender, *Plain and Simple: A Woman's Journey to the Amish* (San Francisco: HarperSanFrancisco, 1989).

9. Pamela Piljac, *You Can Go Home Again* (Portage, IN: Bryce-Waterton, 1985), 86.

10. Ella May Miller, *The Joy of Housekeeping* (Old Tappan, NJ: Spire, 1975), 25–26.

Week 19 *(May)*—**Drudgery, Schmudgery**

1. Gladys Taber, *Still Cove Journal* (Boston: G. K. Hall & Co., 1981), 340.

2. Ann McGee-Cooper with Duane Trammell, *Time Management for Unmanageable People* (New York: Bantam, 1994), 136–37.

3. Dorothy Lehmkuhl and Dolores Cotter Lamping, *Organizing for the Creative Person* (New York: Crown, 1993), 97.

4. Laura Ingalls Wilder, *Little House in the Ozarks: The Rediscovered Writings*, ed. Stephen W. Hines (Nashville: Thomas Nelson, 1991), 206–207. Originally written in 1916.

5. Linda Weltner, *No Place Like Home: Rooms and Reflections from One Family's Life* (New York: Arbor House, 1988), 71.

6. Rita Konig, *Domestic Bliss* (New York: Simon and Schuster, 2003), 247.

7. William Gordon, Episcopal bishop of Alaska, *Time*, 19 November 1965, quoted in James B. Simpson, Simpson's Contemporary Quotations, 1988. www.bartleby.com.

Week 20 *(May)*—**Mother's Day**

1. James Bemis, CatholicExchange.com, copyright 2001, "Mothers Day Overcomes P.C."

2. Ruth Bell Graham and Gigi Graham Tchividjian, *Mothers Together* (Grand Rapids: Baker, 1998), 40.

3. Beverly Nye, *Everyone's a Homemaker* (New York: Bantam, 1982), 156.

4. Barbara Bush, *Barbara Bush: A Memoir* (New York: St. Martin's, 1994), 570.

Week 21 *(May)*—**Here Comes the Sun: Warm-Weather Homemaking**

1. Vicki Lansky, *The Taming of the C.A.N.D.Y. Monster* (New York: Bantam, 1978).

2. Beverly Nye, *A Family Raised on Rainbows* (New York: Bantam, 1981), 100.

3. Encyclopaedia(sic) Britannnica, Inc., copyright 1999–2000, from search.ebi.eb.com/ebi/article, s.v. "bleaching."

4. Helen Mather, *Clotheslines U.S.A.* (Garden City, NY: Doubleday, 1969).

5. Cheryl Mendelson, *Home Comforts* (New York: Scribner, 1999), 335.

6. Ann Hodgman, *Beat That!* (Shelburne, VT: Chapters, 1995), 104–105.

7. Amy Dacyczyn, *The Tightwad Gazette III: Promoting Thrift as a Viable Alternative Lifestyle* (New York: Villard, 1996), 20.

8. Chantal Coady, *Real Chocolate* (New York: Rizzoli International Publications, 2003), 22.

Week 22 *(May/June)*—**Dream On: Planning for Summer**

1. Michael J. Weiss, "The New Summer Break," *American Demographics*, August 2001, 49.

2. Kathy Peel and Joy Mahaffey, *A Mother's Manual for Summer Survival* (Pomona, CA: Focus on the Family, 1989), 5.

3. Ibid., 5–6.

4. Dean and Grace Merrill, *Together at Home* (Pomona, CA: Focus on the Family, 1988), 59.

5. Cheryl Mendelson, *Home Comforts* (New York: Scribner, 1999), 597.

6. Gladys Taber, *Stillmeadow Sampler* (Philadelphia: J. B. Lippincott, 1959), 26.

7. Douglas Groothuis, "Another Kind of Fast," *Moody*, May/June 2000, 44.

Week 23 *(June)*—**School's Out!**

1. Henry David Thoreau, *Walden* (Princeton, NJ: Princeton University Press, 1971), 173. Originally published in 1854.

Week 24 *(June)*—**Father's Day**

1. Karen Mains, *Open Heart, Open Home: The Hospitable Way to Make Others Feel Welcome & Wanted* (Downers Grove, IL: InterVarsity Press, 1976), 98. (Note: this changed because there is a revised edition with new publisher)

2. Rick Bundschuh and Dave Gilbert, *Dating Your Mate: Creative Dating Ideas for Those Who Are Married or Those Who Would Like to Be* (Eugene, OR: Harvest House, 1987).

3. General Douglas MacArthur, as quoted in Robert Byrne and Teresa Skelton, *Every Day Is Father's Day: The Best Things Ever Said About Dear Old Dad* (New York: Atheneum, 1989), 16.

4. Calvin Trillin, *Family Man* (New York: Farrar, Strauss and Giroux, 1998), 3.

5. Dr. James Dobson, *Complete Marriage and Family Home Reference Guide* (Wheaton, IL: Tyndale, 2000).

6. Elizabeth Berg, *Family Traditions* (Pleasantville, NY: The Reader's Digest Association, 1992), 148.

Week 25 (*June*)—**Let the Games Begin: Summer Fun**

1. Jay M. Pasachoff, *Peterson First Guide to Astronomy* (New York: Houghton Mifflin, 1988).

2. Strickland Gillilan, "The Reading Mother," from Hazel Felleman, ed., *The Best Loved Poems of the American People* (New York: Doubleday, 1936), 376.

3. Jim Trelease, *The Read-Aloud Handbook*, 5th ed. (New York: Penguin Putnam, 1979; rep. 2001), 2.

4. Gladys Hunt, *Honey for a Child's Heart: The Imaginative Use of Books in Family Life* (Grand Rapids: Zondervan, 2002).

5. Gladys Hunt, *Honey for a Teen's Heart* (Grand Rapids: Zondervan, 2002).

6. Mark Twain, *Mark My Words*, ed. Mark Dawidziak (New York: St. Martin's, 1996), 52.

7. Cheryl Lightle and Rhonda Anderson, with Shari MacDonald, *The Creative Memories Way* (Colorado Springs: Waterbrook, 2002), 48.

Week 26 (*June*)—**Chore Time: Training the Children**

1. Sandra Felton, *The Messies Manual* (Grand Rapids: Revell, 1981), 119, 121.

2. Dru Scott Decker, *Finding More Time in Your Life* (Eugene, OR: Harvest House, 2001), 42.

3. Franklin Roosevelt, *Looking Forward* (New York: John Day Company, 1933), 51.

4. Tim Kimmel, *Little House on the Freeway: Help for the Hurried Home* (Portland, OR: Multnomah, 1987), 170.

5. Kathleen A. Kendall-Tackett, *The Hidden Feelings of Motherhood* (Oakland, CA: New Harbinger, 2001), 99.

6. James Thornton, *Chore Wars: How Households Can Share the Work and Keep the Peace* (Berkeley, CA: Conari, 1997), 134.

7. Kathy Peel, *The Family Manager* (Dallas, TX: Word, 1996), 75.

8. James Thornton, *Chore Wars*, 148.

9. James Thorton, *Chore Wars*, 135.

10. Sandra Felton, *The Messies Manual*, 122.

Week 27 (*July*)—**Trippity Doo Dah: The Family Vacation**

1. Margaret Horsfield, *Biting the Dust: The Joys of Housework* (New York: St. Martin's, 1998), 37.

2. The Proverbs 31 Ministry, July 1998 newsletter.

3. Canadian Brass, *Red, White and Brass* (New York: Philips, 1991).

4. Adapted from Jane Breskin Zalben, *To Every Season* (New York: Simon and Schuster, 1999), 65.

Week 28 (*July*)—**Shh! The Queen Is Rejuvenating: Nurturing Ourselves**

1. Pam Young and Peggy Jones, *The Sidetracked Sisters' Happiness File* (New York: Warner Books, 1985), 218.

2. James Cross Giblin, *Thomas Jefferson: A Picture Book Biography*, illus. Michael Dooling (New York: Scholastic, 1994), 38.

3. Debbie Barr, *A Season at Home: The Joy of Fully Sharing Your Child's Critical Years* (Grand Rapids: Zondervan, 1993), 169.

4. Anne Morrow Lindbergh, *Gift from the Sea* (New York: Pantheon, 1955; rep. 1975), 50.

Week 29 (*July*)—**Feasting on Fruit**

1. Gladys Taber, *Still Cove Journal* (Boston: G. K. Hall, 1981), 111.

2. Susan Branch, *The Summer Book* (Boston: Little, Brown, 1995).

3. Irma S. Rombauer and Marion Rombauer Becker, *The Joy of Cooking* (Indianapolis: Bobbs-Merrill, 1953), 843.

Week 30 (*July*)—**Flea Markets**

1. Deniece Schofield, *Confessions of an Organized Homemaker* (Cincinnati, OH: Betterway, 1982, rev. 1994), 179.

2. Lynda Millner, *The Magic Makeover* (Santa Barbara: Fithian, 1997), 144.

3. James Beard, *The Armchair James Beard*, ed. John Ferrone (New York: The Lyons Press, 1999), 19–20.

4. Dorothy Lehmkuhl and Dolores Cotter Lamping, *Organizing for the Creative Person* (New York: Crown, 1993), 128.

5. Sharon Tyler Herbst, *The Food Lover's Guide to Chocolate and Vanilla* (New York: Morrow, 1996).

Week 31 (*July/August*)—**God's Recipe for Wives**

1. Glenda Revell, *With Love from a Mother's Heart: Creating an Extraordinary Home* (Lincoln, NE: Back to the Bible, 1998), 185.

2. Walter Wangerin Jr., *As for Me and My House* (Nashville: Thomas Nelson, 1987), 81–82.

3. Helen B. Andelin, *Fascinating Womanhood* (Santa Barbara: Pacific, 1965), 62.

4. Washington Irving, "Rip Van Winkle," published in *The Sketch Book* of Geoffrey Crayon, Gent., written in 1819–1820.

5. Helen B. Andelin, *Fascinating Womanhood*, 76.

6. Gigi Tchividjian, *Thank You, Lord, for My Home* (Minneapolis: World Wide Publications, n.d.), 52–53.

7. Phyllis McGinley, *Sixpence in Her Shoe* (New York: Dell, 1965), 40.

Week 32 (*August*)—**The Bountiful Garden**

1. Marian Morash, *The Victory Garden Cookbook* (New York: Knopf, 1982), 270.

2. Alice Gordon and Vincent Virga, eds., "The Heart of the Seasons," *Summer*, (Reading, MA: Addison-Wesley, 1990), 35.

3. Rosalind Creasy, *The Gardener's Handbook of Edible Plants* (San Francisco: Sierra Club, 1986), 284.

4. Barry Bluestein and Kevin Morrissey, *The Bountiful Kitchen* (New York: Penguin, 1997), 113.

5. Rosalind Creasy, *The Gardener's Handbook of Edible Plants*.

6. Marian Morash, *The Victory Garden Cookbook*.

7. *Sunset's Home Canning* (Menlo Park, CA: Sunset, 1993).

8. www.plimoth.org.

Week 33 (*August*)—**Too Hot to Cook: Summer Food Ideas**

1. Julee Rosso and Sheila Lukins with Sarah Leah Chase, *The Silver Palate Good Times Cookbook* (New York: Workman, 1984, 1985), 148.
2. James Beard, *The Armchair James Beard*, ed. John Ferrone (New York: The Lyons Press, 1999), 324.
3. Mable Hoffman, *Crockery Cookery* (Tucson, AZ: H. P. Books, 1975), 3.
4. Jennifer Crichton, *Family Reunion: Everything You Need to Know to Plan Unforgettable Get-Togethers* (New York: Workman, 1998), 127.

Week 34 (*August*)—**The Job of Queen: Homemaking As a Profession, Part 1**

1. Darcie Sanders and Martha M. Bullen, *Staying Home: From Full-Time Professional to Full-Time Parent* (Boston: Little, Brown, 1992), 73.
2. Dorothy Kelley Patterson, *Where's Mom? The High Calling of Wives and Mothers* (Wheaton, IL: Crossway, 2003), 21.
3. Ann Crittenden, *The Price of Motherhood: Why the Most Important Job in the World Is Still the Least Valued* (New York: Metropolitan, 2001), 58–59.
4. Caitlin Flanagan, "Leaving It to the Professionals," *The Atlantic Monthly*, March 2002, www.theatlantic.com/issues/2002/03/flanagan.htm.
5. Michael H. Minton and Jean Libman Block, *What Is a Wife Worth? The Leading Expert Places a High Dollar Value on Homemaking* (New York: McGraw Hill, 1984).
6. Ann Crittenden, *The Price of Motherhood*, 132.
7. Ibid., 8.
8. Dorothy Kelley Patterson, *Where's Mom?*, 18–19.
9. Pam Young and Peggy Jones, *Sidetracked Home Executive*™ authors. www.shesintouch.com.
10. Phyllis McGinley, *Sixpence in Her Shoe* (New York: Dell, 1965), 19–20.
11. Ann Crittenden, *The Price of Motherhood*, 17.

Week 35 (*August*)—**The Job of Queen: Homemaking As a Profession, Part 2**

1. Linda Weltner, *No Place Like Home: Rooms and Reflections from One Family's Life* (New York: Arbor House, 1988), 70.
2. Jill Savage, *Professionalizing Motherhood* (Grand Rapids: Zondervan, 2001), 29.
3. Ibid., 209.
4. Kathy Peel, *The Family Manager's Guide for Working Moms* (New York: Ballantine, 1997), 11.
5. Jill Savage, *Professionalizing Motherhood*, 199.
6. Phyllis McGinley, *Sixpence in Her Shoe* (New York: Dell, 1965), 11–12.
7. Peter Jaret, "Be Your Own Boss," *Health*, October 1994, 71.
8. Henry D. Thoreau, *Walden* (Princeton, NJ: Princeton University Press, 1971), 27. Originally published in 1854.
9. Ann Hodgman, *Beat That!* (Shelburne, VT: Chapters, 1995).

Week 36 (*September*)—**The Party's Over: School Days**

1. Dr. Mary Manz Simon, *The Year-Round Parent* (Ann Arbor, MI: Vine, 2001), 83.
2. Patrick Kavanaugh, *Raising Musical Kids: Great Ideas to Help Your Child Develop a Love for Music* (Ann Arbor, MI: Vine, 1995), 32.

3. Vicki Lansky, *The Taming of the C.A.N.D.Y. Monster* (New York: Bantam, 1982), 19.
4. Vicki Lansky et al, *Feed Me! I'm Yours* (New York: Bantam, 1974; rev. 1981), 41.

Week 37 (*September*)—**Schedules (or, Which of the 568 Volunteer Opportunities Should I Sign Up For?)**

1. Sandra Felton, *The Messies Manual: The Procrastinator's Guide to Good Housekeeping* (Grand Rapids: Revell, 1981), 115.
2. Annie Dillard, *The Writing Life* (New York: HarperPerennnial, 1989), 32.
3. Pat Ennis and Lisa Tatlock, *Becoming a Woman Who Pleases God* (Chicago: Moody, 2003), 186.
4. Iris Krasnow, *Surrendering to Motherhood* (New York: Hyperion, 1997), 206.
5. Jackie Wellwood, *The Busy Mom's Guide to Simple Living: Creative Ideas and Practical Ways for Making the Most of What You Have* (Wheaton, IL: Crossway, 1997), 32.

Week 38 (*September*)—**Grocery Shopping and Meal Planning**

1. Catharine E. Beecher and Harriet Beecher Stowe, *American Woman's Home* (Hartford, CT: Harriet Beecher Stowe Center, 1869; rep. 1998), 119.
2. Lila Perl, *What Cooks in Suburbia* (New York: E. P. Dutton, 1961).
3. Pat Ennis and Lisa Tatlock, *Becoming a Woman Who Pleases God* (Chicago: Moody, 2003), 220.
4. Sandy Hall, "What Supermarkets Know About You," *An Encouraging Word*, issue #34, 2001, 19.
5. Ibid.
6. Ibid.
7. Amy Dacyczyn, *The Tightwad Gazette* (New York: Villard, 1993), 31–32.
8. Rebecca Low and Georgia C. Lauritzen, Utah State University Extension, "A Management Plan for Home Food Storage," June 1995, www.ext.usu.edu/publica.
9. *Cooking Light*, July/August 1999, 30.

Week 39 (*September*)—**How Can I Make Dinner When I'm Always in the Car? Dinnertime Solutions**

1. P. B. Wilson, *God Is in the Kitchen Too* (Eugene, OR: Harvest House, 2003), 7.
2. Ibid., 48–49.
3. One study done by the National Center on Addiction and Substance Abuse—CASA®, at Columbia University, as quoted on www.menusolutions.com; a study of more than five hundred teenagers done by the Cincinnati Children's Hospital Center, as quoted in Dr. James Dobson's *Focus on the Family Bulletin*, April 2001.
4. Doris Christopher, *Come to the Table: A Celebration of Family Life* (New York: Warner, 1999), 2–3.
5. Donna Fletcher Crow, *Seasons of Prayer* (Kansas City, MO: Beacon Hill, 2000), 33.
6. Rhonda Barfield, *15-Minute Cooking* (St. Charles, MO: Lilac, 1996), 5.
7. Ibid., 7.
8. Catharine E. Beecher and Harriet Beecher Stowe, *American Woman's Home* (Hartford, CT: Harriet Beecher Stowe Center, 1869; rep. 1998), 167.

9. Ruth Marcus, *Washington Post,* 3 March 1999.
10. Rhonda Barfield, *15-Minute Cooking,* 28.
11. Adapted from *Better Homes and Gardens All-Time Favorite Casserole Recipes* (Des Moines, IA: Meredith Corporation, 1977), 69.
12. *Taste of Home Annual Recipes* (Greendale, WI: Taste of Home Books, 1997).

Week 40 *(September/October)*—**The Joys of Leftovers**

1. Coralie Castle, *Leftovers* (San Francisco: 101 Productions, 1983).
2. Ibid., v.
3. Ibid., 152–53.
4. Jay Jacobs, *Cooking for All It's Worth: Making the Most of Every Morsel of Food You Buy* (New York: McGraw-Hill, 1983), 27.
5. Ibid., 28.
6. Irma S. Rombauer, *The Joy of Cooking* (Indianapolis: Bobbs-Merrill, 1946), 766.
7. Cynthia Yates, *1,001 Bright Ideas to Stretch Your Dollars* (Ann Arbor, MI: Vine, 1995), 45.

Week 41 *(October)*—**The Seasons Are Changing: Homemaking in the Fall**

1. Beverly Nye, *A Family Raised on Rainbows* (New York: Bantam, 1981), 125–27.
2. Rosalind Creasy, *Cooking from the Garden* (San Francisco: Sierra Club, 1988), 124.
3. Idea from *Family Fun* magazine.
4. Christine Allison, *365 Days of Gardening* (New York: HarperCollins, 1995), 191.
5. Ibid., 236-37.

Week 42 *(October)*—**Friendship**

1. Alan Loy McGinnis, *The Friendship Factor* (Minneapolis: Augsburg Publishing House, 1979), 182.
2. Dee Brestin, *The Friendships of Women* (Colorado Springs: NexGen, 1987, 2004), 85–86.
3. Gordon MacDonald, *Ordering Your Private World* (Nashville: Thomas Nelson, 2003), 104–105.
4. Gigi Tchividjian, *Thank You, Lord, for My Home* (Minneapolis: World Wide Publications, 1980), 125.
5. Jill Savage, *Professionalizing Motherhood* (Grand Rapids: Zondervan, 2001), 82.

Week 43 *(October)*—**Old-Fashioned Homemaking**

1. Anne Mendelson, *Stand Facing the Stove: The Story of the Women Who Gave America the Joy of Cooking (The Lives of Irma S. Rombauer and Marion Rombauer Becker)* (New York: Henry Holt, 1996).
2. Joanna L. Stratton, *Pioneer Women* (New York: Simon and Schuster, 1981).
3. Ibid., 61, 63, 70.
4. Judith M. Fertig, *Prairie Home Breads* (Boston: Harvard Common Press, 2001), 42–43.
5. Laura Shapiro, *Perfection Salad: Women and Cooking at the Turn of the Century* (New York: Random House, 2001), 12.
6. Maxine L. Margolis, *Mothers and Such* (Berkeley, CA: University of California Press, 1984), 127.
7. Anne Mendelson, *Stand Facing the Stove,* 107.

8. Laura Ingalls Wilder, *Little House in the Ozarks: The Rediscovered Writings,* ed. Stephen W. Hines (Nashville: Thomas Nelson, 1991), 43. Originally written in 1916.
9. Catharine E. Beecher and Harriet Beecher Stowe, *American Woman's Home* (Hartford, CT: Harriet Beecher Stowe Center, 1869; rep. 1998), 181.

Week 44 *(October)*—**Planning Ahead for a More-Relaxed Christmas**

1. *The Columbia World of Quotations* (New York: Columbia University Press, 1996), #2282.
2. Gladys Taber, *Still Cove Journal,* 267–68.
3. Alice Chapin, *Great Christmas Ideas: Hundreds of Ways to Bring Christ Back into Christmas and Discover New Joy in the Holidays* (Wheaton, IL: Tyndale, 1992), 229–32.

Week 45 *(November)*—**Keeping Christ in Christmas**

1. James Montgomery Boice, *The Christ of Christmas* (Chicago: Moody, 1983), 111.
2. Martha Zimmerman, *Celebrating the Christian Year: Building Family Traditions Around All the Major Christian Holidays* (Minneapolis: Bethany House, 1994), 15.
3. Alice Chapin, *Great Christmas Ideas: Hundreds of Ways to Bring Christ Back into Christmas and Discover New Joy in the Holidays* (Wheaton, IL: Tyndale, 1992), 3.
4. James Montgomery Boice, *The Christ of Christmas,* 103.
5. Martha Zimmerman, *Celebrating the Christian Year,* 37.
6. Martha Zimmerman, *Celebrating the Christian Year,* 33.
7. Walter Wangerin Jr., *Preparing for Jesus: Meditations on the Coming of Christ, Advent, Christmas, and the Kingdom* (Grand Rapids: Zondervan, 1999), 186.
8. Ibid., 90.

Week 46 *(November)*—**Company's Coming! Hospitality**

1. Doris W. Greig, *We Didn't Know They Were Angels: Discovering the Gift of Christian Hospitality* (Ventura, CA: Regal, 1987), 46.
2. Lauren F. Winner, *Mudhouse Sabbath* (Brewster, MA: Paraclete Press, 2003), 50.
3. Karen Mains, *Open Heart, Open Home: The Hospitable Way to Make Others Feel Welcome& Wanted* (Downers Grove, IL: InterVarsity Press, 1976), 175-76.
4. Ibid., 176.
5. Doris W. Greig, *We Didn't Know They Were Angels,* 163–64.
6. Karen Mains, *Open Heart, Open Home,* 29-30.
7. Miriam Huffman Rockness, *Home, God's Design: Celebrating a Sense of Place* (Grand Rapids: Zondervan, 1990), 167.
8. Doris W. Greig, *We Didn't Know They Were Angels,* 22–23.
9. Laurie Colwin, *Home Cooking: A Writer in the Kitchen* (New York: HarperPerennial, 1993, rev. 2000), 43.
10. Lauren F. Winner, *Mudhouse Sabbath,* 45.

Week 47 *(November)*—**Thanksgiving, Part 1**

1. Julia Child, with Louisette Bertholle and Simone Beck, *Mastering the Art of French Cooking, Volume One* (New York: Knopf, 1998), x.
2. Robb Forman Dew, *A Southern Thanksgiving: Recipes and Musings for a Manageable Feast* (Reading, MA: Addison-Wesley, 1992), 9–10.
3. Sarah Ban Breathnach, *Mrs. Sharp's Traditions* (New York: Scribner, 1990), 216.

4. Carolyn Freeman Travers, quoted on www.plimoth.org.
5. Robb Forman Dew, *A Southern Thanksgiving*, 16.

Week 48 *(November)*—**Thanksgiving, Part 2**

1. Ray C. Stedman, *Book of Job* (Ventura, CA: Joy of Living Bible Studies, 2004), 16.
2. *Table Graces for the Family*, rev. ed. (Nashville: Thomas Nelson, 1984), 51.
3. Meg Cox, *The Heart of a Family: Searching America for New Traditions That Fulfill Us* (New York: Random House, 1998), 108.
4. *A Classic Thanksgiving: Songs of Praise* (Franklin, TN: Naxos Family Classics, 2000).
5. Adapted from Brenda Poinsett, *Celebrations That Touch the Heart* (Colorado Springs: Waterbrook, 2001), 72.
6. Carolyn Freeman Travers, quoted on www.plimoth.org.
7. Robb Forman Dew, *A Southern Thanksgiving: Recipes and Musings for a Manageable Feast* (Reading, MA: Addison-Wesley, 1992), 86.
8. Adapted from *Better Homes and Gardens New Cook Book* (Des Moines, IA: Meredith Corporation, 1976).
9. Idea from Leanne Ely, author of *Saving Dinner*; see www.savingdinner.com.
10. Rick Rodgers, *Thanksgiving 101* (New York: Broadway, 1998), 42.
11. Frank Donovan, *The Benjamin Franklin Papers* (New York: Dodd, Mead, 1962), 231.
12. www.flylady.net.

Week 49 *(December)*—**Christmas Is Here! Last-Minute Ideas**

1. Elizabeth Berg, *Reader's Digest Family Traditions: Celebrations for Holidays and Everyday* (Pleasantville, NY: The Reader's Digest Association, 1992), 216.
2. Amy Dacyczyn, *The Tightwad Gazette II* (New York: Villard, 1995), 192.
3. E. B. White, *One Man's Meat*, 3rd. ed. (New York: Harper, 1944), 335–36.

Week 50 *(December)*—**Slow Down**

1. Dean and Grace Merrill, *Together at Home* (Pomona, CA: Focus on the Family, 1988), 28.
2. Stuart Briscoe, *What Works When Life Doesn't* (Monroe, LA: Howard, 2004), 155.
3. Dennis Mammana, *The Night Sky* (Philadelphia: Running, 1989).
4. Claudia Arp, *Beating the Winter Blues: The Complete Survival Handbook for Moms* (Nashville: Thomas Nelson, 1991), 159.
5. Nancy Parker Brummett, *It Takes a Home* (Colorado Springs: Cook Communications, 2000), 168.
6. Rick Rodgers, *Fondue: Great Food to Dip, Dunk, Savor, and Swirl* (New York: William Morrow, 1998).

Week 51 *(November)*—**Eating Our Way Through the Holiday: Christmas Foods**

1. James Beard, *The Armchair James Beard*, ed. John Ferrone (New York: The Lyons Press, 1999), 323.
2. Beverly Nye, *A Family Raised on Rainbows* (New York: Bantam, 1981), 166.
3. www.epicurious.com.
4. Shona Crawford Poole, *The Christmas Cookbook* (New York: Atheneum, 1979), 170.

5. Mimi Sheraton, *Visions of Sugarplums*, rev. and expanded ed. (New York: Harper & Row, 1968, 1981), 15.
6. Shona Crawford Poole, *The Christmas Cookbook*, 42.

Week 52 *(December)*—**Bringing in the New Year**

1. Bobbie Kalmar, *We Celebrate New Year* (New York: Crabtree, 1985).
2. Gladys Taber, *Stillmeadow Sampler* (Philadelphia: J. B. Lippincott, 1959), 236–37.
3. Mable Hoffman, *Chocolate Cookery* (New York: Dell, 1978), 34.

If you have ideas or comments about homemaking, Lynn would love to hear them.

You can e-mail her at:

queenofthecastle@truevine.net.